Trading Systems EXPLAINED

How to Build Reliable Technical Systems

Martin J. Pring

MARKETPLACE BOOKS®
COLUMBIA, MARYLAND

Library of Congress Cataloging-in-Publication Data

Pring, Martin J.
[Breaking the black box (2008)]
Trading systems explained : how to build reliable technical systems / by Martin J. Pring.
p. cm.
Includes index.
Reprint. Originally published as: Breaking the black box : learn how to design, test, and apply mechanical trading systems using profitable examples. New York : McGraw-Hill, c2003.
ISBN-13: 978-1-59280-335-4 (pbk.)
ISBN-10: 1-59280-335-0 (pbk.)
1. Investment analysis–Data processing. I. Title.
HG4529.P7463 2008
332.63'2–dc22
2008025033

Published by Marketplace Books Inc.

Originally Published in 2003 by The McGraw-Hill Companies.

Printed in the United States of America.

To my son-in-law Chris

Contents

Trading Systems Explained: How to Build Reliable Technical Systems

Introduction

This book is based on the script for the 4-hour audio-visual CD tutorial, contained inside the back cover. It stands on its own as an introductory work on designing and testing mechanical trading systems, but is best used as a companion study guide with the CD. The tutorial is primarily intended for traders who want to design and follow their own trading systems. However, it also provides useful guidelines and principles for anyone who actively trades in the markets but does not utilize mechanical systems in their day-to-day or intraday activities. For those who do not have the time or inclination to design their own systems, I have included several of my own favorites. None are perfect, but all have been rigorously tested, and several offer excellent results — no guarantees for the future, of course.

The popular MetaStock program was used for the testing process, which is where the data have been derived.

As the research for this book and CD unfolded, three important principles regarding the nature of automated systems stood out. First, the simplest ones work best. This is not to say that every complex system will fail and every simple one will offer profitable results. However, I do think we can generalize and say that complex systems are often crutches for curve fitting—when a more simplified, well-thought-out system performs better over a wider set of markets and time periods. Also, we have the tendency to strive for perfection and therefore tinker with perfectly good models, introducing complex rules to gain that extra margin of profit. Ask any successful trader and he will tell you that perfection is impossible. You should be striving for *small but consistent* profits instead. In this regard, the old adage "cut losses and let the profits take care of themselves" comes to mind.

The second principle is that systems based on intermarket relationships generally offer the best results. These systems rely on a proven relationship between two markets such as interest rates and equities, bonds and commodities, and gold and the CRB Composite. This relationship is then used to qualify whether a market is in a favorable or unfavorable environment. If it is favorable, the system trades from the long side; if unfavorable, from the short side. For example, if the trend of interest rates is down, this offers a positive backdrop for equities. Normally, we might use moving average crossovers of the S&P Composite to go long or short. However, when interest rates are defined by the system as being in a declining mode, this is used as a filter just to ignore negative moving average crossovers or whatever triggering method we may be using. The intermarket relationship is used as a cross check for the market being traded, thereby avoiding a substantial number of whipsaws.

The third principle, which will come as a disappointment for many, is that the longer the time span, the greater the odds of success. I could have written a book including a lot of intraday systems with great results. This would certainly have increased sales, but frankly, I could not find anything that worked consistently. There are a few systems that appear to work well with short-term trading based on daily data. However, the best ones operate on the monthly and weekly charts. On the one hand, this is good because it means the average person does not have to spend all of their time closely watching markets and wasting money on undue transaction costs. On the other hand, few people in this day of instant news and information have the patience and discipline to wait out significant corrections. They will either become discouraged as things go temporarily against their position, or they become bored at the lack of stimulation from watching the tape. There are several systems in this tutorial that have worked incredibly well over a long period of time, and that I have the utmost confidence in. I will also bet the farm though, that few readers will have the patience and discipline to follow them. This is where a reality check of your personal trading practices must come into play.

The book has been divided into three separate parts: Part I deals with the basics of designing and testing systems; Part II presents individual systems based on specific markets; Part III offers some reliable intermarket approaches. This book also includes an Appendix, which provides updated information about some of the systems described in the chapters; the interactive quiz found on the CD, reproduced to help you test your knowledge of material already covered; a glossary of terms; and an index.

Please be aware that the majority of tables used within this text are taken directly from actual screen shots from the MetaStock charting software. Reproduction quality is not as clear as a typeset table, but I wanted to show actual examples, as you would see it on your own computer. I felt a "real life" approach was more important.

With all this in mind, enjoy the material, learn the rules and principles that are covered here, and most of all, good luck and good charting!

Martin J. Pring

PART I

Guidelines for Designing, Testing, and Applying a System

Chapter 1
The Holy Grail?

INTRODUCTION

We all have dreamed of the perfect system that catches tops and bottoms of every move almost to the last tick. Chart 1-1 is an example of what I mean. The arrows indicate the buy and sell points. Beautiful, is it not? Unfortunately, this is a deliberate fix on my part. A system this accurate does not exist and never will. In his book, *The Trading System Toolkit*, Joe Krutsinger states the best systems perform about 50 percent of the time. This does not sound like very good odds. Remember though, he was talking about the *best* systems. The trick is to make sure profitable signals are allowed to run and losing signals are cut short very quickly. There is a well-known market saying, "Let profits run and cut losses short." This applies in spades when designing a trading system.

In the last 20 years, there has been a substantial increase in the use of personal computers in the application of technical analysis. It is easy and quite inexpensive to acquire charting packages, which allow individual traders and investors to devise their own mechanical, or automated, trading systems. These systems can be helpful as long as they are not used as a substitute for sound judgment and thinking. In all of my CD tutorials, videos, and books, I emphasize that *technical analysis is the art of interpreting a number of different and reliable scientifically derived indicators.* Mechanical systems, in this case, are the scientifically derived indicators. First, you get a concept and test it with back data. Then you retest it with more historical data, and finally apply it in the marketplace. Still it must continually be monitored to make sure the underlying assumptions are still valid, because even the best systems inevitably break down. This fine-tuning process is the art. Since no

Chart 1-1 NYSE Composite

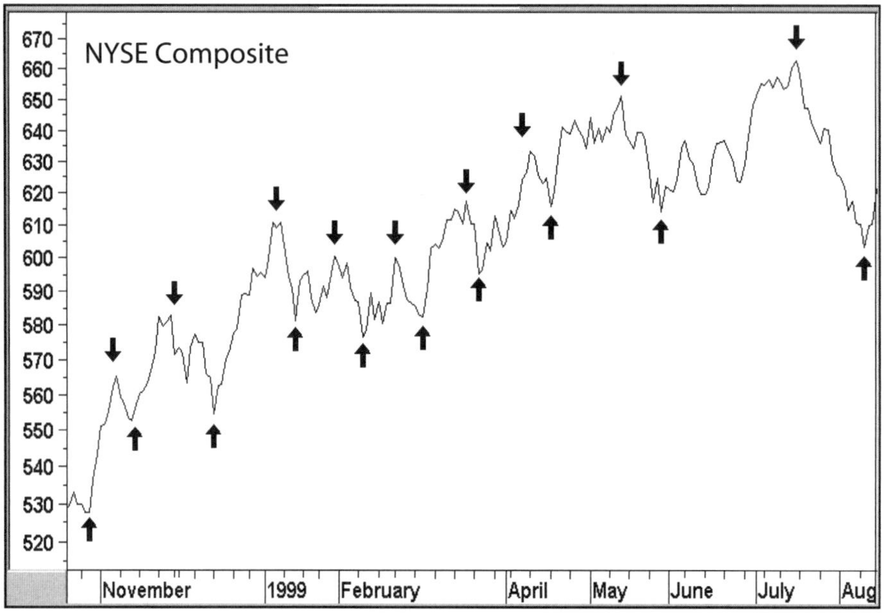

(Source: pring.com)

system is perfect, the process also involves selecting and trading several different systems over different markets for diversification. Then if one or two systems fail, others will pick up the slack.

This course will not reveal a perfect mechanical trading system (the Holy Grail). Parts II and III of this course do, however, offer some actual systems that have been tested in the marketplace. Remember, there never has been and never will be a perfect system. These systems should be viewed as starting points and not the Holy Grail.

USING A SYSTEM AS A FILTER

I believe mechanical trading systems should be used in two ways. The first method is to incorporate a well-thought-out system in conjunction with other indicators to alert the trader or investor that a trend reversal has probably taken place. In this method, the mechanical trading system is an important filter, but it represents just one more indicator in the overall decision-making process. It has alerted you that the market may be a buy or sell, but it is your interpretation of the other indicators that result in the final decision.

Chart 1-2 NYSE Composite

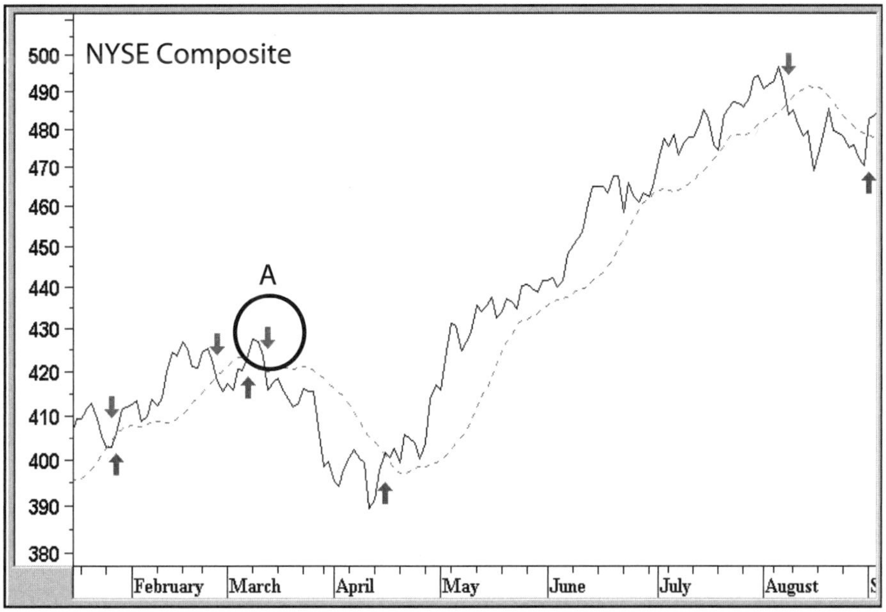

(Source: pring.com)

Chart 1-2 shows buy and sell signals that have been generated from a 10-day moving-average crossover. This approach will inevitably trigger meaningless signals, but it sometimes alerts us to some good opportunities. For instance, the buy and sell signals triggered in February and March did not amount to much since this was a trading range. However, the sell signal at A was quite interesting. It alerted us to the possibility that the New York Stock Exchange (NYSE) was in the terminal process of forming a small top. All we had to do was construct a trendline joining the lows. When the line was penetrated, it represented a more reliable signal to sell than the 10-day crossover on its own.

The same sort of thing developed at the low in Chart 1-3. The mid-April buy signal was the alert to look around for more evidence of a trend reversal. Then, in late April, the price broke above a small trendline, which was the signal to buy. In both instances, the 10-day crossover acted as our alert. From there, we were able to take a closer look at the technical evidence and decide whether the trend was about to reverse. We were using the evidence from other indicators, in these cases, trendlines, to decide whether the alert generated from the moving-average crossover warranted further investigation. What you should *not* do is pick and choose which signals to follow without reference to other indicators. If you do, you are guaranteed to run into trouble.

Chart 1-3 NYSE Composite

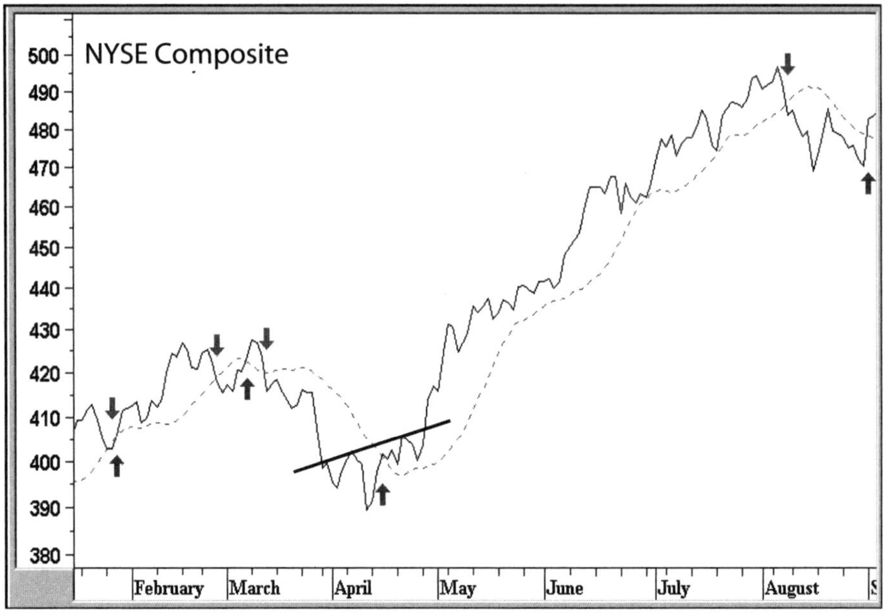

(Source: pring.com)

ACT ON EVERY SIGNAL

The second way a mechanical trading system can be used is to *take action on every signal.* This is the approach on which we will be concentrating here. If the system is well thought out, it should generate profits over the long term. However, if you pick and choose which signal to follow without considering other independently based technical criteria, you run the risk of making emotional decisions and losing the principal benefit of the mechanical approach. Mechanical systems are designed to remove emotion and bias from your decision-making process. If you can choose which signals to go with, then a high degree of subjectivity has been introduced into the equation.

Unfortunately, most mechanical trading systems are based on historical data. They are constructed from a more-or-less perfect fit with the past, in the expectation that history will be repeated in the future. This expectation will not necessarily be fulfilled, because market conditions can, and do, change. A well-thought-out and well-designed mechanical system, though, should do the job reasonably well. In this respect, it is better to design a system that gives a less-than-perfect fit, but more accurately reflects normal market conditions. Remember, you are interested in future profits, not perfect historical simulations. If special rules have to be invented to improve results, chances are the system will not operate successfully when extrapolated to future market conditions. One other housekeeping point: I am using the term "security" to include any freely traded entity, be it a stock, market, currency commodity option and so forth. This is because mechanical trading systems can be devised for any freely traded entity and using the word "security" in this sense avoids repetition.

A WORD OF CAUTION

One fact many people overlook is that the mind deceives us into believing *what is not actually there,* but what we would *like* to be there. The wish, in this case, fathers the thought. For instance, when you first look at Chart 1-4 of DuPont and a Chande Momentum Oscillator (CMO), it looks as though the overbought/oversold crossovers trigger pretty good buy and sell signals, as flagged by the arrows. However, if you study the July 1997 signal more carefully, you can see the indicator actually crossed its overbought line some time earlier in June. It was a very short crossover, but was a penetration nonetheless. Now look at the October 1997 arrow pointing at the oversold crossover. Close examination reveals the indicator did not reach its oversold

Chart 1-4 DuPont and a Chande Momentum Oscillator (CMO)

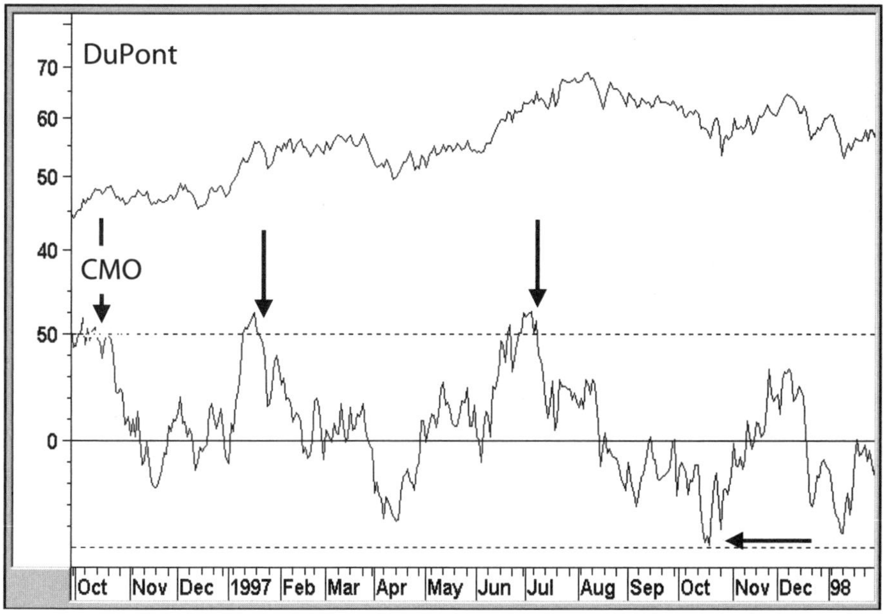

(Source: pring.com)

zone, so there never was a crossover. This is the type of situation that will bring you back to reality when a system is rigorously tested, because test results give us the cold hard facts of when an indicator actually triggered a signal, not when we would have liked it to trigger one. This is one of the reasons a tested result rarely lives up to our initial expectations.

Finally, you should never be satisfied with good initial test results. There are many factors that are different in a real-time application from a simulated test. In fact, there is a special section later which offers pointers on how to make simulated tests better match the real-time application. Always bear in mind that setting up and designing a system is not an easy matter, so make sure you test and test again before committing money to your ideas. It is even a good idea to run through a real-time test, placing the orders but not actually having any money in the account or calling your broker. A few opportunities may be lost, but I can assure you, most people using most systems will avoid costly initial losses, which will more than outweigh the lost profit opportunities. Only when you have complete confidence in the system should it be traded.

Chapter 2
Advantages of Mechanical Systems

INTRODUCTION

Before we delve into the principles of devising an automated system, I would like to spend a little time on their strengths and limitations. Let us start with the advantages.

REMOVE EMOTION AND APPLY DISCIPLINE

A major advantage of a mechanical system is that it automatically decides when to take action, thereby removing emotion and prejudice. There is a rule of thumb in the futures industry that 90 percent of all traders quit as losers in the first year. Unfortunately, this is true because most neophytes trade on emotional, knee-jerk responses to news. Here is an example: the earnings news is bad, so they go short. This is already factored into the price because other seasoned market participants had anticipated this response. Next, the trend reverses against them. If the news is good, they go long and are again tripped out of a position. After enough losing trades they either lose heart, or their trading capital. Mechanical systems help us overcome these problems. The news may be atrocious, but when the system moves into a positive mode, a purchase is automatically made. When it appears that nothing can stop the market from going through the roof, the system will override all possible emotions and biases and quietly take us out.

Take a look at Fig. 2-1, which features four headlines for the U.S. stock market that appeared in November 1997. One gets the impression from these articles that the end of the world was at hand. I remember at the time thinking there had been more media coverage of the Asian crisis than I saw at the time of the 1987 crash. The market eventually moved lower, but not until it had experienced an advance to significant new recovery highs. This type of headline is always associated with sharply falling prices, which create the kind of environment that makes stock purchases unappetizing. The headlines would not be there unless emotions had been roused by declining prices. The arrow on Chart 2-1 shows the S&P Composite at the time of the articles. It is fairly obvious this was a great buying opportunity, but it would have been extremely difficult for the average investor to pick up the phone, call his broker and place a buy order. The advantage of a mechanical system is, when a signal is given, you do not need to worry about the news because it has already been tested under all kinds of conditions. The signals themselves indicate the market has already taken the news into consideration and is now looking ahead to a different scenario than expected by the crowd.

The next advantage is that mechanical systems make it easier to apply discipline to your trading. Most traders and investors lose in the market-

Figure 2-1 Cover Stories of November 1997 Asian Crisis

Chart 2-1 S&P Composite

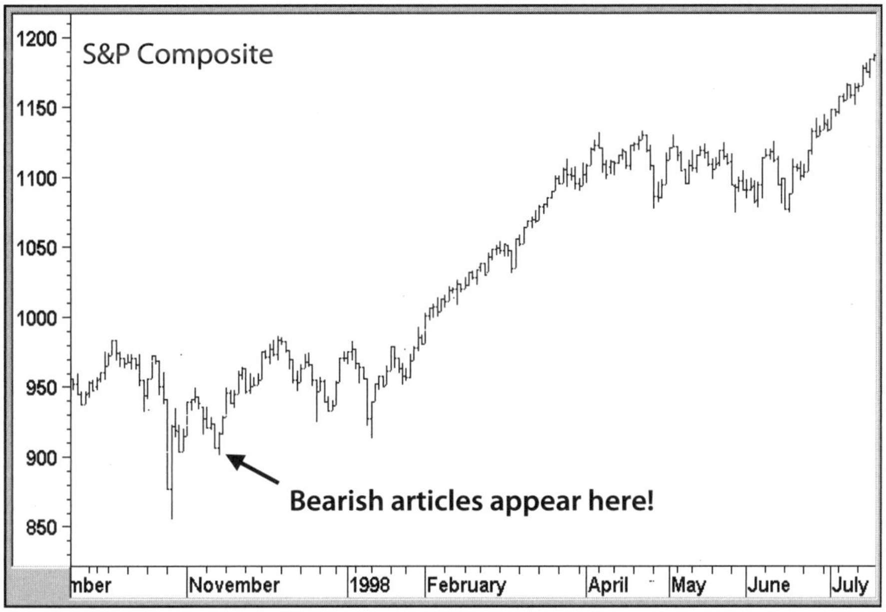

(Source: pring.com)

place because they lack discipline. Mechanical trading requires only one aspect of discipline—the commitment to follow the system. This can be very difficult at times. Look at Chart 2-2. The arrows represent buy signals, the flags represent the sells, and the upper line represents the equity from the system. You can see there were several *whipsaws,* or losing signals, in a row. Also, notice how the equity line is declining.

What you could not have known was that the January 1995 signal was followed by a very strong move. If the system had been properly tested, and you made the commitment to follow it, you would have certainly experienced a few frustrating trades, but the losses would have been recouped with the strong trend following the move shown in Chart 2-3.

GAIN CONSISTENCY AND MANAGE RISK

A well-defined mechanical system is more consistent than a system where buying and selling decisions are left to the individual. The consistency develops in controlling losses as well as profits and is one of the major factors in risk control. If you cannot define risk, how can it be managed?

Chart 2-2 DJ Utility Average

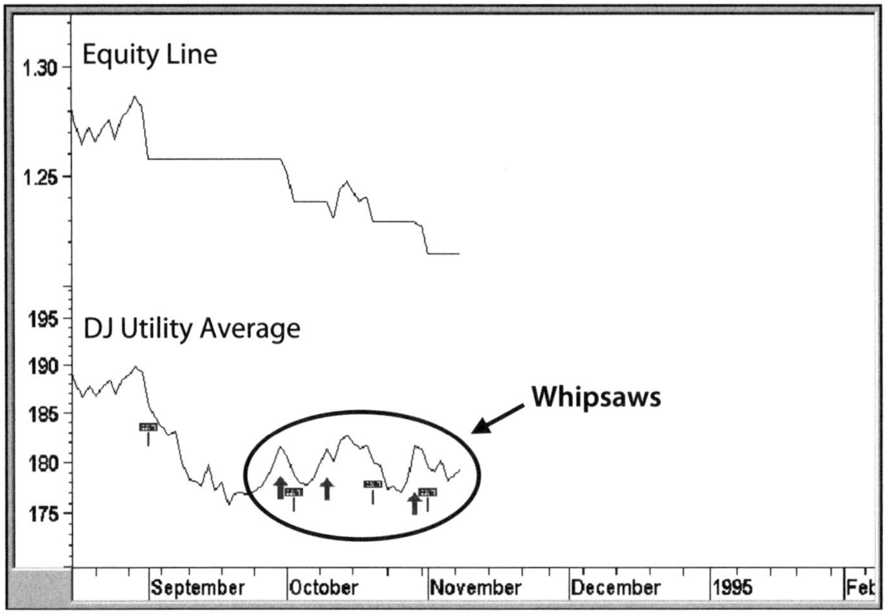

(Source: pring.com)

Chart 2-3 DJ Utility Average

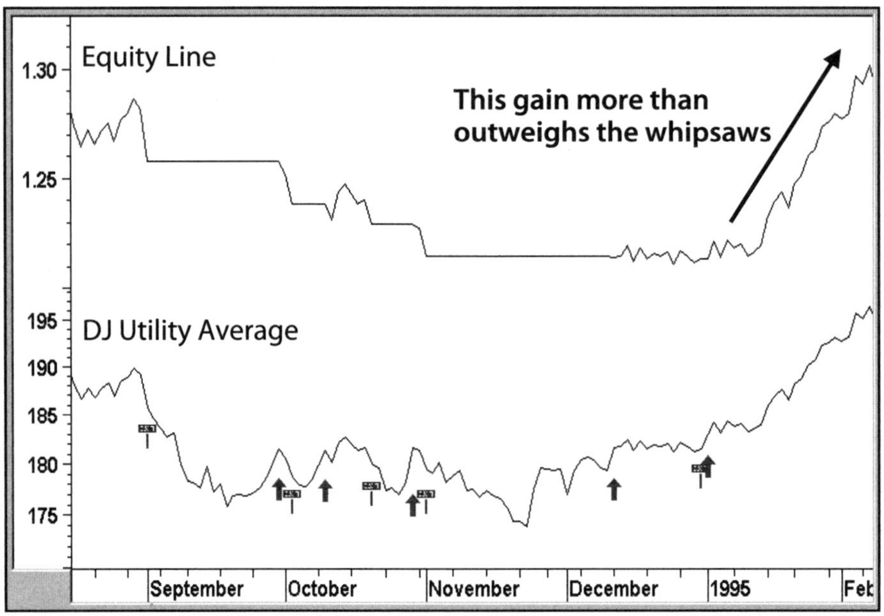

(Source: pring.com)

Automated systems help us do this successfully. The consistent results of a well-tested system also allow us to know in advance how we should react in any situation to the operation of pre-established and tested rules.

A mechanical system will let profits run in the event there is a strong uptrend but will automatically limit losses if a whipsaw signal occurs. Looking again at Chart 2-3, we see several whipsaws are followed by a strong move. When you think about it, the whipsaws represent uncertainty in the battle between buyers and sellers. The more whipsaws, the greater the uncertainty. Consequently, when one side or the other wins, the following move is that much greater because the losing side is exhausted. In this example, the bears certainly had had enough as prices rallied sharply.

Remember, a well-designed model will allow the trader or investor to participate in *every major trend*. A computer-tested system allows profit and risk to be quantified. Trading systems are far from perfect, but they can be used to systematically measure risk. If you do not have a sound risk management program, it is impossible to trade profitably with or without a system. One thing a good, statistically derived system can do is give you an estimate of future profits and risk where it is possible to judge the quality of the return. On the one hand, it is good to earn a $100,000 profit, but if it is earned by risking $100,000, this is not a favorable risk-reward ratio. On the other hand, an exhaustively tested system that returns $100,000 with a maximum drawdown of $10,000, is a much safer bet. It certainly does not guarantee you will only lose $10,000, because there is no reason why the drawdown could not exceed the maximum experienced in the test period. It is unlikely, but can never be ruled out, even with the most exhaustively tested systems.

Chapter 3
Disadvantages of Mechanical Systems

HISTORY DOES NOT ALWAYS REPEAT ITSELF

Although I believe the advantages of mechanical systems outweigh the disadvantages, we still need to consider their disadvantages in order to come to a balanced conclusion. The first is that no system will work all the time, and there may be long periods when it fails to work. Indeed, many people regard systems as being successful if they offer as many losing as winning trades, provided, of course, the winning trades beat the losing ones, and the losing trades do not experience any serious drawdowns.

Using past data to predict the future is not necessarily a valid approach because the character of the market often changes. Look at Chart 3-1 for instance. During the 1993—1996 period, the buy signals generated by the Relative Momentum Index crossing above its oversold zone triggered some good signals for the Commodity Research Bureau (CRB) Composite. Each one, with the exception of the late 1994 signal, was followed by a pretty good rally. However, when we move to the 1997—1998 period, shown in Chart 3-2, the signals are not so good. This is because the first period was a primary bull market and the second a primary bear market. Chart 3-3 shows

Chart 3-1 Commodity Research Bureau (CRB) Composite and a Relative Momentum Index

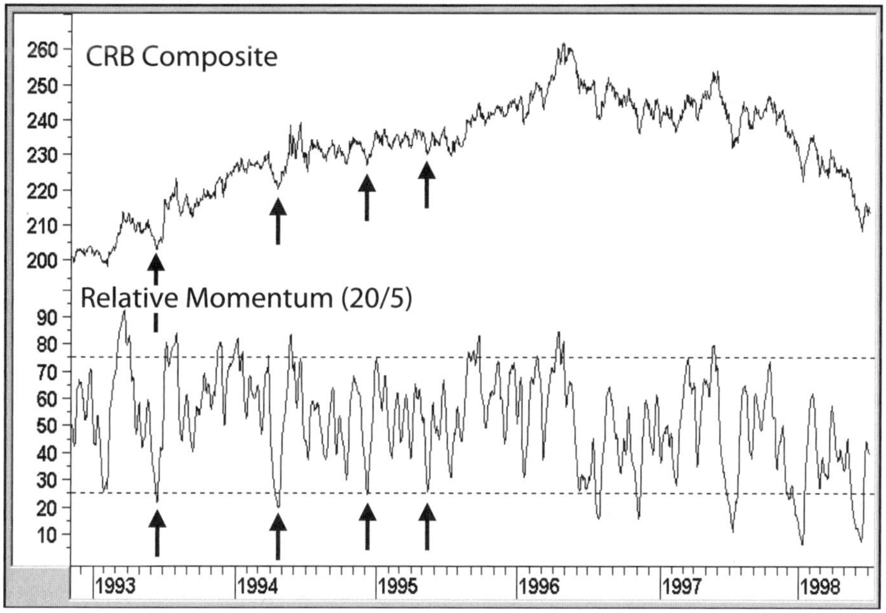

(Source: pring.com)

Chart 3-2 CRB Composite and a Relative Momentum Index

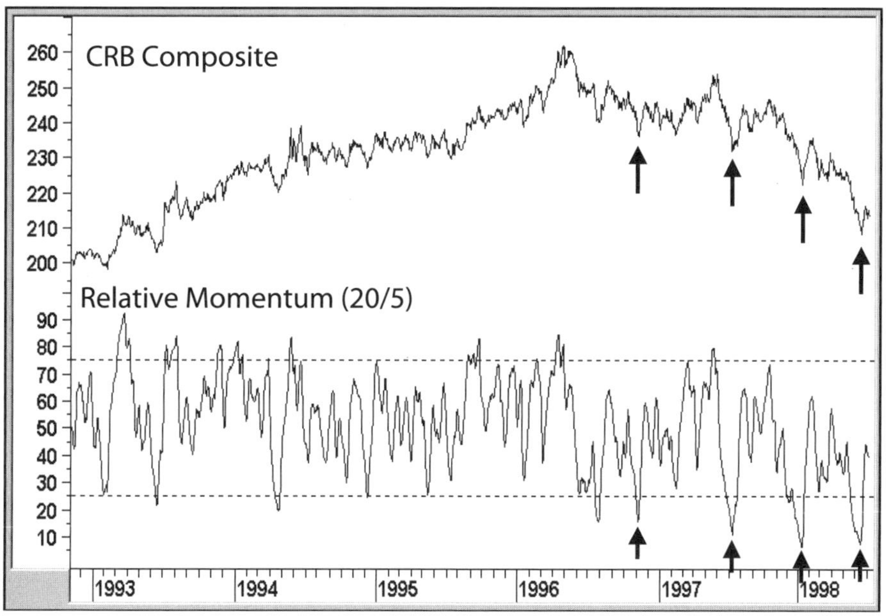

(Source: pring.com)

Chart 3-3 CRB Composite and a Relative Momentum Index

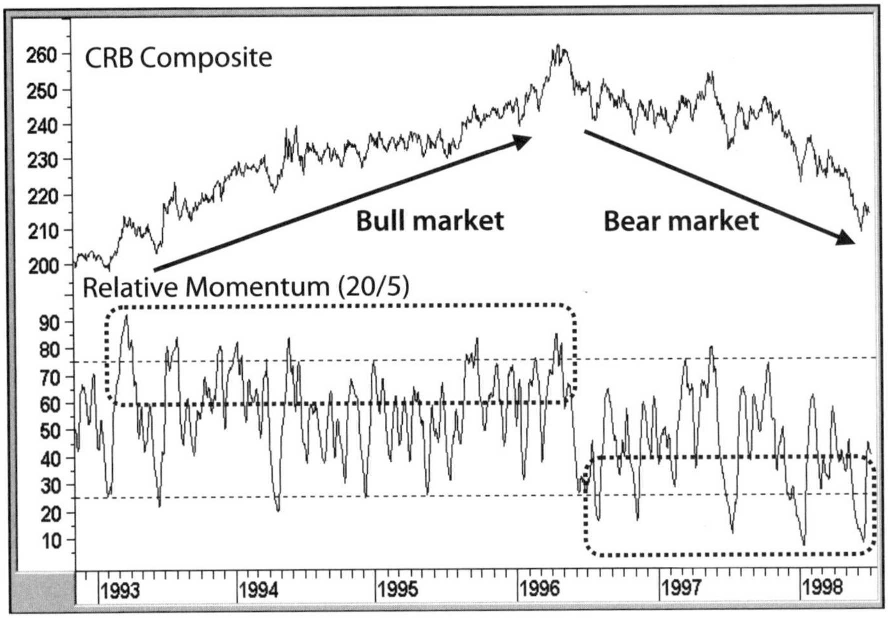

(Source: pring.com)

both periods. You can see there is a distinct difference between the bullish and bearish environments. See how the oscillator reaches and stays in an overbought condition during the bull phase. Now look at the bear market in closer detail. The relative momentum indicator stays in the oversold area most of the time. Also, the oversold readings do not generate the kind of rallies they did during the bull phase. As we will later learn, markets react differently in bull and bear markets.

Most people try to get the best or optimum fit when devising a system, but experience and research tell us a historical "best fit" does not usually translate into the future. One of the most common mistakes people make is to try to get the best results historically when designing a system. We should be interested in the future, not the past. In the process of obtaining the best fit for past data, we may be forced to make compromises and invent all kinds of rules. This type of approach will almost guarantee that the system will not work in the future.

RANDOM EVENTS AND CHANGING CONDITIONS CAN BE MAJOR PROBLEMS

Random events can easily jeopardize a badly conceived system. Chart 3-4 shows a classic example that occurred in Hong Kong during the 1987 crash. Because the market was closed for seven days, there would have been no opportunity to get out, even if a sell signal had been triggered. True, this was an unusual event, but it is surprising how often special situations upset the best rules. The chart also shows the 1989 Tiananmen Square massacre was followed by a sharp drop. A nimble system based on short-term criteria may get you out on a timely basis, but one assuming intermediate time-frames will not. You may say to yourself, "It is always advisable to trade short-term systems because of this example." Bear in mind, however, that a substantial amount of short-term volatility is caused by unexpected news

Chart 3-4 Hang Seng Index

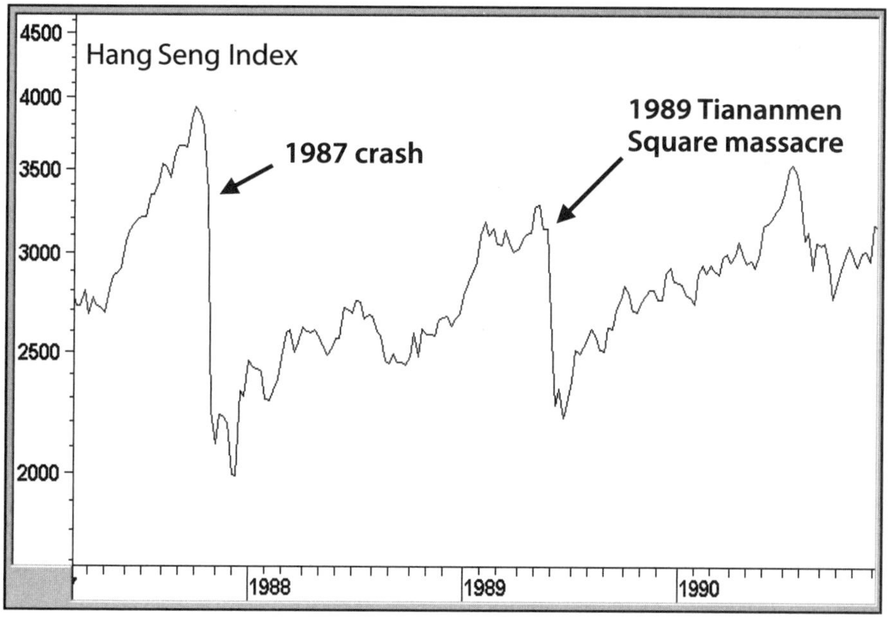

(Source: pring.com)

events that affect markets for a day or two at the most. In these instances, it is unlikely that systems based on longer-term trends will be affected unless the random event is the start of a new trend. Regardless of the frame in which you are working, it is impossible to avoid random events. While they do not occur very often, their existence is, nevertheless, a disadvantage of mechanical trading systems that must be recognized — a sharp reminder of the importance of using a diversified approach. If you have confidence in a system, and it works well with several different securities, trade it in those markets. If one of them experiences an unusual event, the overall results will be more stable.

The most successful mechanical systems are trend following in nature. However, every security experiences periods of ranging action. Chart 3-5 features trade in live cattle between 1979 and 1984, a great trading range. Had we known ahead of time the nature of this trading action, it would have been relatively easy to design a system based on the overbought/oversold oscillators. Most systems are based on trend-following devices, so this commodity would have represented a difficult challenge, unless based on extremely short-term timeframes.

Backtesting will not necessarily simulate what actually happened. For example, it is not always possible to get an execution at the price indicated

Chart 3-5 Live Cattle

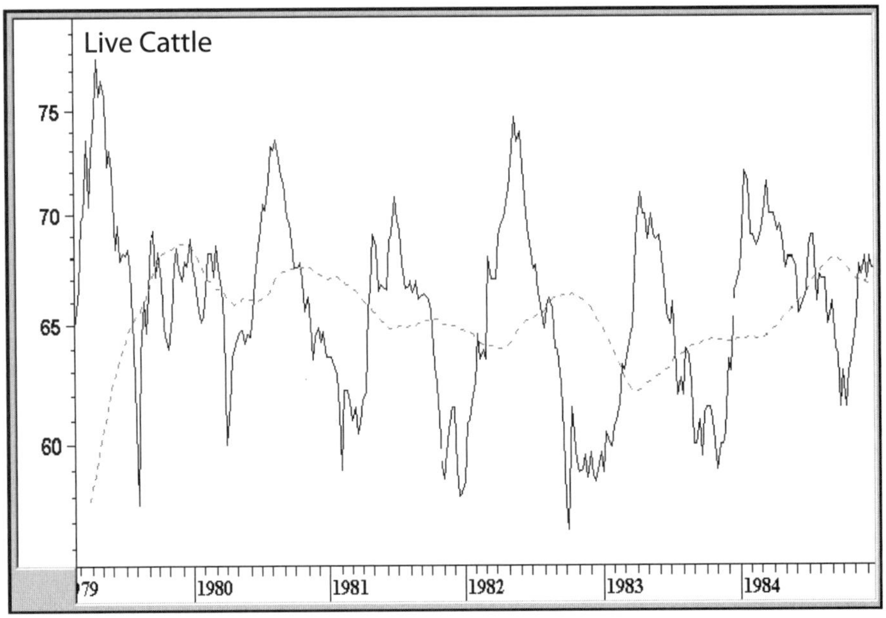

(Source: pring.com)

Chart 3-6 Newmont Gold

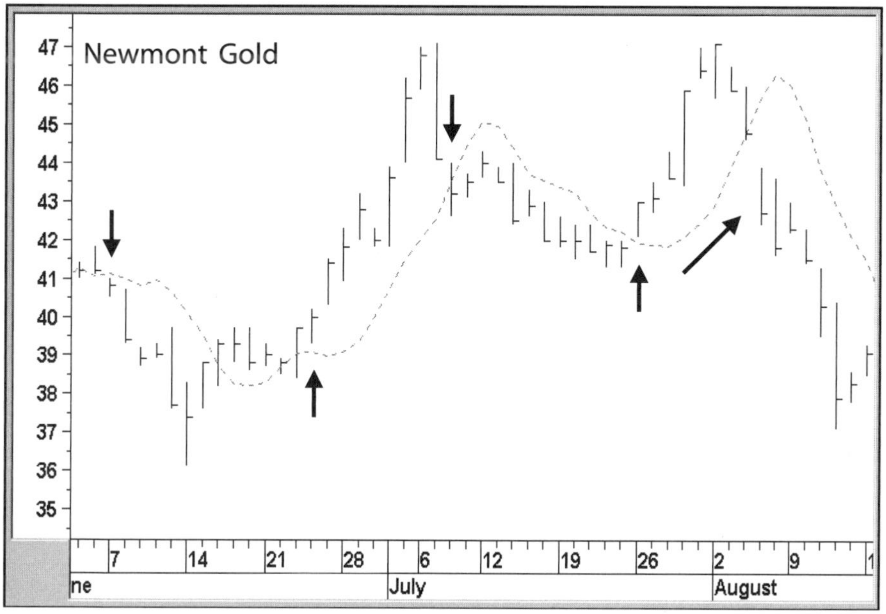

(Source: pring.com)

by the system, because of illiquidity, failure of your broker to execute orders on time, and so forth. Look at Chart 3-6—a bar chart of Newmont Gold. The arrows show the buy and sell points where the closing price crosses above and below the moving average. The system appears to work quite well. The August sell signal called for the liquidation of the position. However, immediately after, the price crosses the moving average. In reality, you can see there was no opportunity to do this since it experienced a huge gap. This is an unusual situation, but it is surprising how many unusual things happen when you apply systems to the market.

Chapter 4
Designing a System

TRENDING ENVIRONMENTS

A well-designed system should capitalize on the advantages of the mechanical approach, but provision should also be made to overcome some of the pitfalls and disadvantages discussed earlier. This section describes how this can be achieved. First, we will take a closer look at the two principal trading environments — trending and trading ranges. Because all securities have different characteristics, even specific ones experience character changes over different periods of time.

Chart 4-1 features the yield on 3-month commercial paper. Its characteristics are clearly suitable for moving-average (MA) crossovers and the other types of trend-following systems. Short-term interest rates have traditionally been strong trending markets and crossovers are rarely associated with whipsaws. Obviously, it would be great if all securities acted this way, but, unfortunately, they do not. The approach in Chart 4-1 uses a 12-month MA. For most traders, this represents an unacceptable time length, so it is very important to define the risk because MA crossovers are always a trade-off between timeliness and sensitivity. In Chart 4-2, the maximum distance in the short-term MA (the dashed line) is the maximum risk. Unfortunately, it whips around and gives several false signals. Although the risk of the individual trade defined by the crossover of this MA is small, the chance of an unprofitable signal is much greater.

An MA with a longer timespan offers greater maximum risk, but fewer whipsaws. In Chart 4-3, the longer-term average is represented by the solid line. You can see the maximum distance between the price and this MA is much, much greater, but nonetheless, there are substantially fewer whipsaws.

Chart 4-1 Commercial Paper Yield

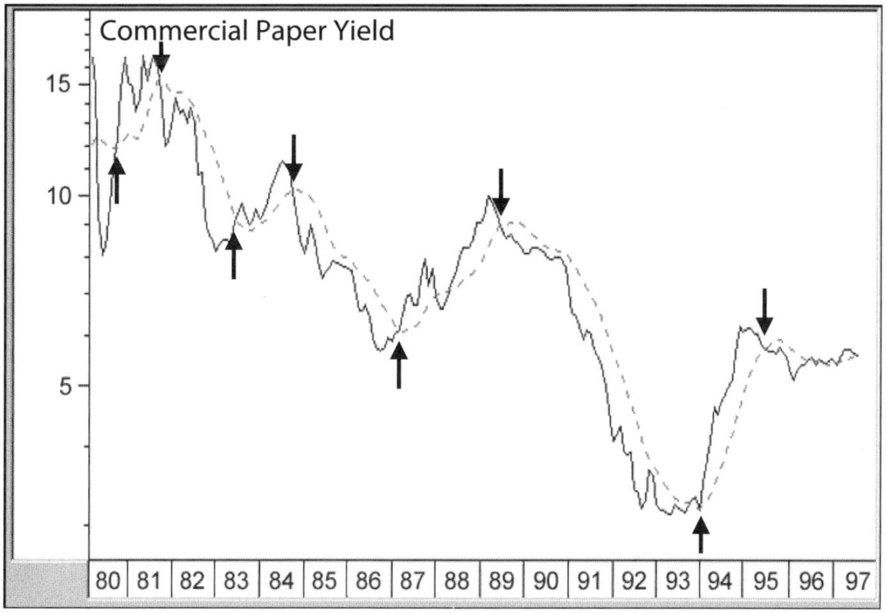

(Source: pring.com)

Chart 4-2 Timeliness Versus Sensitivity

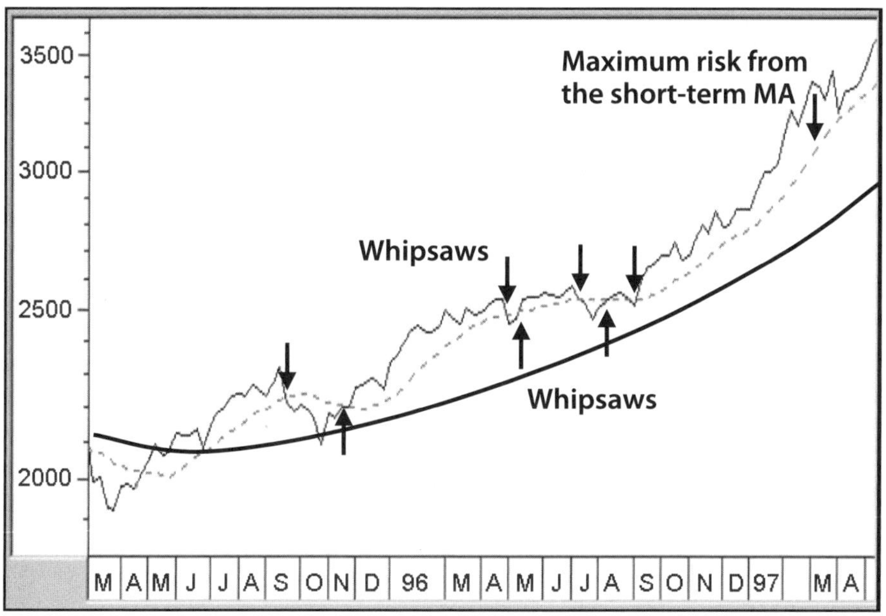

(Source: pring.com)

Chart 4-3 Timeliness Versus Sensitivity

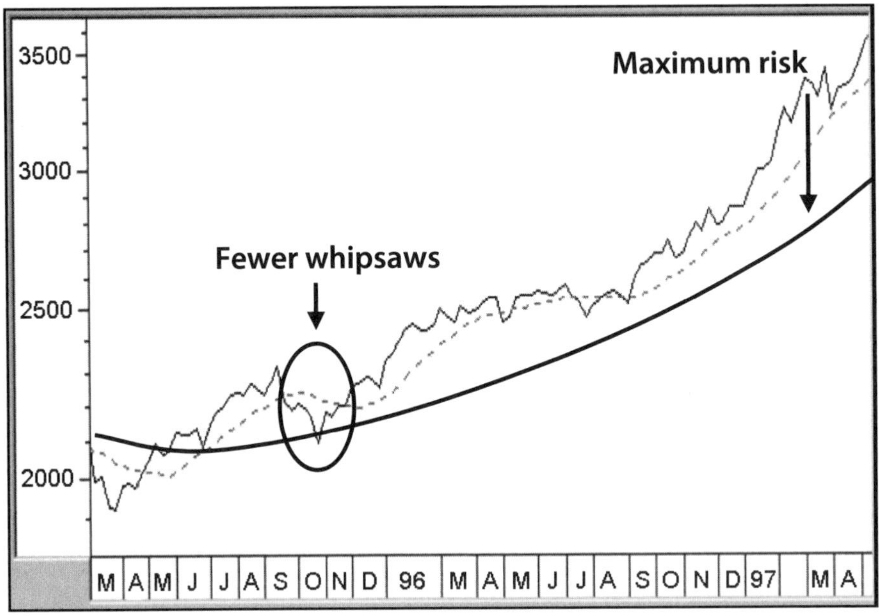

(Source: pring.com)

TRADING RANGE ENVIRONMENTS

Take a look at the trading range shown in Chart 4-4. Here we can see that MA crossovers are virtually useless. Since the average moves right through the middle of the price fluctuations, the crossovers almost always result in unprofitable signals. In this type of environment, oscillators really come into their own because they are continually moving from overbought to oversold extremes, which trigger timely buy and sell signals. If you anticipate a security is likely to experience a trading range, then a mechanical system incorporating an oscillator makes sense. Chart 4-5 is an example of a trading range market between 1989 and 1993. The mark makes very little net progress, but it is possible to use the overbought and oversold crossovers as buy and sell signals. The first buy would be generated in mid 1989 as the ROC rallies back across the oversold zone on its way towards zero. Had the following sell signal been used to initiate a short position, a nasty loss would have resulted because there was no intervening buy signal. The next time the oscillator crossed an extreme zone was late 1990, and it triggered a sell signal. Other signals between 1991 and 1993 also worked out fairly well. The early 1990 sell crossover represents a good example of why a system design should allow for countervailing signals.

Chart 4-4 Live Cattle

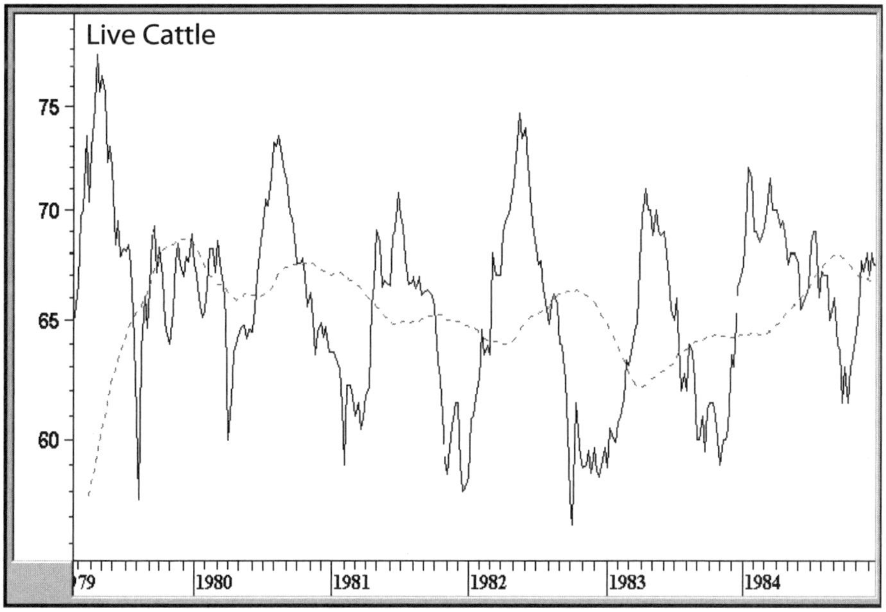

(Source: pring.com)

Chart 4-5 German Mark

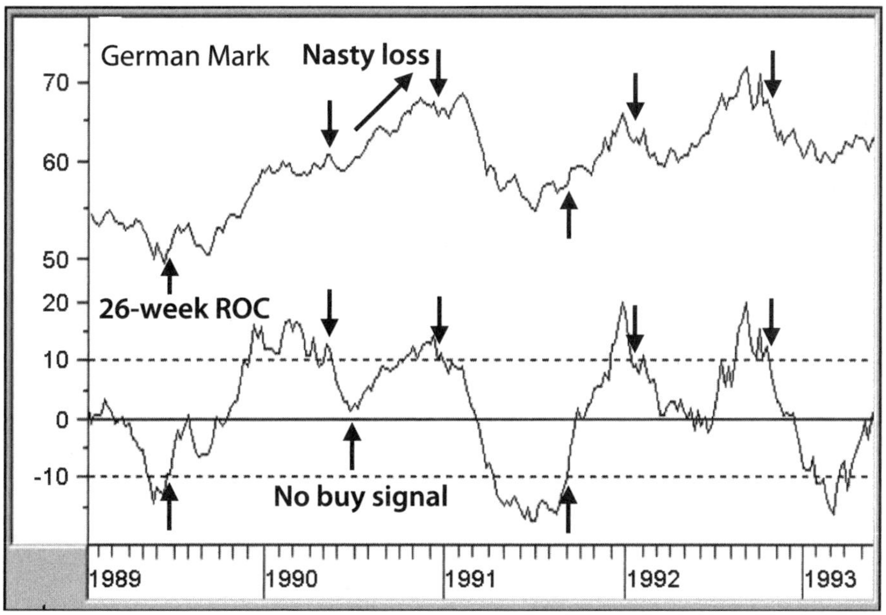

(Source: pring.com)

The risk and reward for oscillator-type signals generated from overbought and oversold extremes are shown in Fig. 4-1. The number of potential trading opportunities is represented on the horizontal axis and the risk on the vertical axis. There are very few times when an oscillator is extremely overbought or oversold, but these are the occasions when the profit per trade is at its greatest and the risk is at its smallest. Moderately overbought conditions are much more plentiful, but the profits are lower, and the risk higher. Taken to the final extreme, slightly overbought or oversold conditions are numerous, but the risk per trade is much higher and profits are significantly lower. Ideally, a mechanical trading system should be designed to take advantage of a situation where profits per trade are high and risk is low. Therefore, execution of a good system requires some degree of patience because these types of opportunities are limited. During a persistent uptrend or downtrend, the oscillator is of relatively little use because it gives premature buy and sell signals, often taking the trader out at the beginning of a major move.

Also, turning points in price trends are often preceded by a divergence in the oscillator. So, it is a good idea to combine signals from extreme oscillator readings with some kind of MA crossover. This will not result in a perfect indicator, but it might help to filter out some of the whipsaws. By

Figure 4-1 Risk/Reward Versus Opportunity

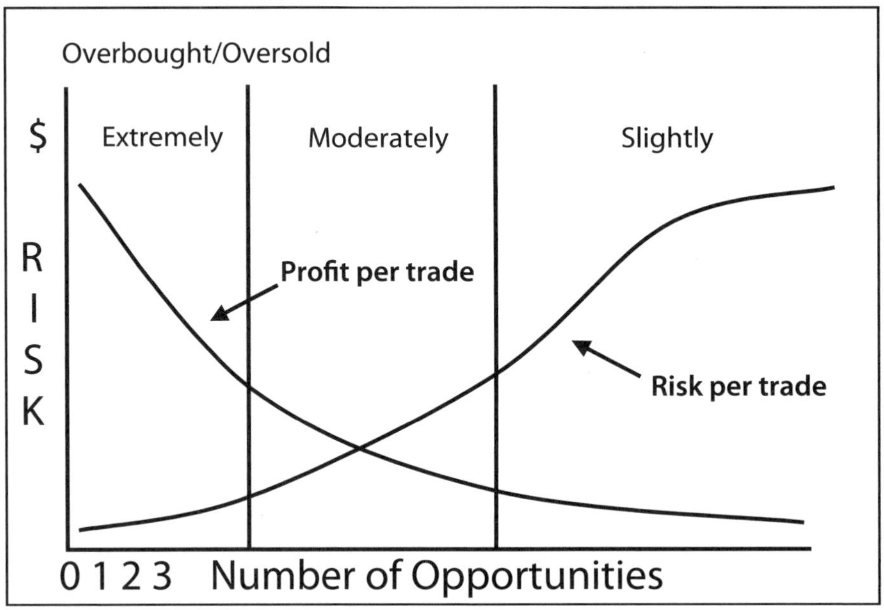

waiting for a confirmation of a trend reversal in the price itself, such a system would allow the trader to ride on the trend for that much longer. The ideal automated system should therefore include a combination of an oscillator and a trend-following indicator. I will have more to say on both of these points in Chapter 13.

ESTABLISH A TIMEFRAME

The next step is to establish a timeframe. First, you have to decide on the span that suits your personality. If you are a day trader, you certainly will not appreciate waiting several months for the next buy or sell signal. Even if you are making money, the action will be too tame. You will invariably start to anticipate signals, losing the discipline the system was supposed to instill. Chart 4-6 features the S&P Composite together with its 12-month MA. The buy and sell signals from the crossovers were good, but many people would not have had the patience to wait for them. This was clearly a very profitable system during the 1990s, but I would be surprised if a short-term trader

Chart 4-6 S&P Composite and a 12-Month Moving Average (MA)

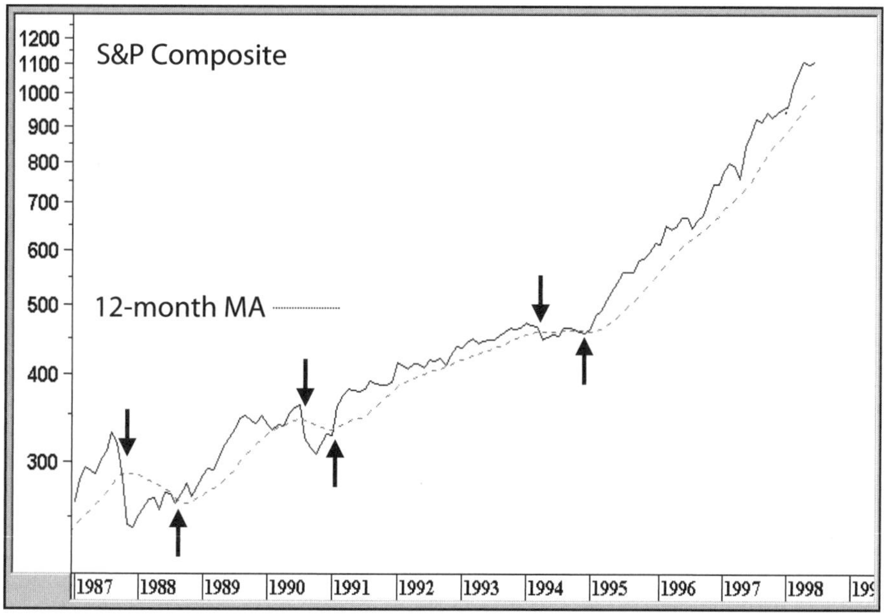

(Source: pring.com)

would have had the patience and discipline to execute it. If you are an investor or a person who does not have the time to devote to day-to-day market activity, you will need to design a system where signals are generated with a Friday close or month-end close.

If you want the excitement of the intraday fracas, then a long-term system will be of no use. Chart 4-7 features a 350-minute MA of the Philadelphia Gold and Silver Share Index (XAU). Buy and sell signals are triggered on a daily basis and you could be in and out several times a day using a shorter-term average.

These monthly and intraday charts represent the two extremes where most people will find themselves falling. I am sure you can see how easy it would be to achieve a mismatch between your personality and the time-frame you choose. Personally, I find the longer-term systems based on monthly, or even weekly, data tend to offer much greater consistency and profits. They also involve far less work. This is not meant to imply they are perfect, because they are not. It also does not mean every short-term system is useless, since that is certainly not the case. Generally, systems based on long-term timeframes work better than those constructed from shorter-term frames. This is because there is a tendency for longer-term trends to

Chart 4-7 XAU and a 350-Minute MA

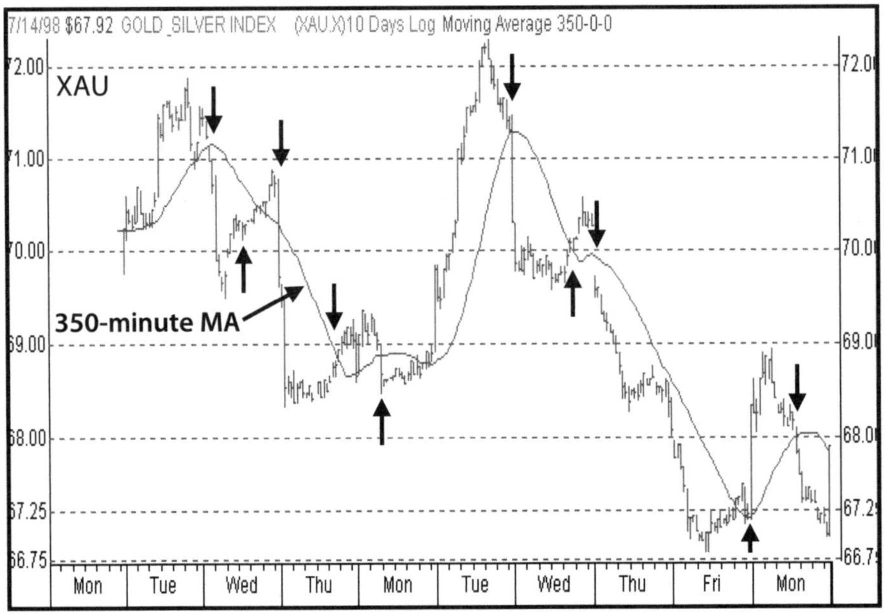

(Source: pring.com)

revolve around emerging economic fundamentals, while random events and noise have a far greater destabilizing effect on systems based on shorter-term trends. Once an acceptable timeframe for your emotional and physical needs has been selected, the next step is to establish a methodology for the system.

ESTABLISH A METHODOLOGY

Choosing and/or establishing a methodology is perhaps the most critical step in designing a system. Often, the methodology is called the *trading strategy* for the system. The process typically starts off with a trading idea, which is tested in a raw form. Later, it is refined and finally optimized.

A strategy is the method that triggers buy and sell signals. A symmetrical trading system is a sell signal, which is the reverse of a buy signal. An MA crossover would qualify as a symmetrical trading system. An asymmetrical system occurs when the sell signal is different from the buy signal. An example would be to buy on a relative strength indicator (RSI) oversold crossover and sell on an MA crossover, as shown in Chart 4-8.

Chart 4-8 Strong Asia Pacific Fund and a 14-Day Relative Strength Indicator (RSI)

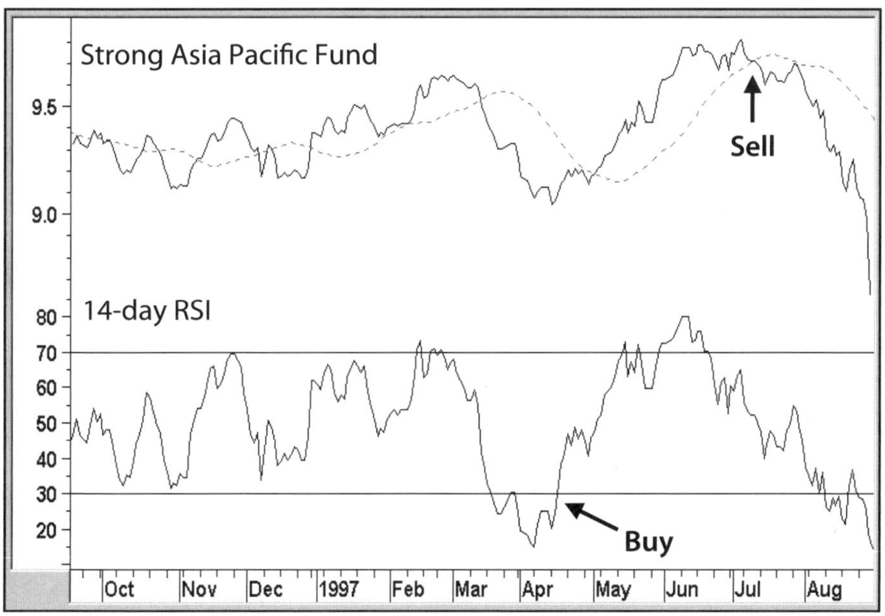

(Source: pring.com)

It is important to come up with an idea you think will work and have confidence in. It could be a technical system based on MA crossovers and oscillators, a value system based on fundamentals, or—my favorite—an intermarket system based on technical relationships. It does not necessarily have to be *your* idea. It could be something you picked up elsewhere, say a modified version of one of the ideas found in this book. The key is, you must have a starting point of some kind. If it does not fit the bill, you can always modify it later.

Chapter 5
Practical Guidelines in System Design

DEFINE THE SYSTEM PRECISELY AND LEARN THE SECURITY'S CHARACTERISTICS

Now it is time for us to turn our attention to several practical guidelines of system design. One of the most important steps in implementing the trading strategy is to define the system precisely. This is meaningful for two reasons. First, if the rules occasionally leave you in doubt about their correct interpretation, some degree of subjectivity is bound to creep in. Second, for every buy signal, there should be a sell signal, and vice versa. If a system has been devised using an overbought crossover as a sell and an oversold crossover as a buy, it might work quite well for a time. There could be long periods, though, where a countervailing signal is not generated simply because the indicator does not move to the other extreme. Failure to precisely define the system can result in significant losses. An example is shown in Chart 5-1, which features the Nikkei and a 39-week rate of change (ROC).

There is a nice buy signal shown in late 1990, which proves to be temporarily profitable. This is a bear market, though, and the price quickly declines again, subsequently falling to a new low. In this instance, there is no countervailing sell signal because the oscillator never moves to an overbought condition. These are the kinds of problems that can easily arise in complicated systems, incorporating many rules and indicators, and certainly justifies the principle of keeping things as simple as possible. Another

Chart 5-1 Nikkei and a 39-Week Rate of Change (ROC)

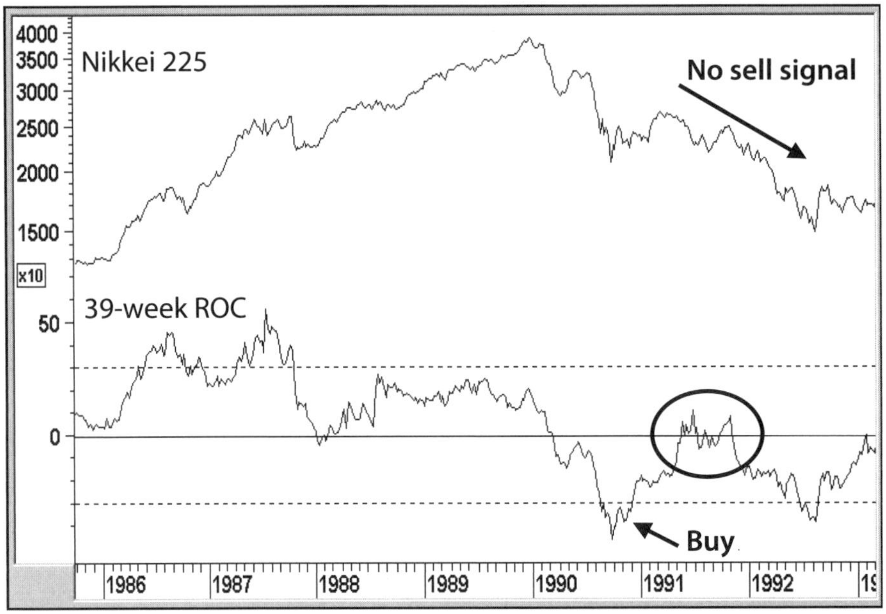

(Source: pring.com)

word of warning — never introduce a subjective rule into the system because it will totally eliminate any sense of objectivity the system was designed to achieve in the first place.

Try to get a fix on the characteristic of the security being traded. Although this is easier said than done, you will find that some markets have strong trending characteristics while others do not. Those that do not will lend themselves to trend-following systems incorporating MAs. Chart 5-2 shows a good example using a 25-day moving average advanced by five days. The Wilshire Target Large Company Growth Fund tends to be in stocks with a relatively predictable earnings trend. Since it is a mutual fund, it consists of a portfolio of stocks, and a diversified portfolio tends to experience greater trending characteristics than an individual stock. This is because individual stocks can be subject to corporate events, such as earnings surprises, and so forth. In Chart 5-2, there are a few whipsaws that are flagged by the two ellipses, but by and large, the trending characteristics of this fund offer good buy and sell signals as flagged by the arrows.

Alternatively, some securities experience strong price moves, which are invariably retraced. This usually happens with most stocks where earnings trends are erratic, such as mines. In Chart 5-3, you can see there were some excellent swings, such as the two marked with the up arrows. Unfortunately, the reversals were so sharp the MA approach missed much of the move.

Chart 5-2 Wilshire Target Large Company Growth

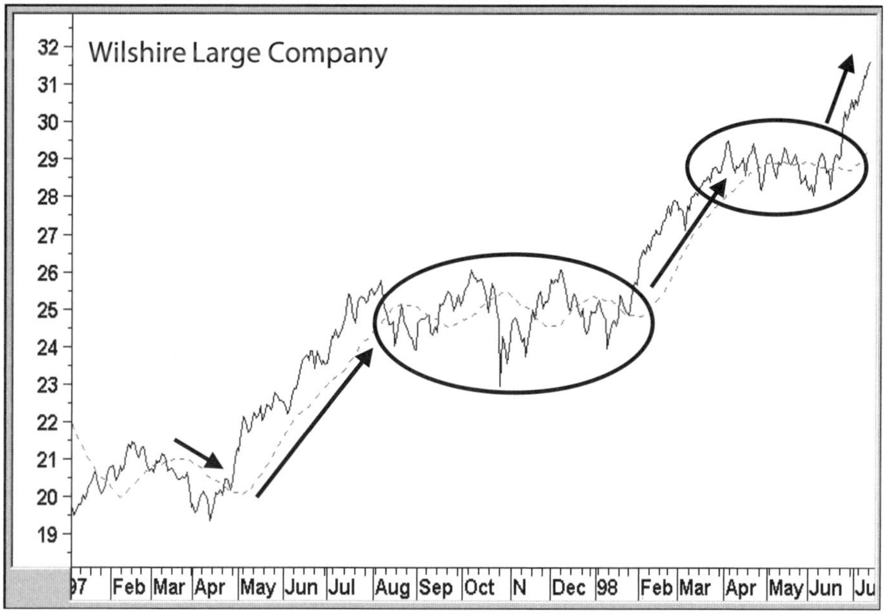

(Source: pring.com)

Chart 5-3 Newmont Mining

(Source: pring.com)

The two horizontal arrows joining the buy and sell crossovers in Chart 5-4 show there were not any worthwhile profits to be made. If we take this same period using an overbought/oversold crossover approach, as I did in Chart 5-5, we can see it worked much better. This is an interesting example. Here, I am using a 14-day RSI flagged by the vertical buy and sell arrows. The two arrows (A and B) joining the buy and sell signals are sloping up in a positive way. In this kind of situation, it is often a good idea to design a system that involves an oscillator as well as a trend-following device.

DEVELOP FILTERS AND KEEP THINGS SIMPLE

In Chapter 1, we discussed the idea of using several indicators as a cross check or filter. You may find that a system based on one indicator works very well, but even the best indicators fail from time to time. Therefore, it is a good idea to incorporate several indicators into a system so they can act as a check on each other. I define *technical analysis* as the *art of identifying a trend reversal at an early stage and riding on that trend until the weight of the evidence*

Chart 5-4 Newmont Mining

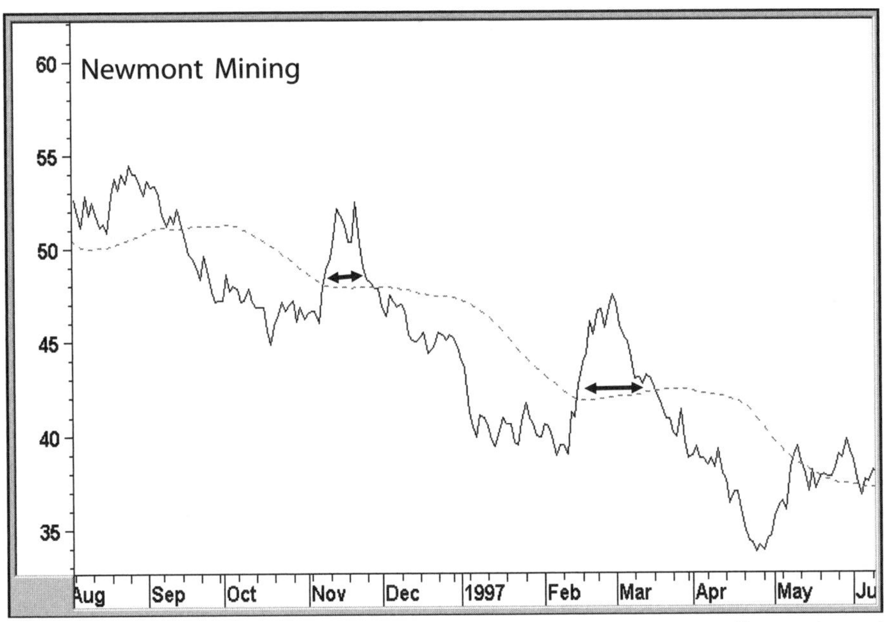

(Source: pring.com)

Chart 5-5 Newmont Mining and a 14-Day RSI

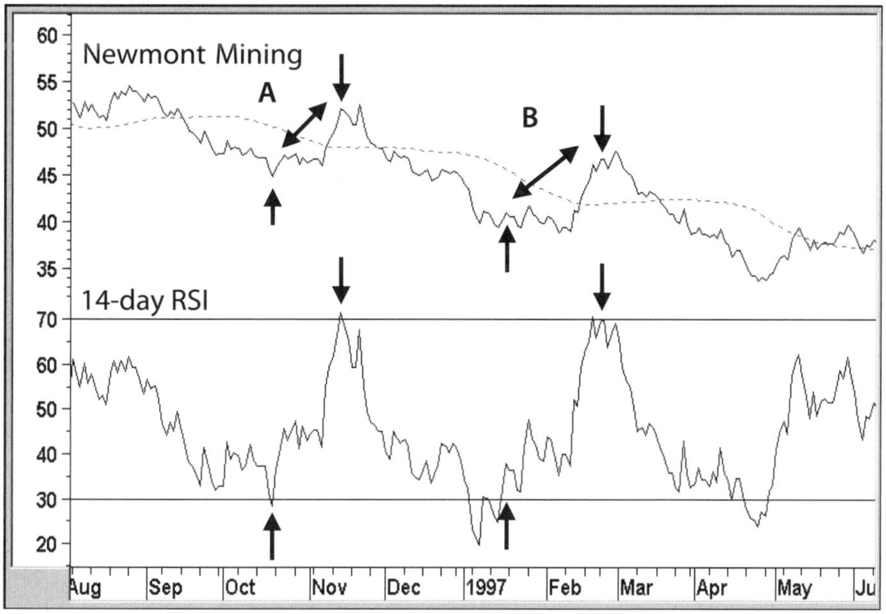

(Source: pring.com)

shows or proves the trend has reversed. I particularly emphasize the words *weight of the evidence* because the more indicators that point in a specific direction, the greater the probability the trend reversal signal is valid. This means if we employ two or more indicators or filters, the system is, other things being equal, likely to be more consistent and reliable. For example, the one featured in Chart 5-6 initiates positions when the price is above its 25-day MA crossover. In this example, we have only one buy and one sell, and the buy signal develops as the price is breaking out from a small pattern. This approach eliminates the many whipsaws that developed in February and early March. The January 1998 peak did not qualify. Although the price was above its moving average, it was not at a 20-day high.

There is no limit to the amount of filters you can introduce into a system. However, I would not recommend more than three or four. Otherwise, things become too complicated. Remember, the best systems are those that are kept as simple as possible. In fact, some of the best approaches I have ever seen incorporate intermarket relationships, where one market is used to predict the course of another. Great results can be achieved by using an MA crossover for each market. This approach is not complicated or sophisticated but is exceptionally effective.

Chart 5-6 Newmont Minng

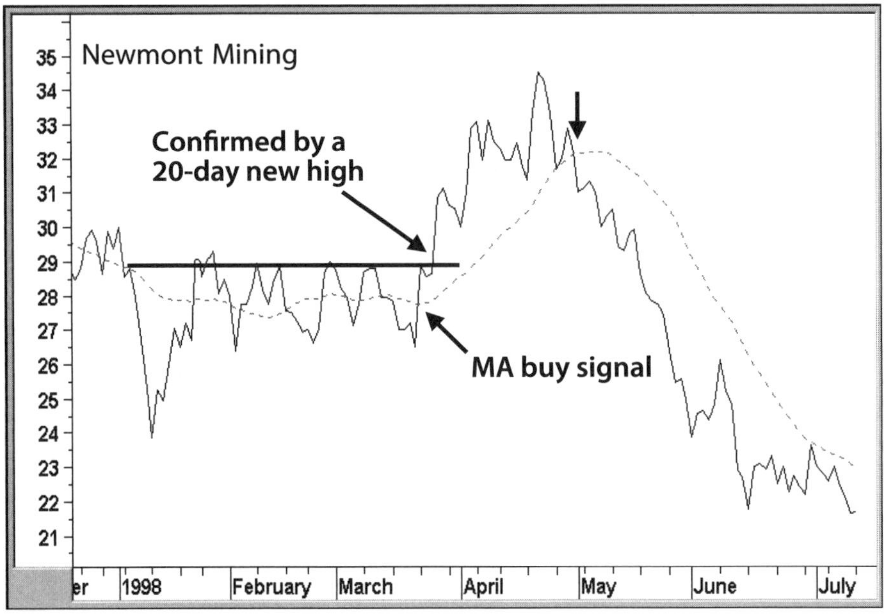

(Source: pring.com)

Keep it simple. Keep the rules simple, few in number, logical, and resist the temptation to invent special rules that make your back testing more profitable. If you do, the results are more likely to be acceptable in the future, when profitability counts. I cannot emphasize enough how important the "keep it simple" rule is.

Chapter 6
Tools for Risk Management

INTRODUCTION

Managing risk typically gets less attention than trying to earn profits but is actually more important. I can tell that any professional worth his salt will concentrate on limiting risk before he worries about getting profits. If you are highly leveraged, losses can quickly become unlimited, whereas profits are typically finite. There are several points here that should be considered.

DESIGN FOR CONSISTENCY

Many people consider a system to be successful if it experiences several profitable trades. Unfortunately, the law of gravity often works too well with such systems, and what goes up comes down equally as fast. Consequently, it is a better idea to design a system that offers slow but consistent profits. In markets, unless you are really lucky, the tortoise always beats the hare. Even when you are lucky, chances are you personally will take the credit rather than putting it down to luck.

Chart 6-1 of the Eurotop Index, comprised of 250 European blue chips, shows a fairly consistent system. You can see this because the equity line slopes up from the bottom left to the top right of the chart with little in the way of dips. As I mentioned before, sometimes you get lucky and do not recognize this fact. This system falls into the "lucky fluke" category because, at first glance, it looks pretty good. After I expanded the history, though,

Chart 6-1 Eurotop Equity Index

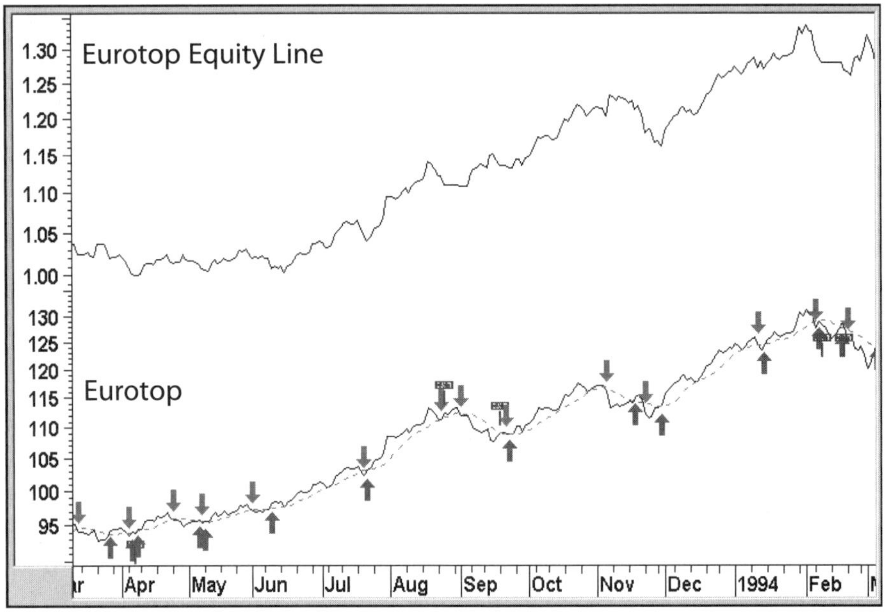

(Source: pring.com)

which is shown in Chart 6-2, the first glance assumption does not look so promising. The price work contained in the triangle was shown in Chart 6-1. Overall, you can see the system experienced a great deal of inconsistency and was not very helpful. Chart 6-1 also shows that it is very important to test over long periods if you are to obtain anything that can be projected profitably into the future. The secret is to design a system that harvests profits slowly, but consistently, over a long period of time. I would always prefer to trade a system that triggers more numerous profitable signals and earns a good, but smaller profit, than one that gives few signals and makes more profit—assuming the number of signals is not so great as to be affected by huge commission and slippage costs. The point is, a system that can consistently generate profitable signals has a better chance of working in real time than one with a few signals. One important assumption—we are comparing two systems of the same timeframe. In other words, it would be unfair to compare a monthly-based system, with a few signals, to a daily based one over the same period because the daily-based system would obviously trigger far more signals. On the other hand, a daily-based signal that triggered 30 signals and returned slightly less profit than one that triggered six signals would, other things being equal, be preferred.

Chart 6-2 Eurotop Equity Index

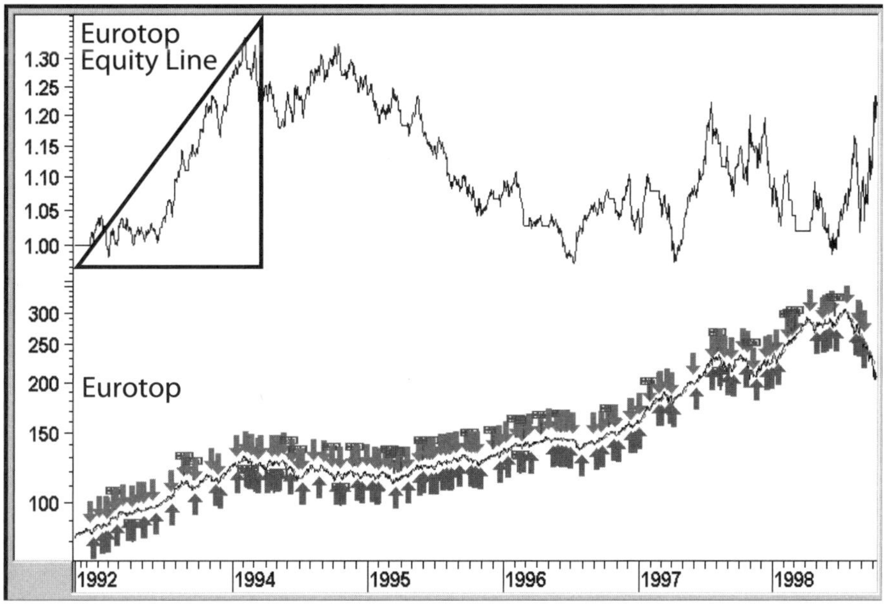

(Source: pring.com)

LIMIT DRAWDOWNS AND PROTECT PROFIT

Another way risk can be better managed is to try to limit drawdowns. *Drawdowns are defined as a loss in equity from a previous equity high.* Let us say you had successfully climbed Mount Everest, a 29,000 foot peak, and then fell down 2,000 feet. Well, the 2,000 feet would be your equivalent of a drawdown. When most traders enter a trade, their eyes are glued to the profit potential. Successful traders look over their shoulders at the potential risk. Remember the old saying mentioned earlier, "Cut losses and let profits run." Designing a system to limit drawdowns is addressing the first part of the equation—cut losses. This is very important because *contra trend moves are usually the ones where losses will be generated.* Consequently, the system you adopt should take this into consideration. The third way risk can be managed is to protect profits.

It is human tendency to register market prices with profits or losses of open positions. However, the profit or loss is not an actual reality until the position is closed. This feeling of joy when a trade is in a profitable situation leads to complacency. We tend to think the profit is already there when it is not—unless we decide to take it by liquidating the position. With some systems, such as those based on MA crossovers, this will not be possible because the price, at the time, will have moved a tremendous distance away from the moving average.

Look at the example of Merrill Lynch in Chart 6-3 of Merrill Lynch. See how the arrow marks the distance between the high for the rally and the level of the moving average. If we wait for the price to move back to the average or for the average to come up to the price, a substantial amount of paper profit will be foregone. For this reason, it is often a good idea to introduce a profit management technique into the system. This could involve a trailing stop, which is moved progressively closer to the current price. Alternatively, the stop could be triggered if the equity falls by a specific amount below the maximum equity in the trade.

Another way profits can be protected is to close out a trade immediately when the price reaches a specific objective. This could be an actual price or a targeted overbought reading in a specific oscillator. In Chart 6-4, the downward-pointing arrows mark when the oscillator reaches an overbought reading.

A fourth way to manage risk is to use a diverse portfolio. Risks are limited if you place smaller bets over several different systems and a num-

Chart 6-3 Merrill Lynch

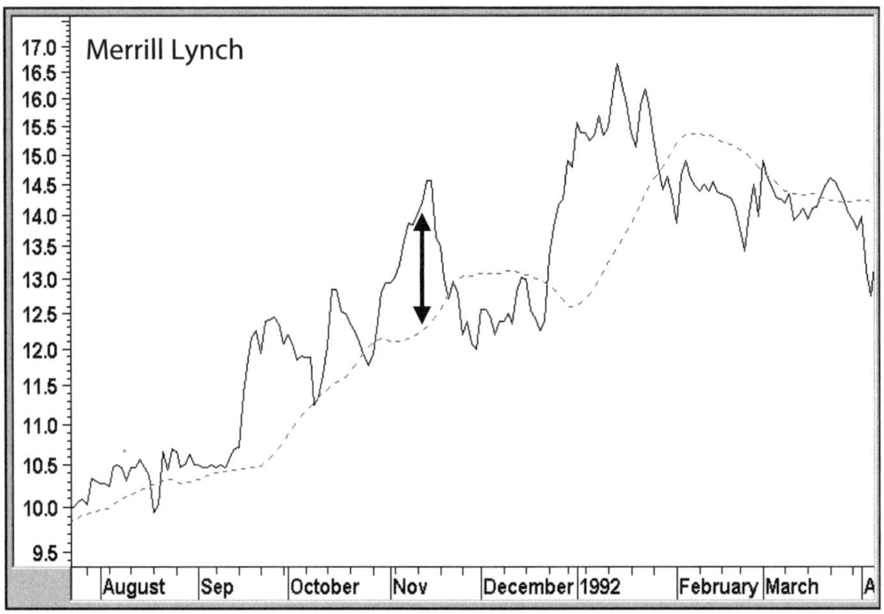

(Source: pring.com)

Chart 6-4 Merrill Lynch

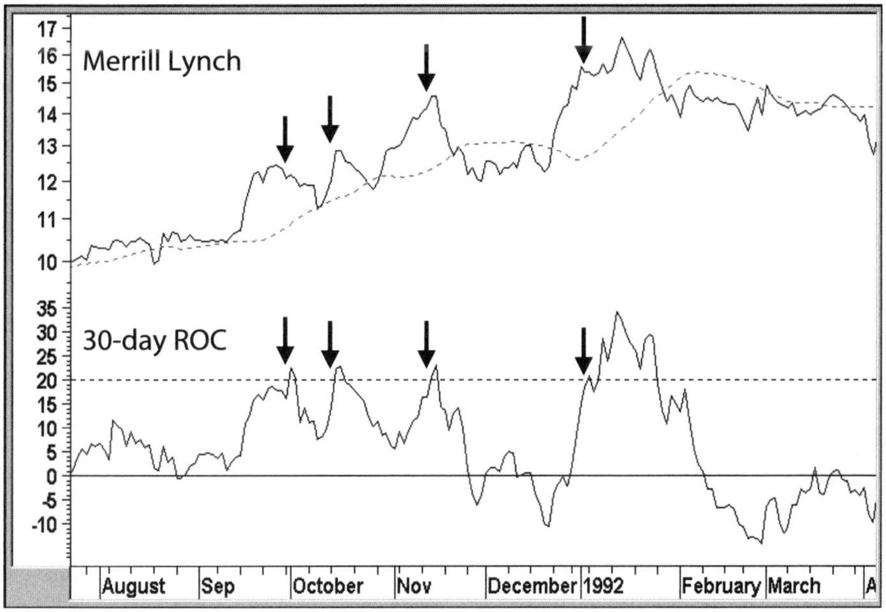

(Source: pring.com)

ber of different securities. If one of your systems fail, or if market conditions cause a specific security to perform far worse than it ever has in the past, the overall results will not be catastrophic because the diversification will bail you out.

ENTERING STOPS AND OTHER MONEY MANAGEMENT TECHNIQUES

When setting up a trading system, it is necessary to define the entry and exit rules first. This can be as simple as an MA crossover or as complicated as waiting for several indicators to be in a bullish or bearish mode before a signal can be generated. Some people prefer to buy only on an entry signal and sell on an exit signal, holding cash until the next morning comes along. This concept is shown in Chart 6-5, which compares the daily closing price of Merrill Lynch with its 45-day MA. Buy signals are identified by the upward pointing arrows. The flags represent sales where the system takes you out of a position and moves you into cash, until the system triggers another buy signal.

Chart 6-5 Merrill Lynch

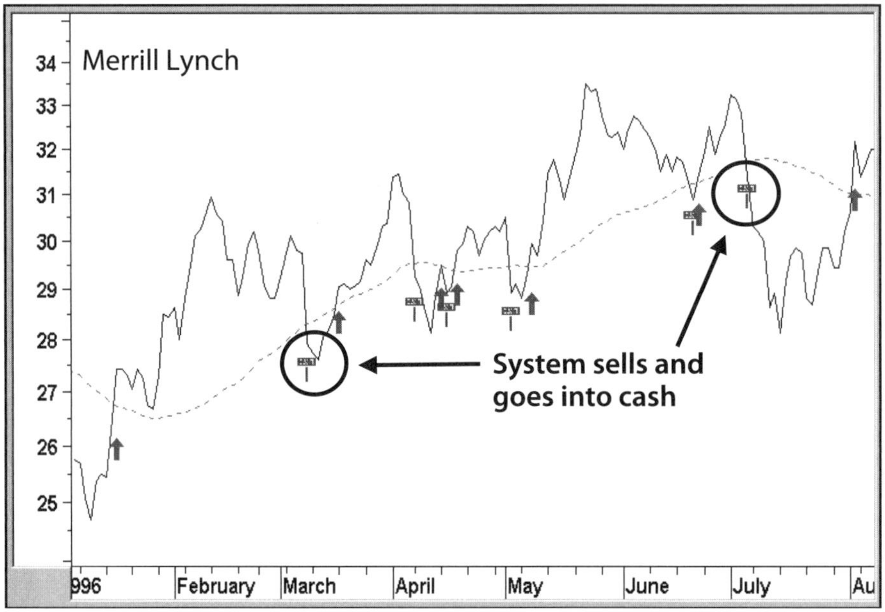

(Source: pring.com)

Many traders prefer to be exposed to the markets at all times. To accomplish this, when the original long position is closed out, a short position is immediately initiated. This is known as a reversal system because positions are reversed each time a signal is given. Chart 6-6 shows the same exercise with Merrill Lynch, but this time, the arrows indicate short positions. This method of flagging buy, short, and cash signals will be used throughout this book.

A *stop loss* is a means of limiting risk, and it is triggered only if certain conditions are met. Of course, setting a stop at a specific level does not guarantee you can get out at that point because the market may move too quickly for the person executing the trade to liquidate it at the price you specified. Alternatively, the market may experience a gap opening and the price runs way through the stop before it can be executed. In Chart 6-7, if you place the stop for a long position at $29.50 based on a 15-day MA crossover, you would expect to get filled at, or close to, your price. This is because Merrill Lynch is a fairly liquid stock. Unfortunately, the market opens at $28.75 on the day after the MA crossover, so there is no way the trade can be executed anywhere near the desired price. Fortunately, these situations are rare, but it must be recognized that *they can and do happen* more often than we like.

Chart 6-6 Merrill Lynch

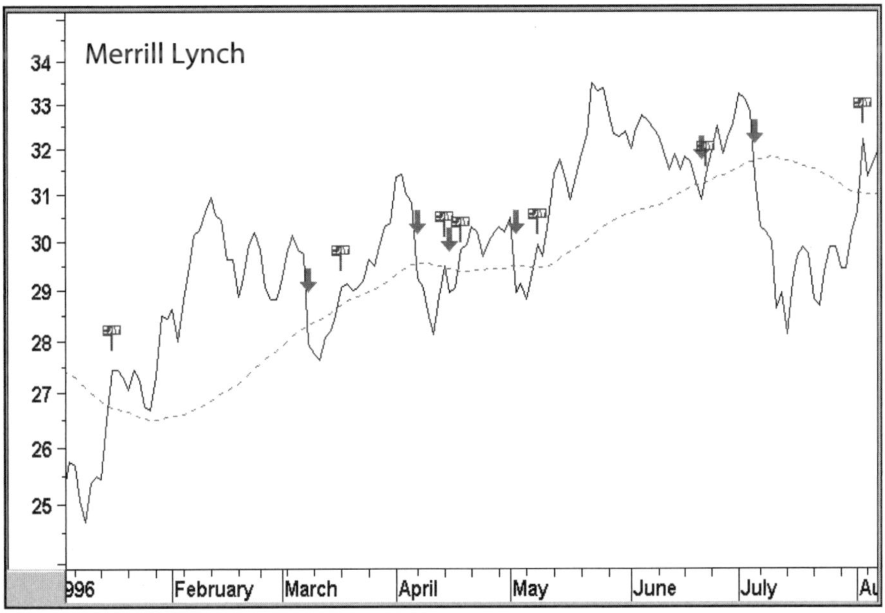

(Source: pring.com)

Chart 6-7 Merrill Lynch

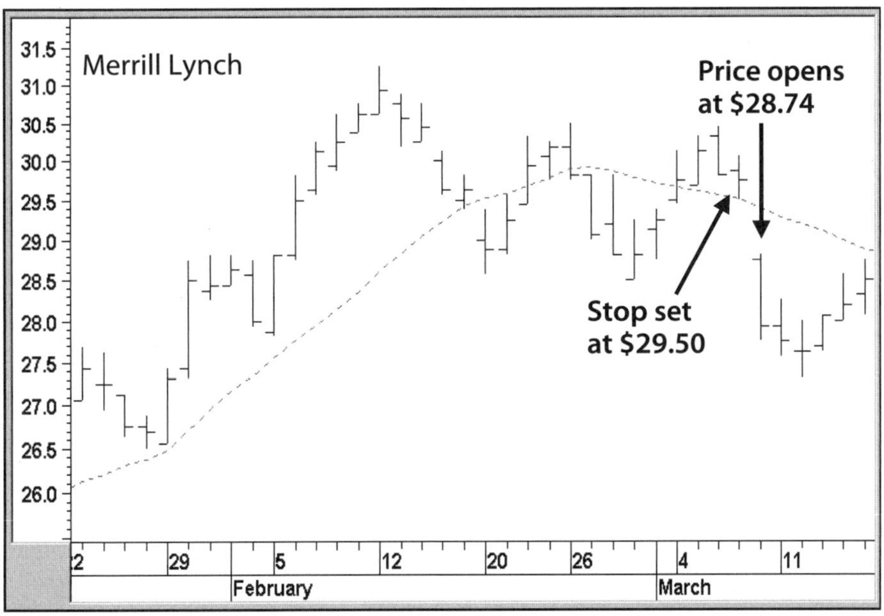

(Source: pring.com)

Before proceeding, we need to cover a few important terms.

- *Trading risk* is the minimum amount of capital to be put at risk in order to be able to trade long enough to establish a profit. It may apply to an individual market or to an entire diversified portfolio.
- *Risk capital* should be greater than the equivalent of *the maximum drawdown* of an established and tested system. The *drawdown* is the largest loss from an established high in the equity.
- The *maximum losing run* is the series of losing trades that has the largest dollar value.
- Finally, *required capital* is the sum of the maximum drawdown margin and a safety factor needed to trade a system profitably.

Since there are various techniques for setting stops, I will first talk about protecting capital and then proceed to protecting profits.

BREAKEVEN STOP

A *breakeven stop* closes an open position when the closed out value falls below the equity amount at the time the trade was opened. It is placed at the price where the trade could be closed, and the proceeds generated would equal the current equity amount. Obviously, a floor must first be established to cover commission costs. Otherwise, every trade would be stopped out as soon as it was initiated. In Chart 6-8, the buy signal is initiated at (A). Once again, I am using a simple 45-day MA crossover based on daily closing prices. The price then rallies and subsequently declines. On the day when the close falls below the breakeven point, the stop icon (B) is displayed. Note how the breakeven stop is triggered before, and at a better price than, the subsequent MA crossover. It was the MA crossover that would have been the triggering point for the sell signal had we not employed the breakeven stop. The late December stop (C) also outperforms the MA crossover. The reason this method has a tendency to work is because we assume an MA crossover will result in a strong trending move. When it does not, and the price returns to the breakeven point, the security is not behaving as expected. In fact, it has lost upside momentum. I am not saying you never see a quick reversal and a rally to new post-crossover highs. You can never say never in this business. However, once a price fails to act in the manner expected, it is just good money management practice to liquidate the position.

One thing to watch for with an MA crossover is that on the day of the signal, the closing price is not substantially above the breakout point. If it is, there is a greater than normal chance the price will react for a couple of days and trigger a breakeven stop. Looking at Chart 6-9, we see a very strong breakout day—so strong, it was necessary for the price to experience a fairly

Chart 6-8 Merrill Lynch

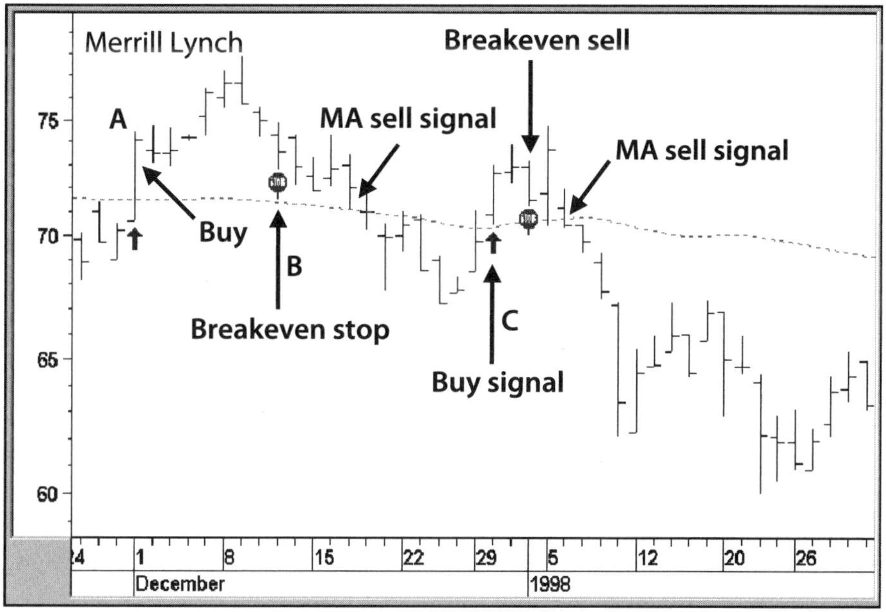

(Source: pring.com)

Chart 6-9 Merrill Lynch

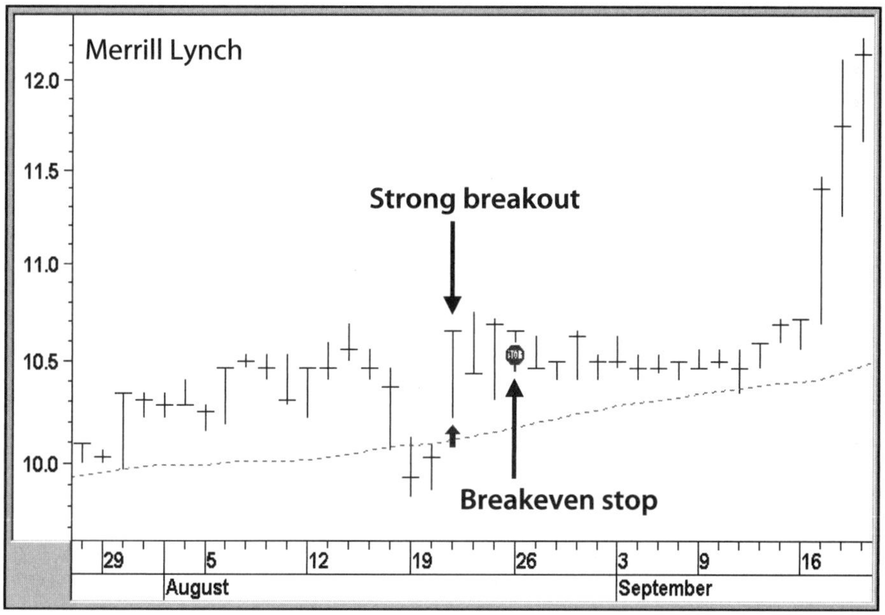

(Source: pring.com)

prolonged period of digestion. In the process, the breakeven stop was triggered. This was a great pity, since the security went on to experience an explosive rally.

INACTIVITY AND MAXIMUM LOSS STOPS

When you enter a position, it is expected the price will move in your favor fairly quickly. The *inactivity stop* closes an open position when the security's price does not generate a minimum positive price change within a specified time period. An inactivity stop is triggered when the price remains relatively inactive, either just after the position is entered or for any period thereafter. A *positive price change* is defined as an upward price movement for long positions and a downward price movement for short ones.

In Chart 6-10, the buy signal is generated at point A. The inactivity stop is triggered when the price fails to rally by .25 percent over a 4-day period, marked point B. Initially there is no problem, as an advance materializes immediately after the MA crossover takes place. Then, as the price reaches the $35 area, it experiences a 3-day decline. The fourth day is a rally (point B) but this still leaves us with no net progress over the 4-day period and certainly not a .25 percent gain. Thus, the position is stopped out.

Chart 6-10 Merrill Lynch

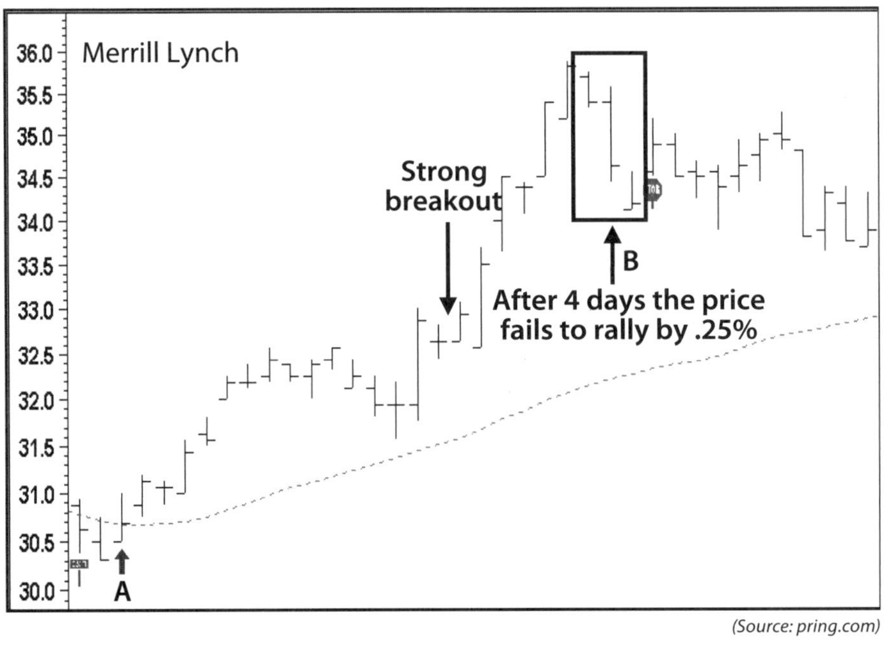

(Source: pring.com)

In the next example, Chart 6-11, the inactivity period has been increased to 6 days. You can see the stop in this instance, labeled point A, occurs well before the MA crossover. Indeed, the crossover signal would have been particularly poor because the close developed around the low of the day. In the next situation, labeled point B, the stop and moving-average sell signal developed around the same time. Finally, at point C, the MA crossover developed at a slightly better price than the inactivity stop.

You can appreciate that sometimes the inactivity stop works better, and at other times the MA crossover gives the superior signal. I particularly like the inactivity stop because it tells us when momentum is starting to flag, and that is often associated with a trend reversal. A great deal depends on the amount of movement and the inactivity time period, so considerable experimentation is required before you will come up with the ideal stop mechanism. So many times we enter a position expecting the price to trend in our favor and when it does not, we still hold on to the position, eventually losing money. The inactivity stop is designed to automatically liquidate the position if things do not go according to plan.

A *maximum loss* stop takes us out of a position when a specific dollar amount, or percentage of losing equity, has been reached. For example, if you knew your system had a maximum loss of 10 percent during the testing period, you might want to use the 10 percent loss level as a stop point because it would indicate the system was not operating according to expectations.

Chart 6-11 Merrill Lynch

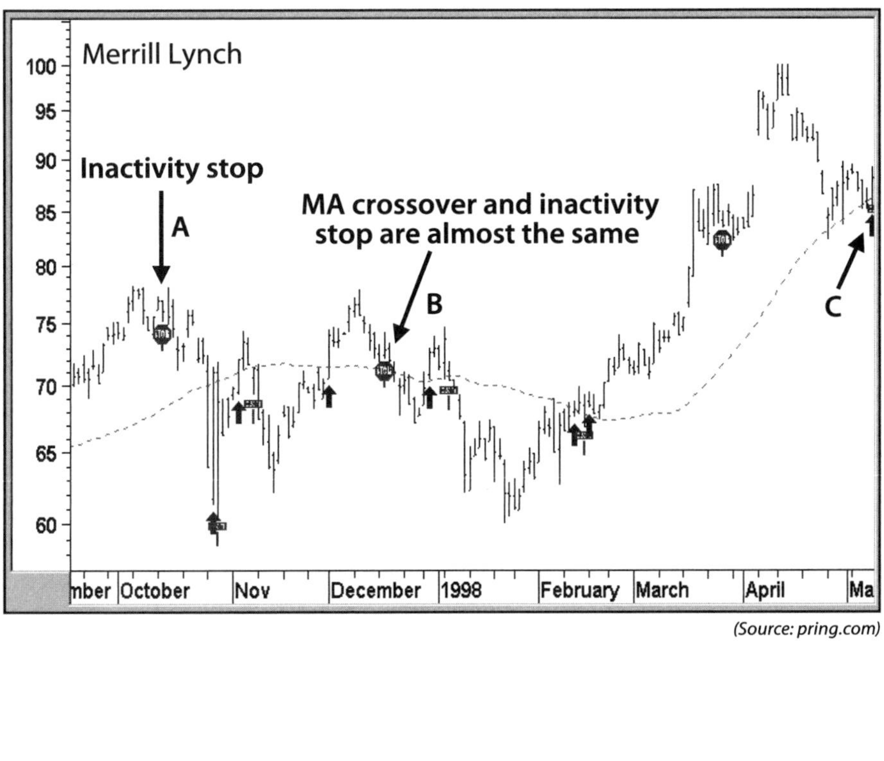

(Source: pring.com)

PROFIT TARGET STOP

Most systems allow profits to run, but there may be a point at which you want to protect some, or all, of the profit in the event the market unexpectedly reverses. A *dollar profit target* is a dollar amount above or below the entry price, depending upon whether the trade is from the long or short side. I am sure you recognize by now that it is impossible to get out at the maximum profit point; that is, at the high for a long position or the low for a short position. Inevitably, some profit will be given up. The dollar profit stop method addresses this point and locks in some profit before the price reaches its maximum profit potential. This can result in a lower profit, since the option of riding with an extended trend is forfeited, but a profit-taking stop will offer a greater consistency of profit; that is, a greater percentage of winning trades.

One way a target profit can be triggered is to set it as a specific amount above or below an MA, or as a percentage above or below the average. In Chart 6-12, a 10 percent profit target was set. The stop would have liquidated the position right at the top, which is a highly desired outcome. Chart 6-13 also uses a 10 percent profit target from the opening position, and also appears to have a timely stop. However, Chart 6-14 shows additional price action. You can see this was only the beginning of a really strong trend and the sell signal from the MA crossover came from much higher levels. My

Chart 6-12 Merrill Lynch

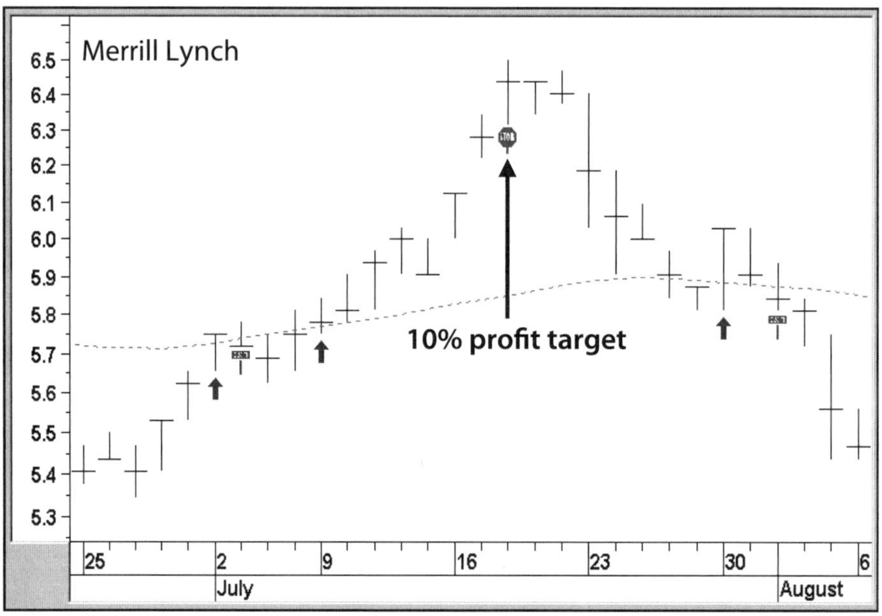

(Source: pring.com)

Chart 6-13 Merrill Lynch

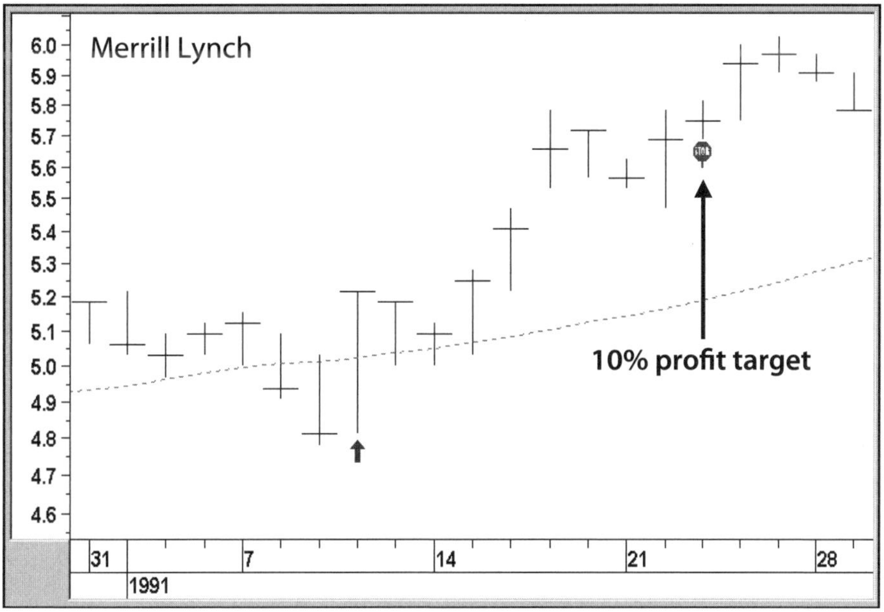

(Source: pring.com)

Chart 6-14 Merrill Lynch

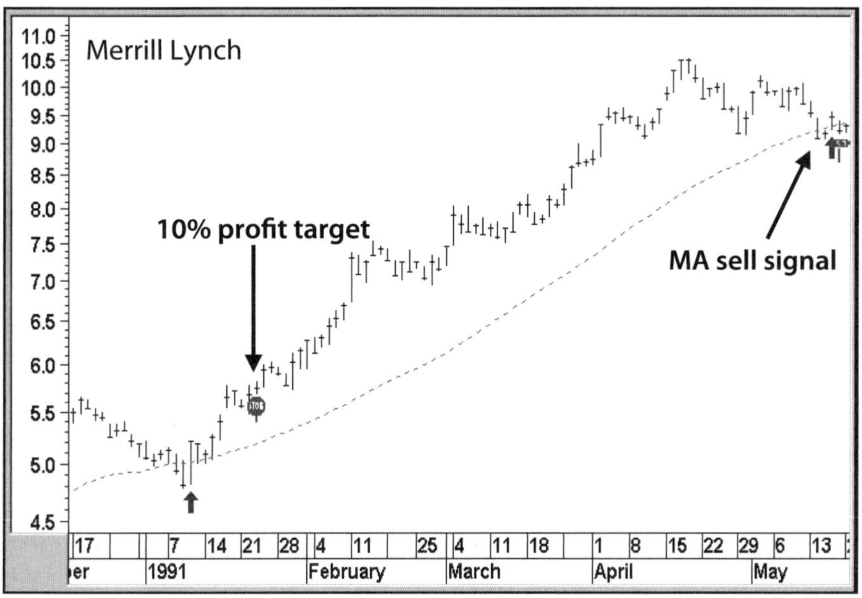

(Source: pring.com)

own preference is to go long with two units. One would be sold with the profit target achievement and the other with the MA crossover.

TRAILING STOPS AND THE PARABOLIC SYSTEM

A *trailing stop* continuously moves in the direction of the position, often at progressively faster rates. The advantage of a trailing stop is that profits are more aggressively protected. The disadvantage is that the position stands a better chance of being stopped out before the trend has had a chance to reach its potential. There are two types of trailing stops. The first sets the stop as soon as the trade has been initiated. This could be as simple as placing it under an MA and waiting for the average to move in the direction of the trade. The second possibility is a little more complex, since it involves waiting until a minimum profit target has been achieved. The rationale is to give the trade some time to allow for possible whipsaws, provided it remains within the tolerance of the system.

The *parabolic system,* a stop technique developed by Wells Wilder, is calculated to move progressively faster in the direction of the trading position currently being held. Hence, the stop becomes tighter and tighter until it is eventually triggered. The parabolic indicator is displayed in Chart 6-15 as the slightly thicker line above and below the price line A. It is really trading on the idea that a price trend gathers momentum as it gets under way. When momentum starts to dissipate, as flagged by a consolidation or a couple of sessions of weakness, it indicates vulnerability and the parabolic stop is triggered.

Wilder devised it as a reversal system, where a trader is always in the market, either being long or short. However, I caution against this policy, preferring to only trade in the direction of the main trend; that is, using the parabolic to exit positions only.

In Chart 6-15, the entry point develops as the price closes above the previous parabolic curve. Please note that for the purposes of this example, I am going against my normal policy and using the parabolic as a reversal system. The initial stop is placed at point B, just where the parabolic curve starts. As the price rallies, the parabolic indicator accelerates to the upside, finally triggering a sell signal at point C. Since I am using this as a reversal system, the sell signal initiates a short position. The parabolic above the price would be used to stop out short positions. Once again, I would caution against shorting into a bull market, however confident you are of a forthcoming drop, because even in this instance the position was stopped out with a small loss.

Chart 6-15 Merrill Lynch

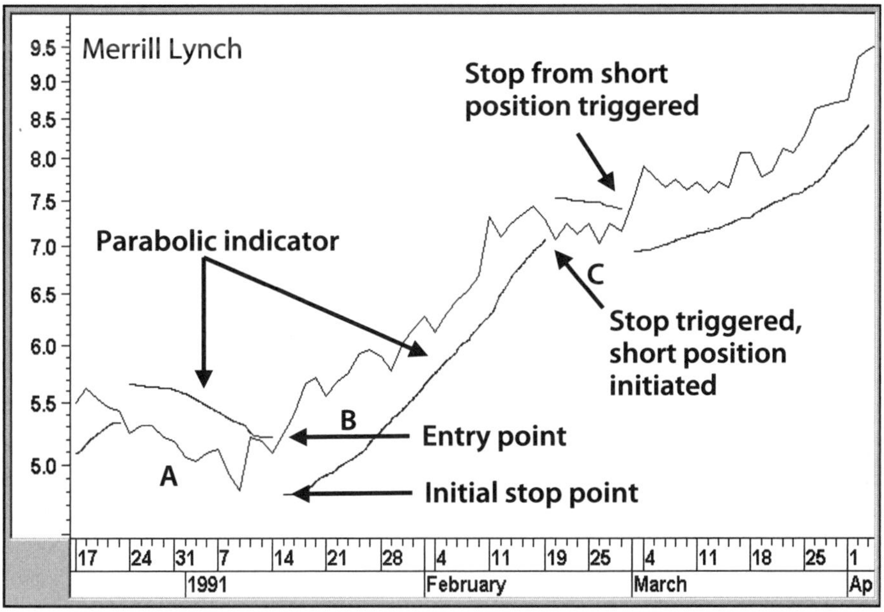

(Source: pring.com)

TRAILING DOLLAR STOP

A *trailing dollar* stop is the second of two methods of setting trailing stops. It is placed at a dollar amount above or below a recent low or high (depending on whether you are short or long) in the equity for the current trade. For example, in Chart 6-16, I have given the stop a value of 10 percent and based it on a closing, rather than an intraday extreme. This means that once 10 percent of the profit is given up, the stop is triggered. You can see in Chart 6-16 that the trade is entered at around $40 in February. Each time the price makes a new closing high, the stop is placed 10 percent below it. Therefore, the stop is being placed progressively higher (trailing the dollar) as the price advances.

It is the opposite on a closing basis. If the price falls to the extent that 10 percent of the profit is lost, the stop is triggered. In this example I have also allowed for a 4-day cooling-off period. This means the stop is actually trailing the market for four days. In effect, if the price lost 11 percent of the profit in the first day, and subsequently rallied to a new high before four days had expired, the stop would not be triggered. Please remember I am talking about the profit and not the price. The profit in this case would have

Chart 6-16 Merrill Lynch

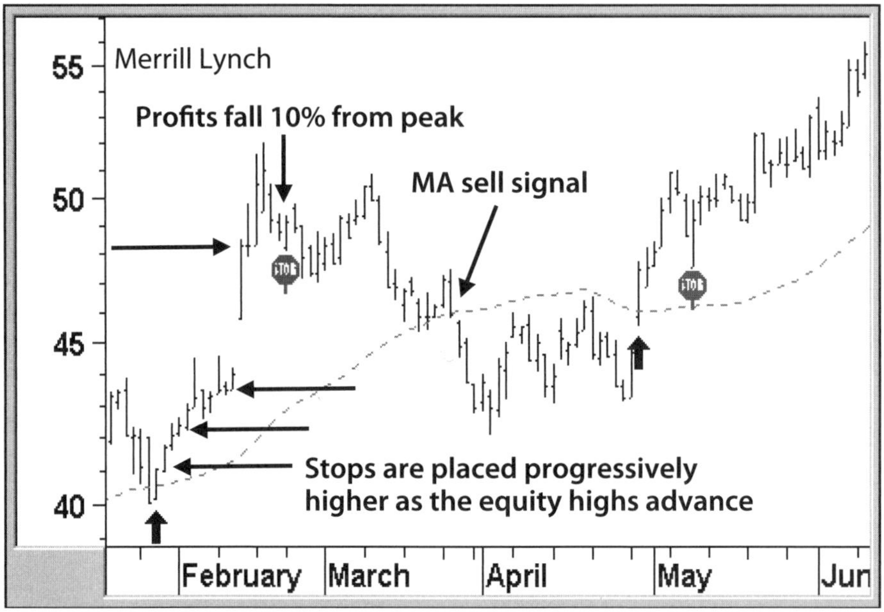

(Source: pring.com)

been about $10, that is, the approximate difference between $41 and $51; consequently, the 10 percent is 10 percent of $10, not $51. In this particular case, the trailing stop did better than the MA crossover shown in Chart 6-16. Of course, I do not guarantee this is always the case.

Chapter 7
The Testing Process

THE FIRST STEP

The first step in the testing process is to run the system through a set of historical data. In Chart 7-1, I am testing the idea that 25-day MA crossovers will generate above average returns for Merrill Lynch. The buy and sell signals are shown in the lower panel and the equity line is featured in the upper one. During the period of the test, the equity line ends at a higher price than it begins, so the system is profitable. In fact, it turns \$1 into \$1.28 by the end of the period. All of the equity lines used in this test start at \$1, and most of them are profitable. By now, I am sure you are wondering, how do they earn their profits and what is the quality and prediction of the system? Studying Chart 7-1, we have to ask ourselves the question: Is 25 days the best timespan, or will something else work better? That is where our second point, optimization, comes in.

USING HISTORICAL DATA AND OPTIMIZATION

Optimization, defined by Robert Pardo in his excellent book, *Design, Testing and Optimization of Trading Systems,* is "the systematic search for the best indicator formula." It involves the testing of a large number of parameters on the same set of price data to find out which set of parameters offers the best results. If we decide to optimize the MA crossovers that exhibit the

Chart 7-1 Merill Lynch and a 25-Day MA Crossover System

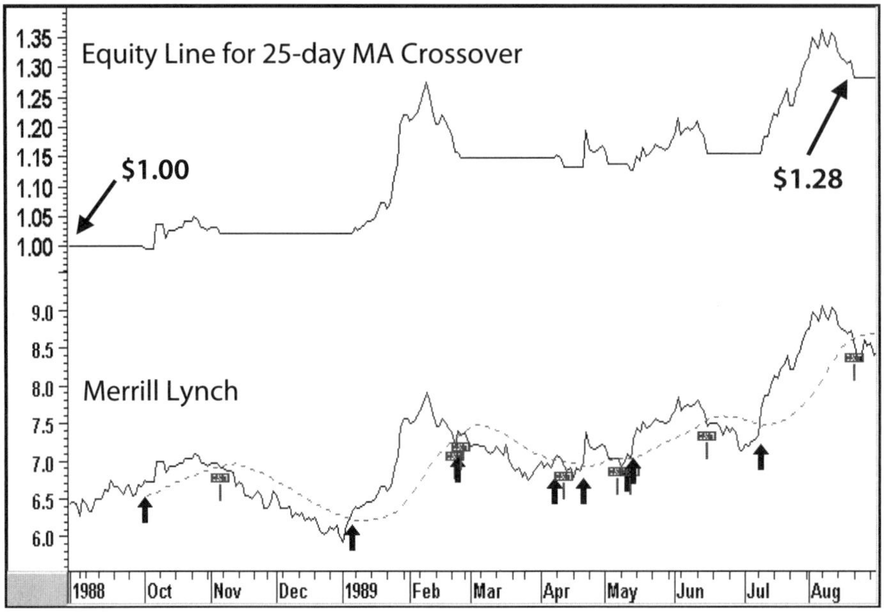

(Source: pring.com)

most profitable signals, the process would consist of establishing a range of timespans and then testing each one. It also requires a lot of computing time to optimize for many variables. For this reason, it is common practice to select steps when undergoing onerous tests. Instead of calculating every conceivable timespan 1, 2, 3, 4, and so on, the test would be conducted in steps of two, or five, so the optimization would be carried out for timespans of 2, 4, 6, 8 or 1, 5, 10, 15, and so forth. Even though the steps reduce the number of calculations being made, the results are not really hampered because we are not interested in the best possible fit, since this is likely to be a fluke. However, if we can get an approximate best answer by testing for every fifth period, this will usually give us a satisfactory result. If the results are not satisfactory, the level of the step can be reduced to limit the overall range of timespans.

Table 7-1 shows an optimization for simple MA crossovers between 1988 and 1990. I tested for a range of 2 to 36 days in one step increments, which means the computer has run 34 tests. As you can see, the best results came from a 13-day timespan.

Chart 7-2 shows the results for the initial period. The series in the lower panel is the price together with a 13-day MA. The arrows represent buy signals and the flags are sell signals. The upper portion contains the

Table 7-1 Merrill Lynch MA Optimization

Best time span is a 13-day MA

MERRILL LYNCH

...	Status	Net Profit	Perce...	Tot...	Win...	Losi...	Avg ...	OP...
	OK	0.4322	43.22	32	10	22	3.9327	13
	OK	0.3247	32.47	29	10	19	3.1337	14
	OK	0.3237	32.37	33	10	23	3.6921	12
	OK	0.2922	29.22	117	35	82	2.8937	2
	OK	0.2862	28.62	29	9	20	3.5846	15
	OK	0.2743	27.43	27	9	18	3.3785	16
	OK	0.2737	27.37	26	9	17	3.2261	17
	OK	0.2626	26.26	18	7	11	3.8806	26
	OK	0.2568	25.68	24	9	15	2.9850	20
	OK	0.2297	22.97	19	7	11	2.5495	27

Chart 7-2 Merrill Lynch and a 13-Day MA Crossover System

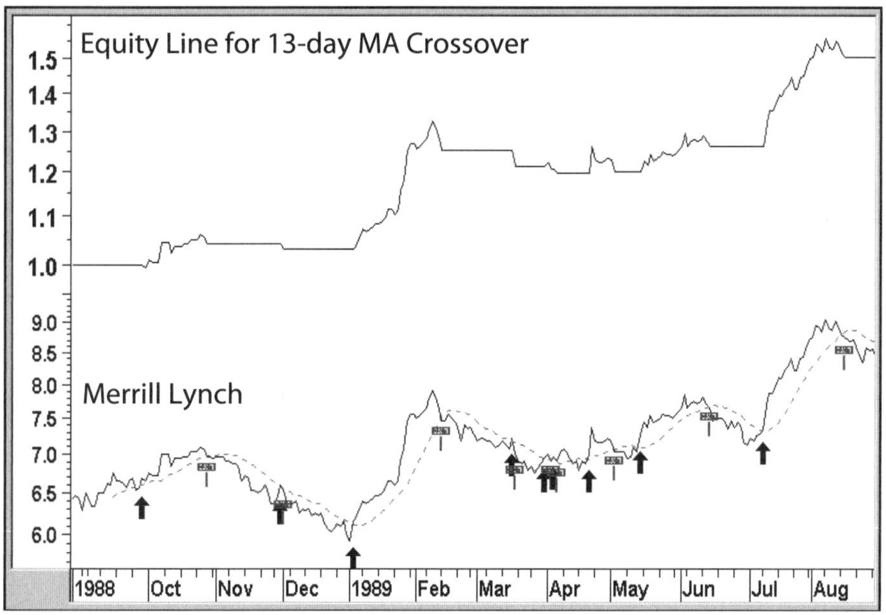

(Source: pring.com)

equity line, which shows the progress of the equity as time passes. The best equity lines show a steady rise from the bottom left-hand corner to the top right, indicating consistency. What we do not want to see is a line sloping from the top left-hand corner to the bottom right, because this means the system lost money.

Another undesirable characteristic is an equity line that experiences sharp declines and volatile rallies, since this indicates inconsistency. Lastly, in Chart 7-3, periods when the line is horizontal are those when the price is below the moving average and the system is in a cash position. For the purposes of this test I have assumed no margin or commissions, nor was any interest earned during the periods when the system called for a cash position. During the period displayed in Chart 7-2, the system acted reasonably well. But what happened later? Well, Chart 7-3 shows the period immediately following. As you can see, the equity line falls between August 1989 and May 1990. This brings us to our third principle of testing—the walk-forward analysis.

Chart 7-3 Merrill Lynch and a 13-Day MA Crossover System

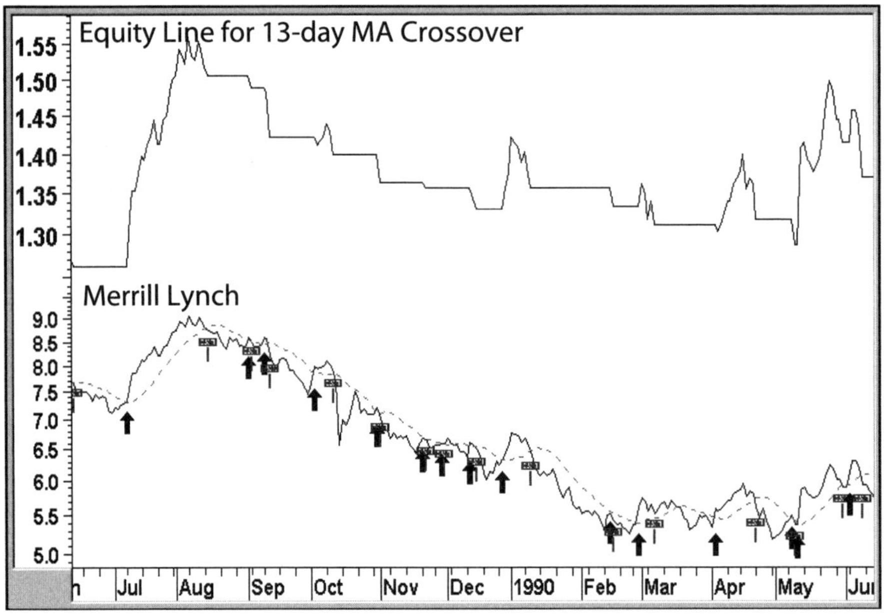

(Source: pring.com)

WALK-FORWARD ANALYSIS

Walk-forward analysis evaluates performance by extrapolating the results of an earlier period. In effect, you take the best parameter of the test period and run it on a later set of data. Instead of "flying blindly" into the future, the system is given a simulated, but thorough testing using actual market data. It is also a good idea to test your ideas on other securities to see if there is any consistency in the results. This out-of-sample process is useful because it moves us closer to an untested, real market environment. Of course, it is not real-time trading where slippage and emotions are involved, but it is the next best thing. If our optimized timespan has not been properly tested, or if the result was a statistical fluke, the out-of-sample testing period is where it will show up.

In Chart 7-4, I merely extrapolated the results of the 13-day MA crossover between 1991 and the end of 1994. It looks as if we have a lot more signals, but remember this is a 4-year period, whereas the previous charts

Chart 7-4 Merrill Lynch and a 13-Day MA Crossover System

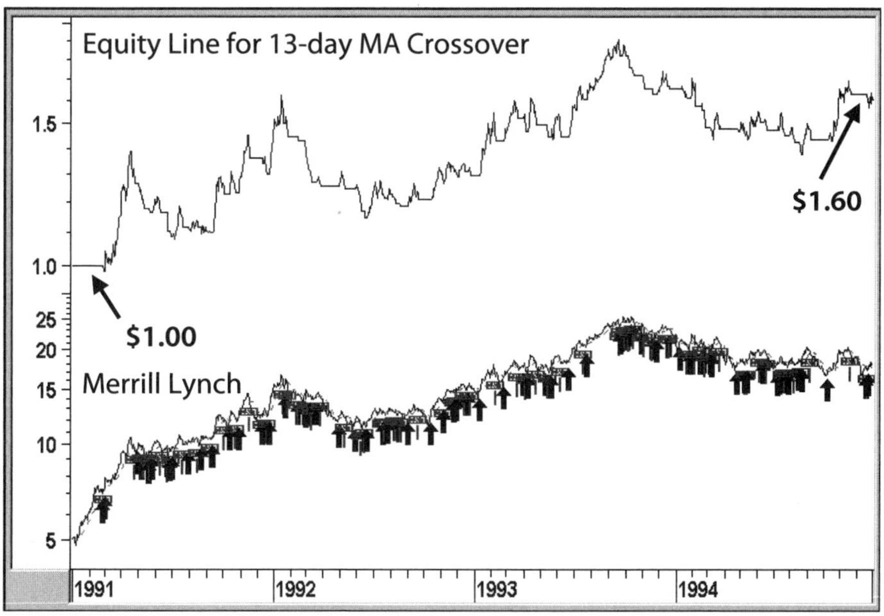

(Source: pring.com)

displayed data for only a few months. Overall, the results were not that great, since this very basic system produced $1.60 for an initial investment of $1. Now you could say this is not as good as the buy-hold approach, which was much better, but that is really no concern to the system trader. His or her only objective is to make a good return on his or her money—not to beat the buy-hold approach. After all, this period encompassed one of the strongest segments of one of the strongest bull markets on record. With the benefit of hindsight, it would have been better to buy and hold, but no one I know can trade with this advantage.

When I did this test, I could have run a period I knew was going to work better, but for the purpose of this book, I blindly forward tested the results for the next few years. The result was not too bad as you can see from the action of the equity line in Chart 7-5. The system returned $7.29 from the original starting equity of $1. Although it still did not compare to the buy-hold approach, we have to remember markets do go down. Shortly after I ran this test in the summer of 1998, Merrill Lynch went from over $100 to less than $40, giving up several years of "profitable" buy-hold investing in a matter of weeks.

Chart 7-5 Merrill Lynch and a 13-Day MA Crossover System

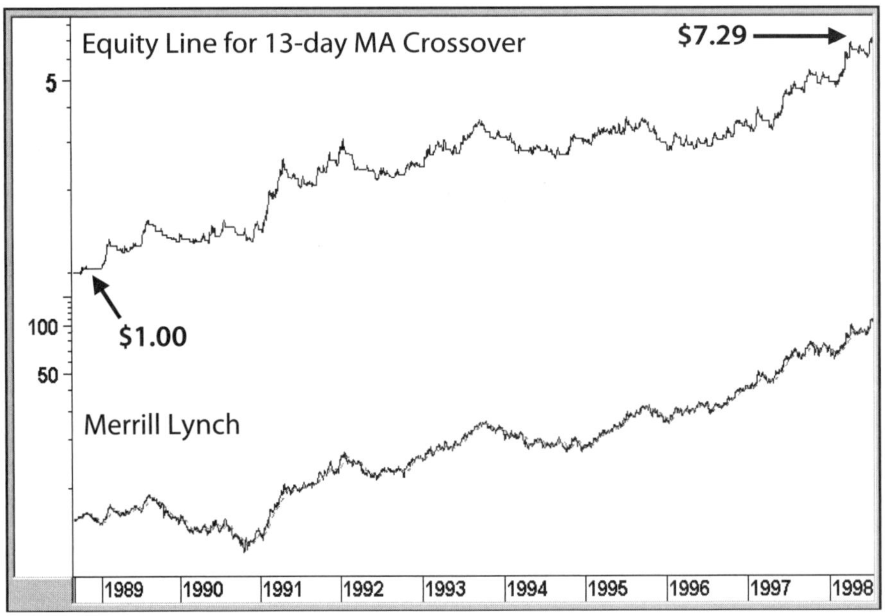

(Source: pring.com)

WALK BACKWARD AS WELL

Chart 7-6 shows the Dow Jones Industrial Average (DJIA) together with an equity line for a simple 45-week MA crossover system. The results were extremely impressive, with very little drawdown and consistent profits. As Chart 7-7 shows, this was a good trending period for the most part and really should have returned a good performance. During the period from the mid 1960s to 1982, the Dow was in a wide-swinging trading range. I thought it would be a good idea to see how well the system performed in this type of market environment (Chart 7-7). As it turned out, it did reasonably well, gaining about 85 percent compared to the buy-hold approach of 20 percent. I do not want to dwell on the comparison of a trading system with the buy-hold approach because the buy-hold result is something we only know with hindsight, and cannot guarantee or repeat. A mechanical system obviously cannot guarantee future results will match past performance either, but at least there is a greater statistical probability if the system has been well tested. Rather than being compared with the buy-hold approach, I think a mechanical system's success should be judged on its ability to earn a satisfactory and consistent rate of return over time.

Chart 7-6 DJIA and a 45-Week MA Crossover System

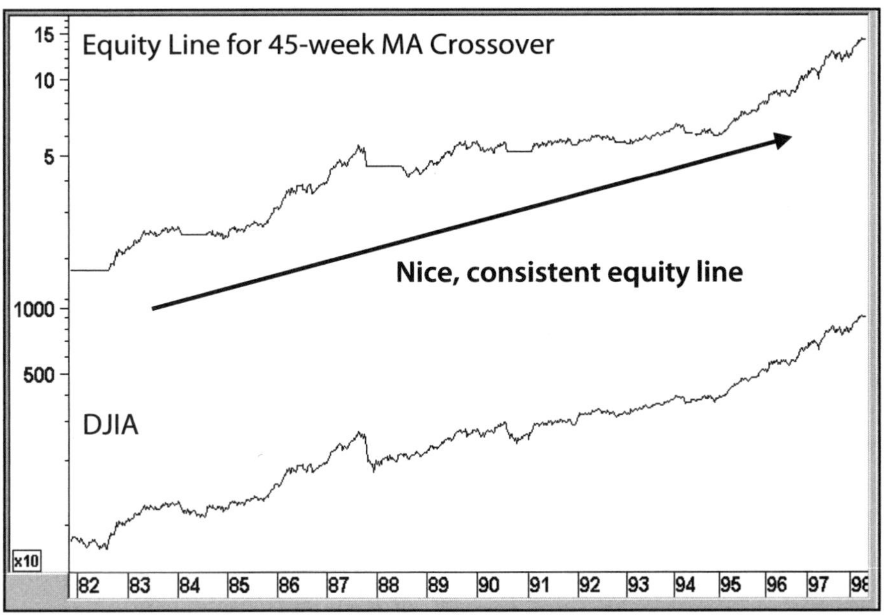

(Source: pring.com)

Chart 7-7 DJIA and a 45-Week MA Crossover System

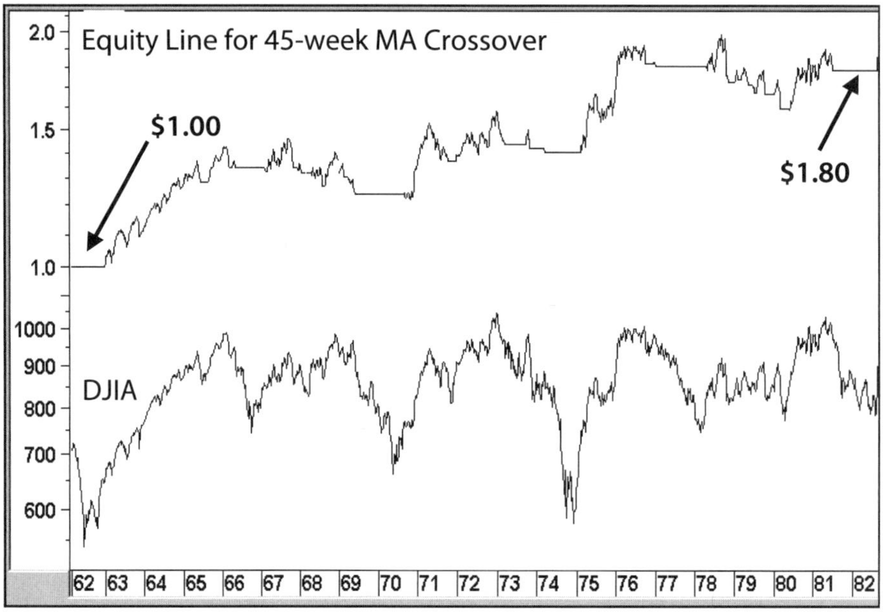

(Source: pring.com)

All in all, the walk-forward testing offers three advantages:

1. A more reliable measure of profit and risk is attained due to the larger data sample.
2. If the model has too many rules that result in "curve fitting," this will quickly be revealed by the walk-forward analysis. A post-optimized system should provide results that are similar to the tested data. If it consistently tests with say 30 percent of the profit of the original test, then it should be dropped or dramatically refined because there are probably too many rules.
3. The final advantage of the walk-through analysis is it will reflect changes in the market environment such as volatility, changes in liquidity and so forth. You can have more confidence in the results of such a system because it will have proven itself to be adaptable to a variety of market conditions.

With modern technology, it is now very easy to find a software package that will test and optimize data for you. I have used Equis International's MetaStock software, but there are many powerful programs, such as AIQ, Telescan, Investors FastTrack, and Omega's Trade Station. Wealth-lab developer (available at *pring.com*) is a new program solely devoted to testing. It has a high learning curve but is arguably the best widely available system testing software available.

BACKTEST OVER MANY YEARS USING MANY SECURITIES

The final point concerning the testing process is to backtest over a sufficiently long period with many different securities. The more data tested, the greater the reliability of future results. This point is obvious because the more data tested, the better the opportunity you have to find a security or environment that does not respond in a profitable way. A system that works over a wide variety of conditions is likely to operate in a similar manner in the future, and it is the future we are interested in.

Chart 7-5 shows the result of extrapolating the 13-day MA system for the whole period between 1988 and 1998 for Merrill Lynch. Overall, the system performed pretty well, turning in a return of 700 percent. This chart is being referenced again because it shows what can happen during a strong linear bull market, where sharp corrections were few and far between. With

Chart 7-8 XAU and a 13-Day MA Crossover System

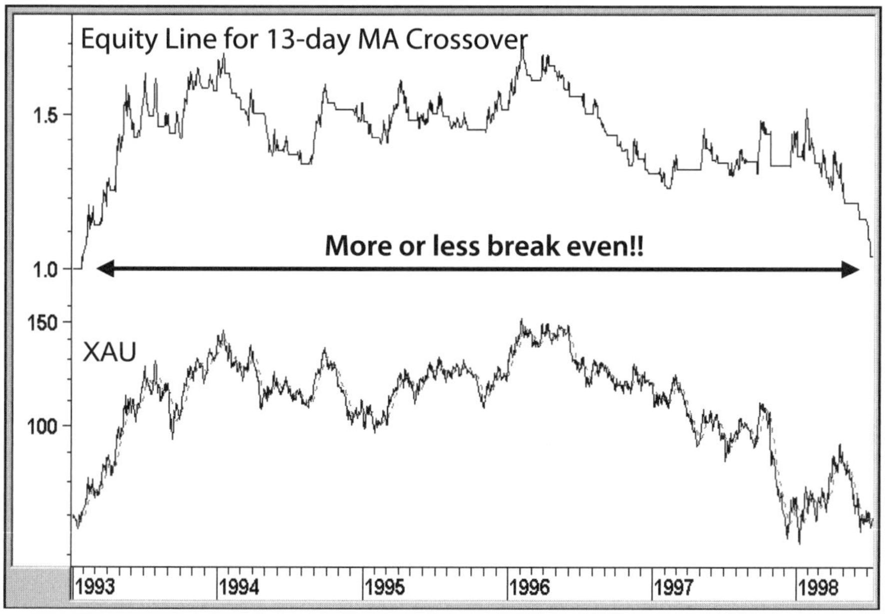

(Source: pring.com)

Chart 7-9 General Motors and a 13-Day MA Crossover System

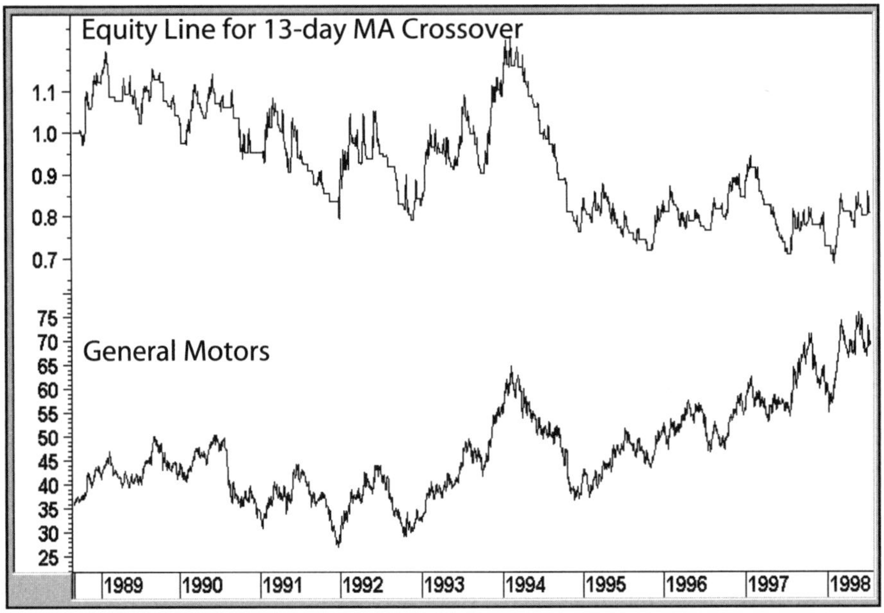

(Source: pring.com)

the benefit of hindsight, we know it is a good system, but what would happen if it were tested in a more volatile period? One sector that was quite volatile in the 1990s was gold shares. Chart 7-8 shows the 13-day MA crossover system did not test at all satisfactorily under such an environment. The results are both volatile and unprofitable. Notice how the ending equity is just about the same as the starting amount. If you think this was bad, just look at the system when applied to General Motors. In Chart 7-9 it actually lost money as the starting amount of $1 in 1989 is reduced to about 80¢ by mid 1998.

This demonstration is not meant to discourage you, but merely to point out what may work for one security in one particular period of time is not guaranteed to work for others. Different markets have different characteristics, which means we must apply systems to carefully appraised characteristics rather than trying to apply the same system to all securities at all times. When we use a system that buys when a price rises by 2 percent from a trough and sells when it declines by 2 percent from a peak, the results will be dramatically different from a futures contract with a relatively low volatility such as T-bills, than an extremely volatile one like lumber. The tolerances for lumber would have to be much greater than 2 percent; otherwise the system would be whipsawing all over the place.

Chapter 8
Reviewing the Results

TOP PROFITS DO NOT ALWAYS INDICATE THE BEST SYSTEM

When reviewing the simulated results of a mechanical system, there is a natural tendency to look at the bottom line to see which one would have generated the most profits. However, top results do not always indicate the best system and there are several reasons for this.

It is possible that most, or all, of the profit was generated by one or two signals. If this is the case, it would place lower odds on it generating good profits in the future, because it lacks consistency. Chart 8-1 shows an example of an inconsistent system using the Hang Seng. It is based on 13-week MA crossovers, but positions are only taken on the short side. In this instance, the timely sell signal just prior to the crash of 1987 was responsible for all of the profit. It is true that other signals also generated profits, but this was a kind of water torture because they all proved to be countercyclical rallies in an ongoing equity line bear market. Had it not been for this one excellent signal, the system would have wiped out the account by the beginning of 1992.

Another consideration involves the identification of the worst string of losses. After all, it is no good having a system that generates a large profit over the long term if you do not have sufficient capital to ride out the worst period. There are two things to look for in this respect: the longest string of losing signals, and the maximum amount lost during these adverse periods. Check to see if losses developed because of sloppy rules. Sometimes a

Chart 8-1 Hang Seng and a 13-Week MA Crossover System (shorts only)

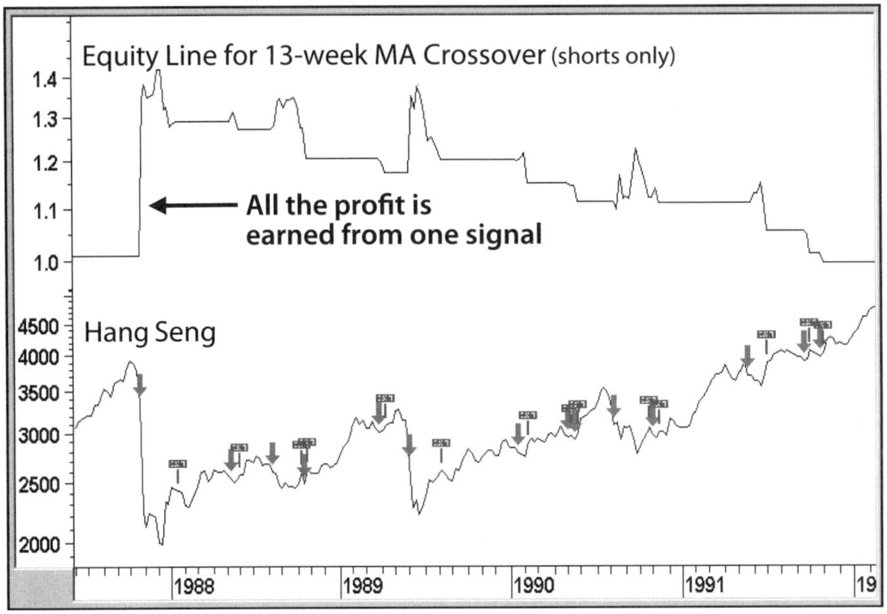

(Source: pring.com)

system will return below average results because the trading rules are lax and do not account for certain market situations. In Chart 8-2 of the Hang Seng I am using Bollinger Bands as the triggering mechanism. Short signals develop when the price crosses over the upper band and then slips below it (A). The position is covered when the price crosses below the neutral band, the dashed line (B). Buy signals develop when the price slips below the lower band (C) and then rises above it. Sell signals develop when the price crosses above the center band (D). In effect, buy and sell signals are being created when the price reverses from an overextended position and closed when they reached neutral. It looks reasonably good during the period shown in Chart 8-2. However, in Chart 8-3, I extended the coverage so you can see that two huge losses were incurred in the 1984–1987 period.

If we look at Chart 8-4, which is the 1986–88 period, a little more closely, we can see the reason. The initial short sale is made in October 1986 as the price slips below the outer band. It almost crosses below neutral in May 1987, but does not quite do it. That signal alone would have resulted in a serious loss, but the actual crossover did not take place until the 1987 crash period. This is an excellent example of why it is extremely important to make sure your systems have some form of countervailing signals that

Chart 8-2 Hang Seng and a Bollinger Band Crossover System

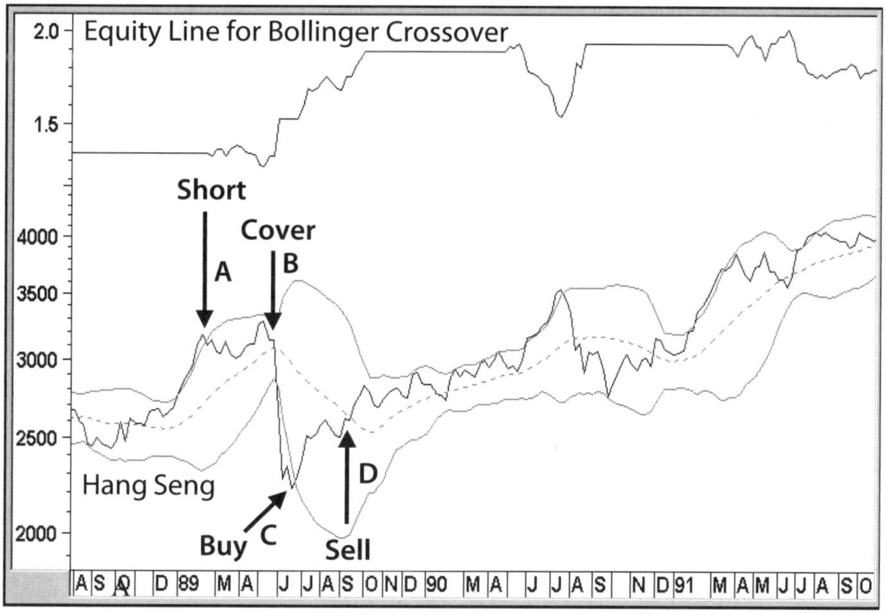

(Source: pring.com)

Chart 8-3 Hang Seng and a Bollinger Band Crossover System

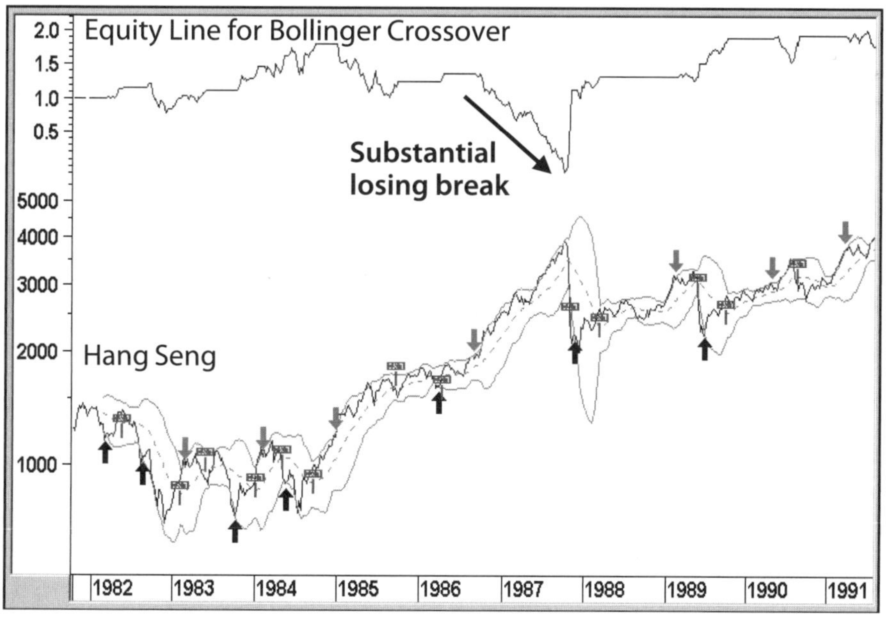

(Source: pring.com)

Chart 8-4 Hang Seng and a Bollinger Band Crossover System

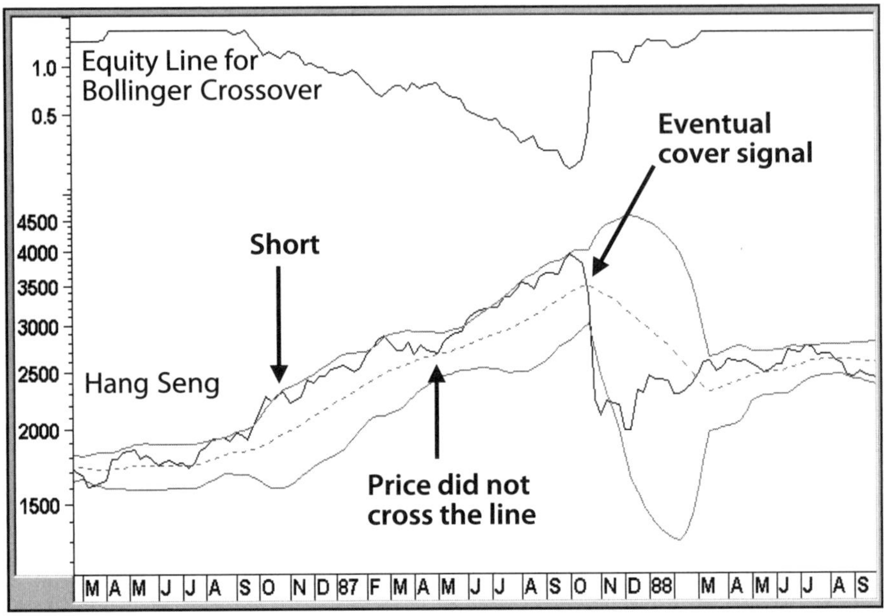

(Source: pring.com)

will limit losses. Under the rules of this system, the law of averages says positions will sooner or later be reversed and in most cases losses will be limited. However, in this specific case we saw the inconvenient exception to the rule because the bull market had extremely strong underlying upside momentum. I should add that my criticism is not of the Bollinger Bands themselves, for they are a fine and innovative technical tool, but is merely of the way my system rules were established. I used this example to illustrate a point.

CHURNING AND SLIPPAGE

Churning will destroy profits because of costly commissions, slippage, and emotional bankruptcy. A system that generates huge profits but requires a significant number of trades is less likely to be successful in the real world than one based on a moderate number of trades. This is true because the more trades that are executed, the greater the potential for slippage through illiquidity, and so forth. More transactions also require more time and involve greater commission costs and so forth. It is very easy to test a system and forget that in the real world we are required to pay commissions.

Some allowance must also be made for slippage. *Slippage* is the difference between the price where the stop was placed and where it gets filled. Also, your system may call for a short-trade when the price crosses below its moving average. However, when the market opens the next day, emotions may be running so strongly the price gaps down, and it is not possible to execute the trade at or near the required price. If provision is not made for such possibilities, either by establishing a rule to buy at the open or actually deflating the trading results by a percentage to allow for such possibilities, the actual results will not reflect the tested data.

In Chart 8-5, there is an equity line for JP Morgan using a 26-week MA crossover. For this example, I have assumed a 6 percent interest rate for cash periods, and a .5 percent commission both in and out. The equity line rises from $1 to $2.30, a respectable, but certainly not great performance. However, if I raise the commission to 2 percent in and out you can see in Chart 8-6 that the profit earned is far less — $1.30 in fact. The point here is to emphasize that the more you trade, the greater the amount of potential profit you will be donating, either to your friendly broker as commissions, or, in the case of stocks, to the specialist on the floor in the form of slippage. The rule, then, is to try to devise a system that is not in the charity business.

Chart 8-5 JP Morgan and a 26-Week MA Crossover System

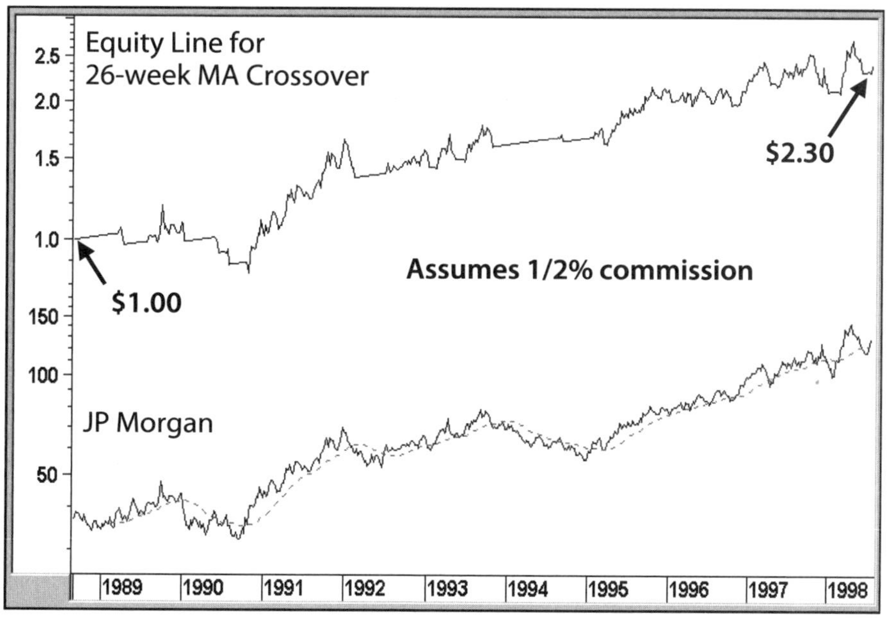

(Source: pring.com)

Chart 8-6 JP Morgan and a 26-Week MA Crossover System

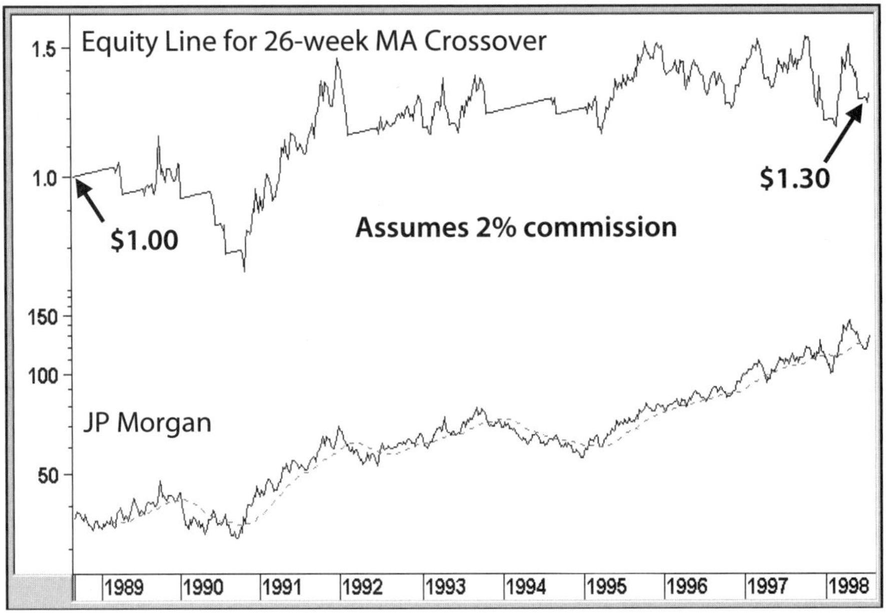

(Source: pring.com)

BALANCE PROFIT VERSUS LOSS AND RISK VERSUS REWARD

Monitoring the average amount of losses and profits will enable you to identify an approximate win or lose ratio. For a profitable system, if average losses exceed average gains by a wide margin, the system is depending on one or two signals to earn a majority of the profits. If there are a lot of losses, but the average is low, then it shows the system is cutting losses fairly quickly and is managing risk quite well.

Most system testing software will give you an indication of whether the profits earned in a system offer a good reward/risk ratio. Sometimes we get great rewards but have to undertake tremendous risks to get them. If that is the case, the high risk associated with the system may result in giving back most, or all, of the profit gained. If we can earn a smaller, but satisfactory profit for a considerably reduced risk, we are far better off.

Chart 8-7 features the American Century 2020 Zero Coupon Fund. Since it is a no load fund, I have assumed zero commissions. The test optimized a 25-day crossover as one of the best systems. As you can see, the equity line is consistent in its slow rise from the lower left hand corner to the upper right. What happened to the reward/risk ratio?

Chart 8-7 American Century (formerly Betham Capital Management) 2020 Zero Coupon Fund and a 25-Day MA Crossover System

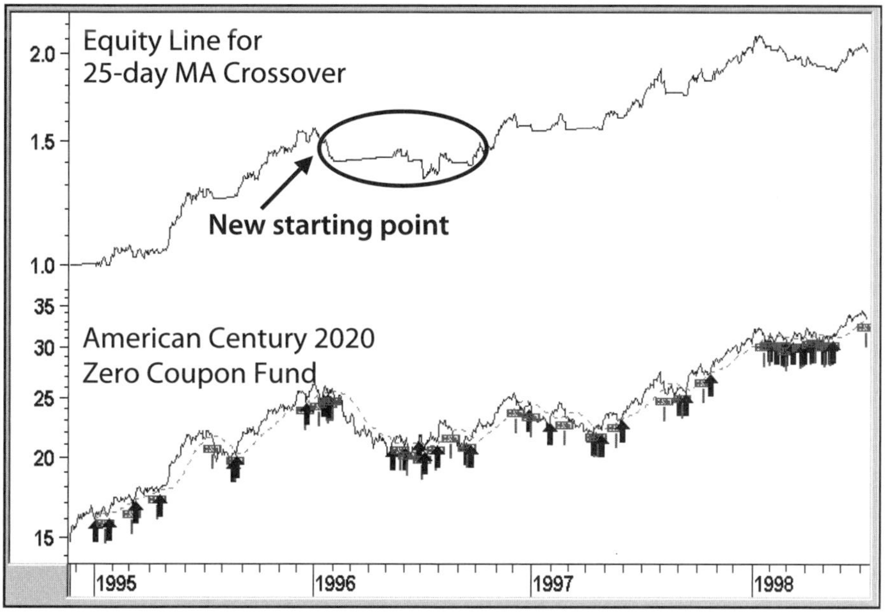

(Source: pring.com)

Table 8-1 shows the reward/risk ratio report calculated by the MetaStock® System Tester is defined as the worst open equity loss. This is the lowest level of profit or loss below the starting equity position, calculated as a ratio of the profit at the latest period or the latest plot on the equity line. When the number is below zero, the risk outweighs the reward; when above, the reward outweighs the risk. The worst number is negative one hundred (−100) and the best is plus one hundred (+100). In this case, the reward/risk is about as good as it gets because the ratio is just under 100. We have to be a bit careful, because the place in the equity line where the losses appear can affect the reward/risk ratio as you can see within the ellipse in the table above. In Chart 8-8, I have started the testing just before this losing period and the equity curve looks very similar. The losing streak is placed within the ellipse.

If the test were stopped at this point, the reward/risk ratio would be negative, because the starting point was followed by a loss. In Table 8-2, you can see the reward/risk was still good, but fell to 78 percent from 98 percent. The average win was certainly much better than the average loss. The report also shows the system was cutting losses and letting profits run because there were only ten wins compared to the 20 losses.

Table 8-1 American Century and a 25-Day MA Crossover System

Winning long trades	16	Winning short trades	0
Total winning trades	16	Total losing trades	22
Amount of winning trades	1.35	Amount of losing trades	-0.46
Average win	0.08	Average loss	-0.02
Largest win	0.24	Largest loss	-0.08
Average length of win	31.88	Average length of loss	4.50
Longest winning trade	80	Longest losing trade	15
Most consecutive wins	5	Most consecutive losses	6
Total bars out	382	Average length out	9.79
Longest out period	69		
System close drawdown	0.00	Profit/Loss index	68.76
System open drawdown	-0.00	Reward/Risk index	99.80
Max open trade drawdown	-0.08	Buy/Hold index	-19.37

Reward/risk

Chart 8-8 American Century and a 25-Day MA Crossover System

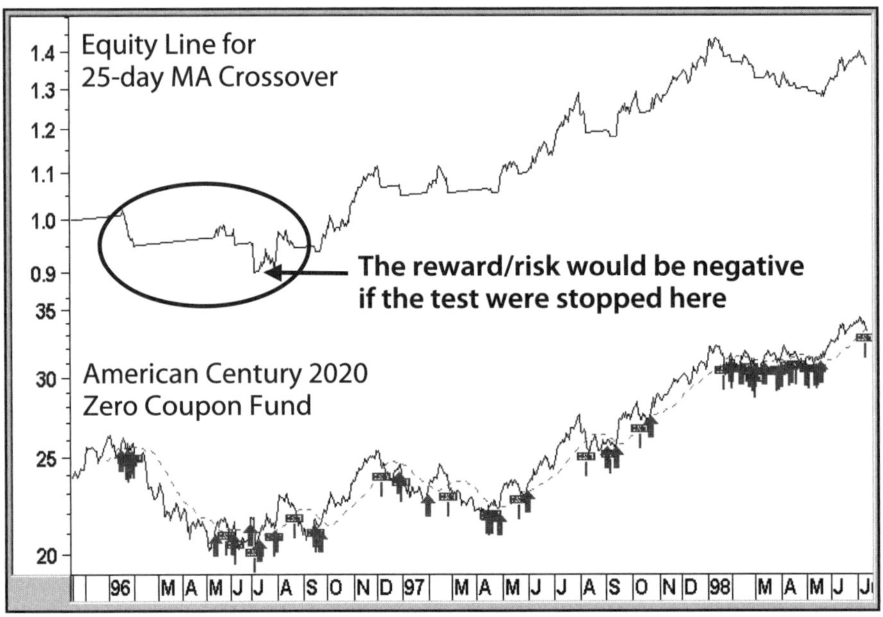

(Source: pring.com)

Table 8-2 American Century and a 25-Day MA Crossover System

Winning long trades	11	Winning short trades	0
Total winning trades	11	Total losing trades	20
Amount of winning trades	0.59	Amount of losing trades	-0.30
Average win	0.05	Average loss	-0.02
Largest win	0.14	Largest loss	-0.05
Average length of win	28.36	Average length of loss	3.55
Longest winning trade	62	Longest losing trade	11
Most consecutive wins	2	Most consecutive losses	6
Total bars out	346	Average length out	10.81
Longest out period	69	Reward/risk	
System close drawdown	-0.10	Profit/Loss index	54.48
System open drawdown	-0.10	Reward/Risk index	78.52
Max open trade drawdown	-0.05	Buy/Hold index	-8.77

COMPARE MARKET ENVIRONMENTS

Pay attention to the market environment during the testing period. It may be great to show a fabulous result from a test, but it is also important to examine the kind of market conditions when the trading took place. If you are testing a trending system in a trending market, such as in Chart 8-9, using a 40-day MA for McDonald's, the results had better be good because the system was meant to operate in that type of environment. But does it test in a trading range environment? Take a look at ellipses A and B, which contain ranging activity. In the case of A, magnified in Chart 8-10, the results are quite good. The arrow connects the start of the trading range to the breakout point. You can also see the arrow for the equity line slopes up, indicating the system did better than the buy-hold approach. Trading range B, magnified in Chart 8-11, was longer. The equity line arrow slopes downward, indicating the actual price beat the system marginally. Overall, in this particular instance, the trend following the MA crossover system did reasonably well in a sideways moving market. I have to say, though, a trending system does not normally do as well as this in a trading range.

When optimizing, look to see if similar combinations test as profitably. When you are optimizing for the best parameters the odds are greater that

Chart 8-9 McDonald's and a 40-Day MA Crossover System

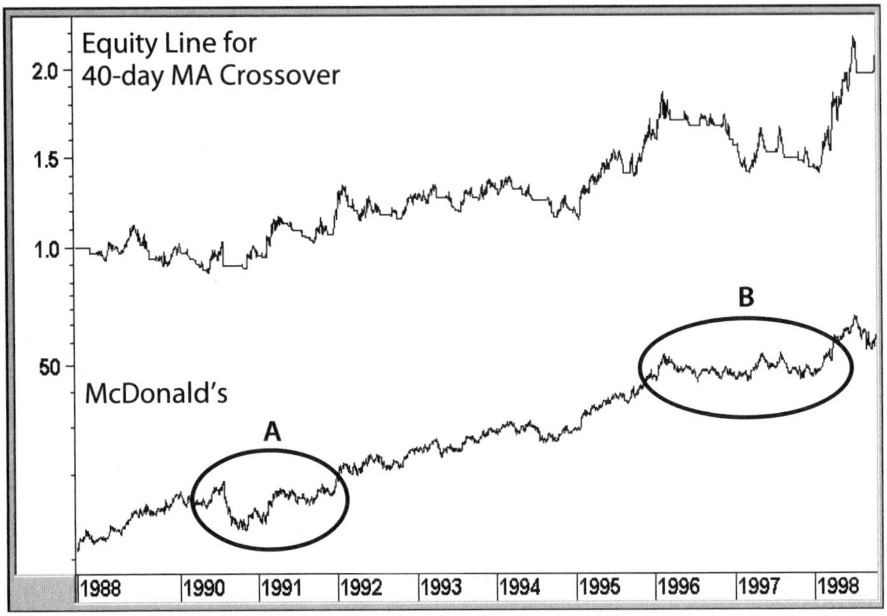

(Source: pring.com)

Chart 8-10 McDonald's and a 40-Day MA Crossover System

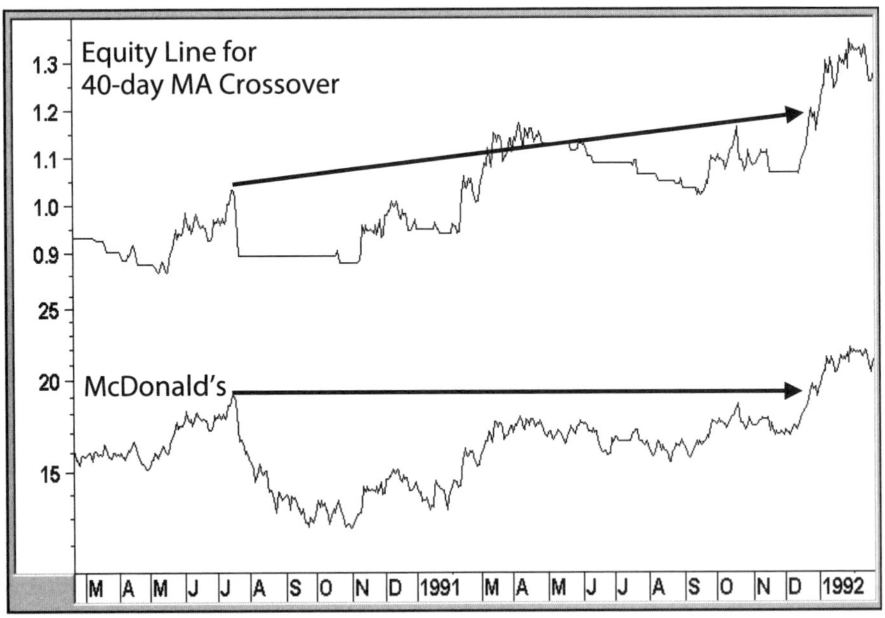

(Source: pring.com)

Chart 8-11 McDonald's and a 40-Day MA Crossover System

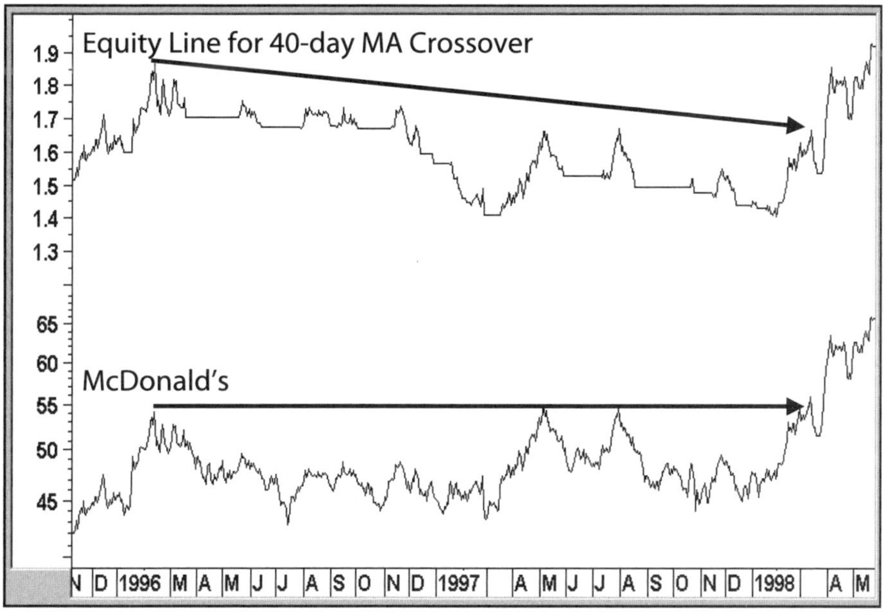

(Source: pring.com)

Table 8-3 Invesco Health Sciences Fund

Consistent cluster

INVESCO STRAT PT HEALTH SCI

Status	Net Profit	Percent...	Tot...	Win...	Losi...	Avg...	OP...
OK	17.6395	1763.95	130	56	74	4.3149	17
OK	16.2705	1627.05	143	65	78	3.8120	15
OK	15.8549	1585.49	126	51	75	4.7651	18
OK	15.3885	1538.85	137	59	78	3.9239	16
OK	15.3865	1538.65	114	47	67	5.0309	21
OK	15.3799	1537.99	119	50	69	4.6175	19
OK	15.0677	1506.77	118	52	66	4.3718	20
OK	13.9308	1393.08	112	46	66	6.1399	22
OK	13.6044	1360.44	171	74	97	3.4844	13
OK	[illegible]	[illegible]	[illegible]	[illegible]	[illegible]	[illegible]	[illegible]

Table 8-4 Matthews Korea Fund

Isolated example

MATTHEWS KOREA

...	Status	Net Profit	Perce...	Tot...	Win...	Losi...	Avg ...	[illegible]...
	OK	0.2919	29.19	64	29	35	1.4042	3
	OK	0.2819	28.19	14	7	7	1.1769	17
	OK	0.2564	25.64	14	7	7	1.1163	18
	OK	0.2563	25.63	11	5	6	1.5407	25
	OK	0.2309	23.09	11	5	6	1.3101	26
	OK	0.2220	22.20	10	4	6	4.0792	55
	OK	0.2176	21.76	8	3	5	4.3120	65
	OK	0.1969	19.69	12	6	6	0.8897	21
	OK	0.1948	19.48	12	5	7	1.1870	27

the results will be more reliable if several timespans of similar duration are among the top performers, as opposed to one isolated incident. Look at the report in Table 8-3, for the Invesco Health Sciences Fund. I tested for MA crossovers from 10 to 65 days. See how all the top results have very similar timespans, since the 15-, 17- and 18-day spans are all in the top four. This means the results are less likely to be a statistical fluke because they reflect a clear-cut pattern. In Table 8-4, of the Matthews Korea Fund, the 3-day span is clearly an isolated example. It is therefore a statistical fluke and less likely to be reliable.

Chapter 9

Enhancing the Results

LET THE TREND WORK IN YOUR FAVOR

Now we turn our attention to the task of enhancing the results of our system. They say a "rising tide lifts all boats." Well, the same is true of markets. Take a look at Chart 9-1, which is a very basic system. Buy signals are generated when the 21-day RSI crosses above 50 and sell signals when it crosses below 50. The thick lines above the price indicate a primary bull and bear market. The areas contained within the ellipses indicate signals that develop in the direction of the main trend. The first three ellipses indicate buy signals in a bull market, and the two on the right, sell signals in a bear market. As you can see, all of these price movements have good magnitude. Now look at Chart 9-2, which shows the sell modes in the bull market. These are the contrary signals and are the ones that experience whipsaw price moves. The same is true for the buy signals in a bear market as featured in Chart 9-3. Generally, they also have a bad track record. I do not wish to leave you with the impression this is true of *every* contratrend signal. In Chart 9-4, for instance, I have highlighted a consolidation within the bull trend when both buy and sell signals resulted in whipsaws. When the trend is in the process of reversing, the odds of a pro-trend whipsaw are higher because the reversal process often involves a trading range as the price traces out a reversal pattern. This is exactly what happened for both the 1992 bottom and the 1994 top as featured in Chart 9-5.

Chart 9-1 General Motors and a 21-Day RSI

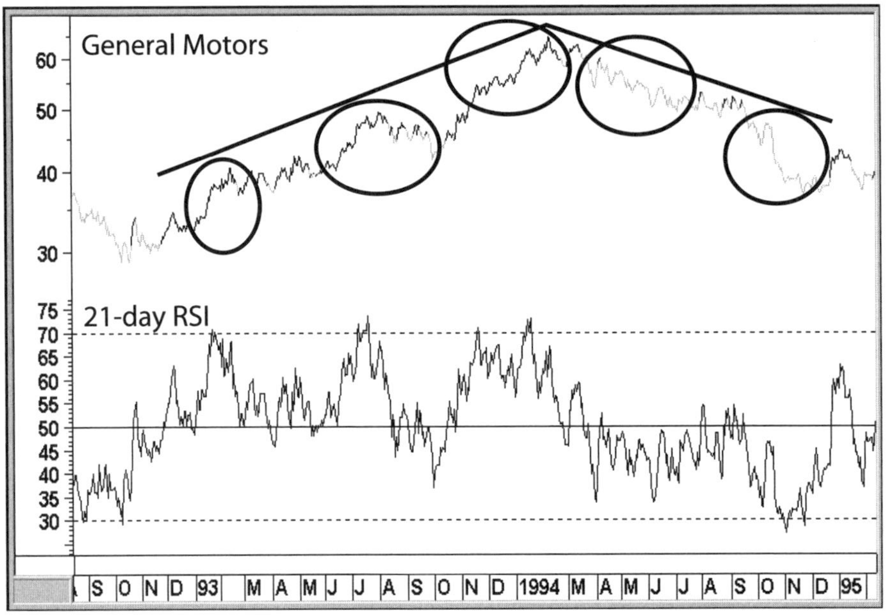

(Source: pring.com)

Chart 9-2 General Motors and a 21-Day RSI

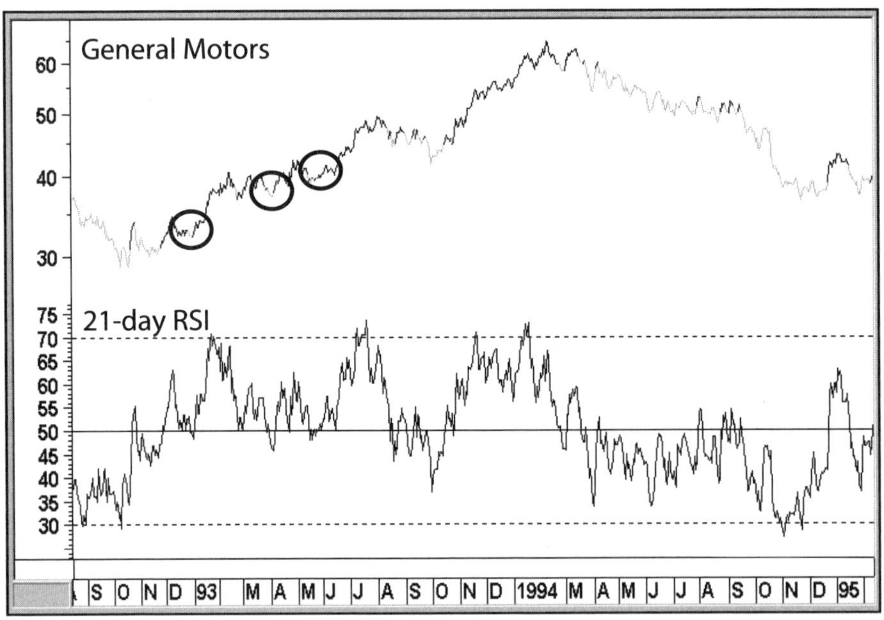

(Source: pring.com)

Chart 9-3 General Motors and a 21-Day RSI

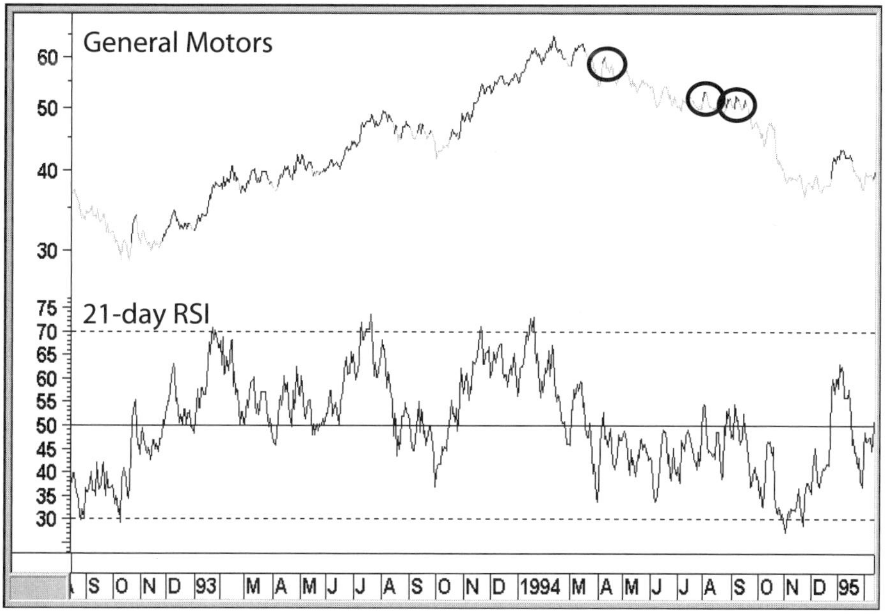

(Source: pring.com)

Chart 9-4 General Motors and a 21-Day RSI

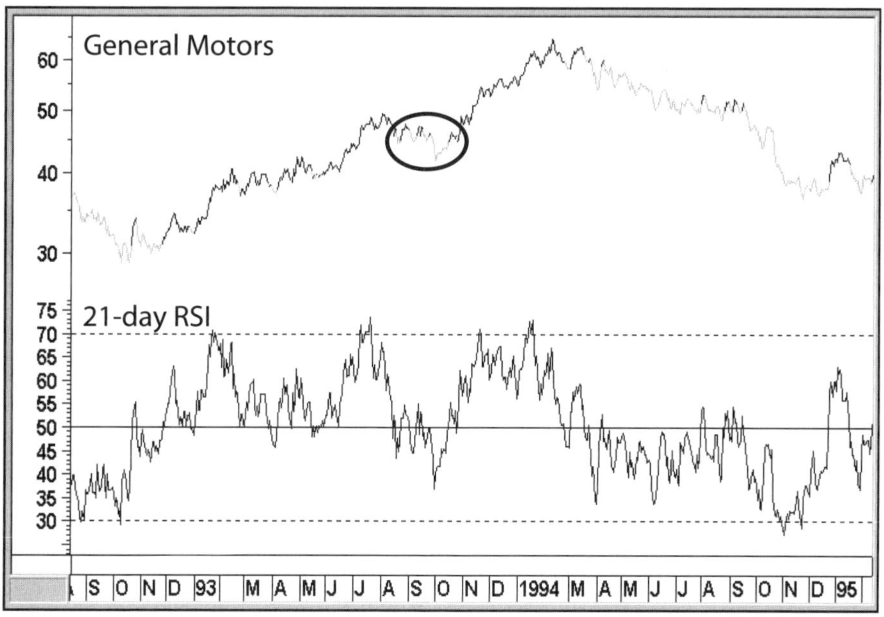

(Source: pring.com)

Chart 9-5 General Motors and a 21-Day RSI

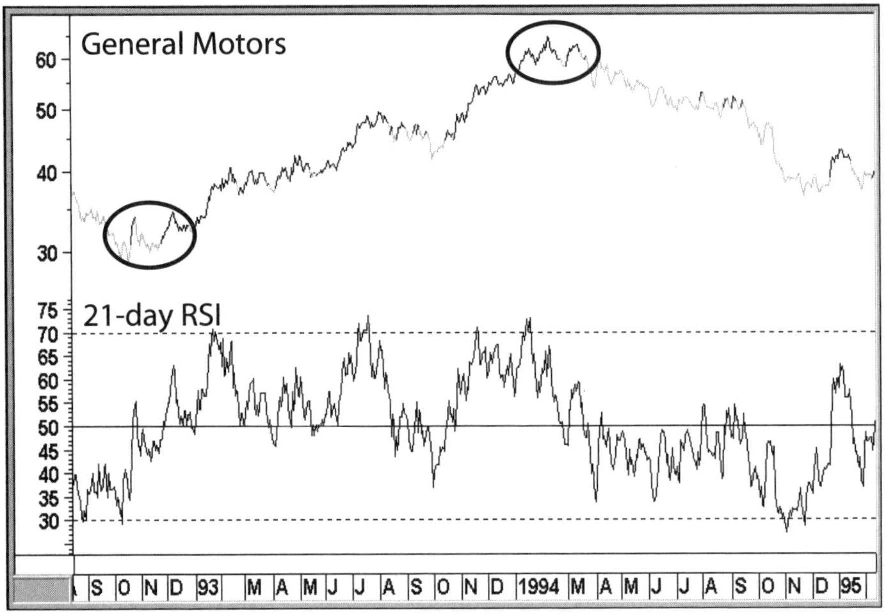

(Source: pring.com)

The point is, if a worthwhile trending short-term move develops, it is much more likely to extend in the direction of the main, or primary trend. It makes sense to develop a system that attempts to identify the direction of the main trend and then only trigger signals for pro-trend short-term moves. Such a system would never go short in a bull market or long in a bear market. This is easier said than done, but I will give you a few additional pointers later on.

TAKE ADVANTAGE OF CARRYING COSTS

In many instances, markets come with a carrying cost. If possible, design a system so it takes advantage of these charges. For example, all options come with a time premium. Buyers *pay* the premium but are offered the possibility of huge gains. Alternately, sellers *receive* the premium, even if there is no change in price, but they accept a theoretical unlimited risk. While the potential for an individual gain from selling an option is not as great as buying one, the odds favor the seller.

Consequently, more consistent profits can be obtained. Look at Chart 9-6. The series in the upper portion of the chart is IBM and in the lower portion is an October 1998 $125 call. The price of IBM is the same at the start of the chart as it is at the end. In fact, it is the strike price of $125. There is no change in price for the stock but there is a significant loss for the option. The starting price in the chart is $10, but the closing price, about 5 months later, is $2.80. Therefore, selling the option offers a pretty large percentage gain but the price paid was a theoretical unlimited risk. However, had we been using a well-tested and reliable system, the erosion of the time premium would have worked in our favor. Obviously, I have used this example to emphasize my point, but I do not wish to leave you with the idea that this approach always results in a profit because it certainly does not. Selling options does put the odds in your favor. Another word of caution: you should always pick securities that are liquid and unlikely to experience unexpected news. For example, a takeover bid can push a stock's price up dramatically. Avoid takeover candidates when selling options if you can. Also, trade this approach over several different stocks so the risk of a major unexpected surprise is well diversified. We also have to remember premiums on options rise and fall with the level of volatility as well as the time element. This factor should be borne in mind.

It is normal for futures contracts to have a carrying cost. If you buy the contract, you have to pay the carrying cost depending on how long you

Chart 9-6 IBM Versus IBM October 1998 $125 Call

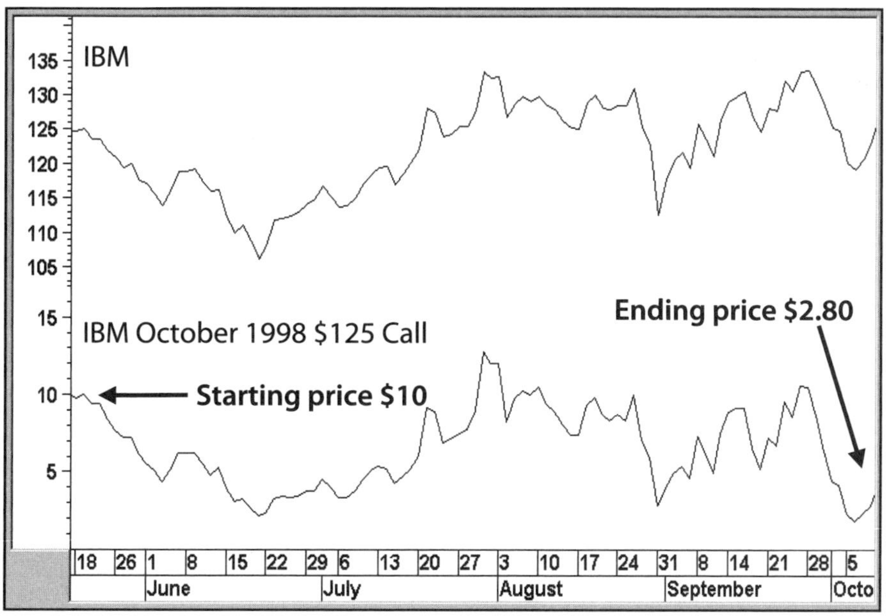

(Source: pring.com)

hold it. Alternately, if you short it, you will receive the carrying cost. It is just a small point, but it is amazing how carrying costs can work for or against you over a long period of time. Look at the two series shown in the Chart 9-7. The upper series is cash gold as reflected by the London PM Fix. The lower series is December 1998 Gold as traded in New York. It is true there will *almost* always be different prices for each series because they close at different times in the day. The major difference, though, is the carrying cost. It is fairly obvious that the futures contract is far weaker than the cash price because the carrying cost built into the price declines as the contract comes closer to expiration. This can be seen in Chart 9-7 as the September low in cash is well above that of July, whereas the price for the futures contract in September was below that of July.

It may not always make sense to short gold to take advantage of this type of situation because the price could well be in a bull market and we do not want to trade in the opposite direction to the main trend. However, if you want to go long, you can always take advantage of the carrying cost by trading a far out or deferred contract. This is because three things determine the price of a futures contract: the underlying cash price, the carrying cost, and the amount of time required to carry. In some markets a fourth factor, expectations, also weighs in. This means if the carrying cost per day,

Chart 9-7 Cash Gold Versus December 1998 Gold

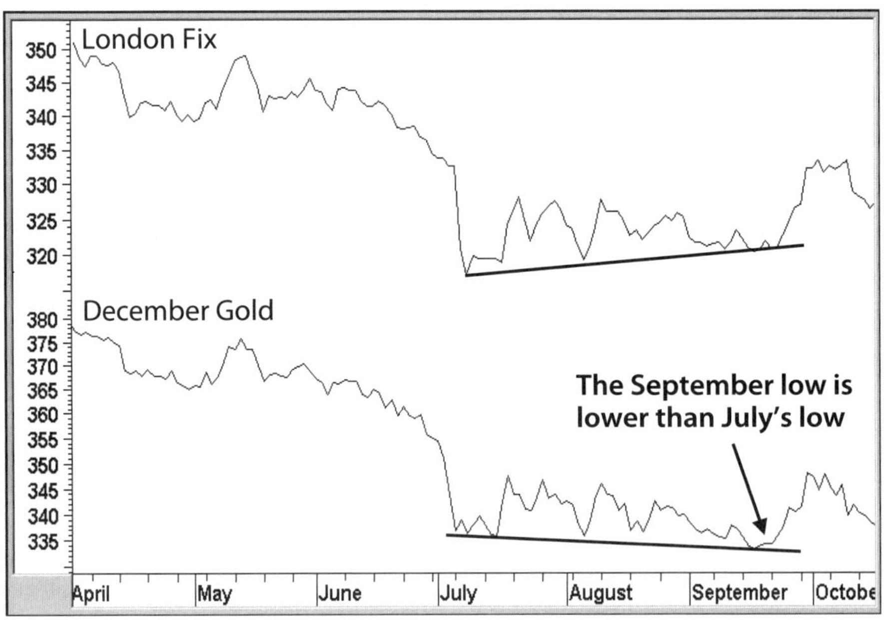

(Source: pring.com)

which is principally the interest rate charge, stays the same and the price goes up, the far out contracts will increase in price more than the nearby months. This is because the higher the price, the greater the interest rate cost (assuming no change in the level of interest rates). If the price and the interest rate go up, then the far out contracts will increase even faster. The principal problem with deferred contracts is they are usually far less liquid, so the spread between the bid and ask can be much greater.

Remember the point I made earlier: not all deferred futures contract prices are perfectly related to the carrying cost because they cannot be arbitraged. Therefore, psychological factors may sometimes affect the relationship between the far out prices and the spot price. Always monitor the open interest in these contracts together with the historical relationship between the cash and delayed contracts prior to basing a trading strategy on these relationships.

Another point to keep in mind is that shortages of product in the cash or spot market can lead to what is known as *backwardation,* where it is the nearby months that trade above the deferred contracts for a temporary period because of a shortage of physical product. Such a swing from a carrying charge market, known as "contango" to "backwardation," could obviously have an effect on a system based on the normal carrying charge relationship. However, the automatic nature of the signals triggered by the system should limit losses on a fairly timely basis, provided the system is well tested.

Chapter 10
Applying Systems and Practical Guidelines

INTRODUCTION

Having learned about the designing, testing, appraising, and enhancing processes, it is now time to take the biggest step: applying the system to the market place. First let's cover several practical guidelines to follow.

EXECUTE PHANTOM TRADES AND ACT ON EVERY SIGNAL WITHOUT QUESTION

It is a good idea to take a system and pretend you are actually placing orders in real time. Then keep a written record of the paper profits or losses. If it is a good system, or if it is a bad one experiencing good returns, you will find this process to be temporarily disappointing since some profits will be given up. However, if it loses money during this phantom period, you will find out that the system is not perfect. If you have the discipline and courage to start trading with it after this series of adversities, you will be in a much stronger position to stay with it the next time it performs poorly. Before actually committing money, be sure that the string of losses did not occur because the system was weak, but because it was a typical period during the testing period. Alternately, if this poor period resulted in a record drawdown, then certainly think twice before entering the market with actual money.

If you have confidence in your system, do not second-guess it. Otherwise, unnecessary emotion and undisciplined action will creep back into the decision-making process. Also, you may miss out on a major move just before it is about to get under way. In the example in Chart 10-1 you can see a series of whipsaws within the ellipse. Such disappointment would have encouraged the average trader to give up, but look what happened—the whipsaws were followed by an extremely strong upside move, and the profits more than offset the previous losses.

Also, make sure you have enough capital to survive the worst losing streak. When you are devising a system, it is always a good idea to assume the worst possible scenario and to make sure that you start off with enough capital to survive such a period. In this respect, it is worth noting that the most profitable moves usually occur *after* a prolonged period of whipsawing, as we just saw. Remember, one of the most important things about applying mechanical systems is to stay the course and be persistent. Often the best signals come at the time when we feel least encouraged to apply them, and this is usually after a string of small losses.

Chart 10-1 CRB Composite and a 54-Day MA Crossover

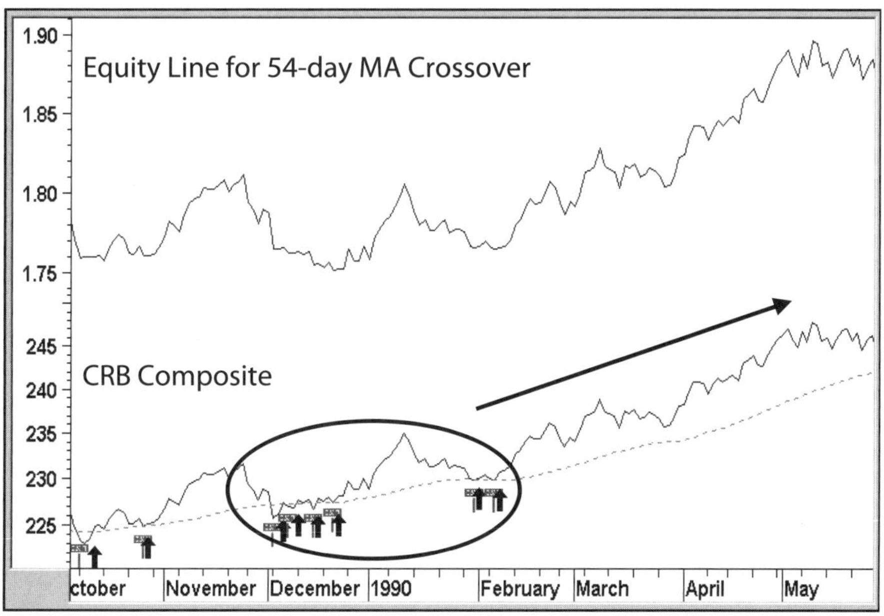

(Source: pring.com)

COMPARE THE ACTUAL WITH THE TESTED

Once a system has been thoroughly tested and applied, it is of paramount importance to compare the actual results to previous performance. Remember, a well-designed system should behave in a similar way to the test. If the tested model produced gains averaging 5 percent per quarter, then a quarter with a 10 percent loss experienced in real time is not consistent. You will find real-time performance can just as easily develop with a profit as with a loss. For psychological reasons, it is probably better to experience a couple of small losses than a large profit in this initial trade. This is because people tend to learn very little when things are going their way, but find it more difficult to deal with taking losses. In fact, the odds of the first trade being a winning one should be about as great as the win/loss ratio in the sample testing period.

It is not a bad idea to set up a table featuring the highlights of the testing period with that of the real-time sessions when evaluating the real-time results. Table 10-1 offers a partial overview, annualized profits, number of trades per year, percentage of winning trades, percentage of largest drawdown, largest winning and largest percent losing streak, and so forth. Then, as time passes, you can enter data for the real-time sessions. Obviously, you do not want to wait for a whole year before entering the average num-

Table 10-1 Comparison of Test to Real Time

Test Results		Real Time Results	
Annualized Profits %	15	Annualized Profits %	10
Number of trades per year	10	Number of trades per year	8
% winning trades	45	% winning trades	55
Largest % drawdown	20	Largest % drawdown	10
Largest % winning streak	20	Largest % winning streak	15
Largest % losing streak	15	Largest % losing streak	8

ber of trades per year, for example, so enter a monthly pro-rata figure. If you find after 3 or 6 months that real time is dramatically underperforming the tested data on a wide number of fronts, then the odds are the system is not living up to expectations. In this case, the real-time results at a 10 percent annualized rate are not quite so good as the test results at 15 percent, but still satisfactory. It does do better, though, in the area of consistency, where 55 percent of the trades are profitable compared to 45 percent for the test period. The largest drawdown is also less at 10 percent compared to 20 percent for the test. By and large, the real-time results at this point indicate there are no fundamental reasons for questioning the validity of the test data.

Occasionally, unexpected random events, such as an earthquake and other acts of God, materialize. Such developments should be recognized as "out of test" experiences and not be used to justify the dropping of a system. Also, if you experience an unusual string of losses, do not give up, provided they are consistent with some poor period during the test. However, if this period of losses far exceeds anything experienced in the test, it is a different matter.

By the same token, you should become equally as wary if the system produces more profits than ever before. This is because the equilibrium between the tested and actual results is out of kilter, but for a positive reason. Normally, the juicy profit picture causes us great pleasure and we overlook such discrepancies. Bear in mind, if a system shows dramatically better profits in real rather than tested time, it is just as likely to move in the opposite direction and throw up far worse profits than the test period. In such cases, it is a better idea to take those unexpected profits and move to the sidelines, continuing to appraise the results as you go. For example, profit may have been earned because of greater volatility, and volatility, just like leverage, can work both ways. Larger profits due to greater volatility can produce equal, if not greater, losses. Since we are interested in consistency with low volatility, this is not such a good idea. My advice in such situations is to closely examine the results. You may have been positioned on the right side of an unexpected and unanticipated event purely by chance. Then examine and compare the actual with the simulated results more closely. If there is great inconsistency, then take the profit and drop the system!

REASONS FOR SYSTEM FAILURE

Obviously, we enter the period of actually trading a new system in real time with a great deal of optimism and hope. However, we must be prepared for the fact that the system will exceed the maximum drawdown established in the testing period. Does this mean that it failed? Probably so, and there are three reasons why a system fails in the real world.

1. It is an inherently poor system.

If you followed the guidelines for design and testing outlined earlier, this is probably not the cause. Perhaps you were a bit careless during the testing process, and did not review the results carefully enough; were satisfied with big profits, but overlooked the huge risk required to achieve them? Alternatively, did you introduce too many rules? Did you overfit the data? Was the system improperly optimized? Or the testing period too short? Did you just choose securities that trended when you should also have considered trading range environments? Perhaps you chose the optimized parameters that offered the greatest rate of return for a specific period rather than tried to find the best average parameters.

2. Market conditions have changed.

If the system was well designed and thoroughly tested, this is the most likely reason for failure. Even here, unusual market conditions such as volatility and liquidity changes adversely influence the results. This is an indication that the system was not sufficiently tested with a wide spectrum of securities in different market environments. Unless the cause is a random event, such as a major political or economic crisis, it is best to go back to the drawing board and retest for the kind of market conditions that were not covered by previous tests.

3. There are problems with simulation.

Whenever we apply a system, it is important to remember a simulation can never duplicate exactly what will happen in real-time trading. The shorter the trading horizon and the number of trades, other things being equal, the greater the discrepancy between the simulated and actual results. If the system fails badly in real time, then the simulation should be examined in great detail to see if it differs from the real-time application. It is also true that the more fallacious the simulation, the greater the trading losses once it is applied in real time. Therefore, it should be examined to make quite sure an allowance is made for any discrepancies that might develop. Following are some of the ways in which simulation can differ from reality.

THE EFFECT OF COMMISSIONS

The cost of commissions is fairly obvious and must be accounted for in any system. If you trade a lot, commissions can easily become a major cost of doing business. This is where systems based on weekly or monthly data have a large advantage. Always make sure you add a realistic amount for commissions when simulating a result. Table 10-2 is reproduced from the *OnTrack Report,* an excellent mutual fund letter published by Michael Price of New Orleans, La. He used it to make the point that commissions can really eat up a lot of your profit if you are not careful. He assumed 100 transactions per year at a fairly modest $27 transaction fee for each side of the trade. The extreme left-hand column shows the size of the account, that is, starting off with $10,000 at the top and working down to $400,000 at the bottom. The top row represents the growth rate, starting from 0 percent and working up to a pretty hefty 40 percent per annum. The point of the table is to show that transaction fees in an active account—even as small as $27 per trade—can have a pretty debilitating effect on a portfolio. It shows, for example, that even a 10 percent growth rate, which is respectable in normal times, loses 44 percent on an account of $10,000. It is only when the account size increases to $125,000 that a return in excess of 5 percent can be earned. Note also that the $10,000 account fails to make money, even when the return increases to a stupendous 40 percent. This compares to a 35 percent rate of return for an account of $125,000.

When it is fully margined at 50 percent the results take on a different meaning (Table 10-3, also from *OnTrack*). You are severely punished if you lose money at a 10 percent growth rate. Allowing for a 7 percent margin charge, the loss is reduced slightly from 44 percent to 41 percent. However,

Table 10-2 Effect of Commissions on Performance

$/ANN	0%	10%	20%	30%	40%
10000	-54.0%	-44.0%	-34.0%	-24.0%	-14.0%
25000	-21.6%	-11.6%	-1.6%	8.4%	18.4%
50000	-10.8%	-0.8%	9.2%	19.2%	29.2%
75000	-7.2%	2.8%	12.8%	22.8%	32,8%
100000	-5.4%	4.6%	14.6%	24.6%	34.6%
125000	-4.3%	5.7%	15.7%	25.7%	35.7%
150000	-3.6%	6.4%	16.4%	26.4%	36.4%
175000	-3.1%	6.9%	16.9%	26.9%	36.9%
200000	-2.7%	7.3%	17.3%	27.3%	37.3%
225000	-2.4%	7.6%	17.6%	27.6%	37.6%
250000	-2.2%	7.8%	17.8%	27.8%	37.8%
275000	-2.0%	8.0%	18.0%	28.0%	38.0%
300000	-1.8%	8.2%	18.2%	28.2%	38.2%
325000	-1.7%	8.3%	18.3%	28.3%	38.3%
350000	-1.5%	8.5%	18.5%	28.5%	38.5%
375000	-1.4%	8.6%	18.6%	28.6%	38.6%
400000	-1.4%	8.7%	18.7%	28.7%	38.7%

Table 10-3 Results Using Margin

$/ANN	0%	10%	20%	30%	40%
10000	-61.0%	-41.0%	-21.0%	-1.0%	19.0%
25000	-28.6%	-8.6%	11.4%	31.4%	51.4%
50000	-17.8%	2.2%	22.2%	42.2%	62.2%
75000	-14.2%	5.8%	25.8%	45.8%	65.8%
100000	-12.4%	7.6%	27.6%	47.6%	67.6%
125000	-11.3%	8.7%	28.7%	48.7%	68.7%
150000	-10.6%	9.4%	29.4%	49.4%	69.4%
175000	-10.1%	9.9%	29.9%	49.9%	69.9%
200000	-9.7%	10.3%	30.3%	50.3%	70.3%
225000	-9.4%	10.6%	30.6%	50.6%	70.6%
250000	-9.2%	10.8%	30.8%	50.8%	70.8%
275000	-9.0%	11.0%	31.0%	51.0%	71.0%
300000	-8.8%	11.2%	31.2%	51.2%	71.2%
325000	-8.7%	11.3%	31.3%	51.3%	71.3%
350000	-8.5%	11.5%	31.5%	51.5%	71.5%
375000	-8.4%	11.6%	31.6%	51.6%	71.6%
400000	-8.4%	11.7%	31.7%	51.7%	71.7%

the 5 percent growth rate can now be achieved with a $75,000 account compared to the previous $125,000. Also, with a $10,000 account, the 40 percent growth rate now achieves a 19 percent profit compared to a 14 percent loss. As it builds in size, so does the return. For example, a $125,000 account can achieve a 65 percent return with margin compared to 35 percent on a cash basis.

I do not want to leave you with the idea that working with margin is always a good thing because it is not. Later on we will see how gearing affects mechanical systems and can wipe you out even though the system itself is profitable. One final point I will keep reiterating is the fewer the number of trades, the smaller will be the transaction costs and the more profitable will be the system, other things being equal.

PLACING ORDERS

I would like to remark on the various ways orders can be placed, since this can also affect the results of the system. A *market order* is immediately executed at the prevailing price. In a "fast" market this will usually be executed at a price somewhat different from that quoted on the quote machine. Chart 10-2 shows a sharp rally in September bonds. Often the bond market reacts

Chart 10-2 September Bonds

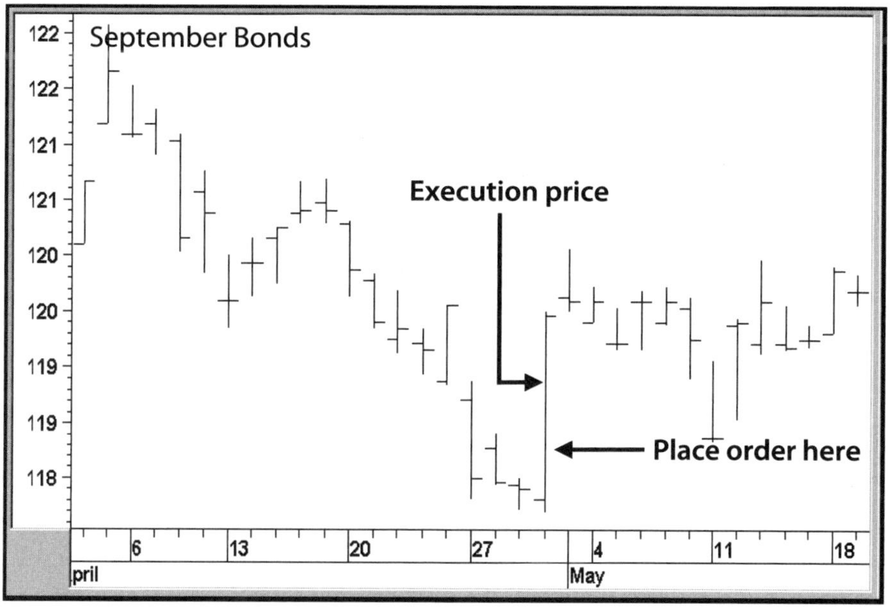

(Source: pring.com)

to the monthly employment numbers with extreme volatility. You may enter your order at a certain price, such as I have indicated on the chart. However, liquidity can really dry up when unexpected news develops. It is possible your broker gives you a quote, but by the time you place the order and get an execution, the price moves considerably. This is obviously an unusual situation but one for which an allowance should be made in the simulation.

A *sell-stop order* is executed as a market order when the price declines to the designated level. A *buy-stop order* is placed at a price below the current level and must be filled at, or below, the price. A *sell limit order* is placed at a price above the current level and must be filled at, or above, the price. Both buy and sell limit orders are ways around the slippage problem. There is no guarantee that they will be executed if the market is fast or only trades at the requested price for a very short period. For example, in Chart 10-3, International Paper, the chances of a buy limit order being filled at $53¹/₄ would be remote. Not only would this have been the low of the day, but the volume bar reveals there was very little activity, especially in relation to the wide spread between the high and the low.

Finally, a *market if touched (MIT) order* becomes a market order as soon as the security trades at the designated price. These orders are useful if, in the case of a long position, the price is briefly touched but not enough trading takes place to ensure a fill. The next best thing at that point is a

Chart 10-3 International Paper

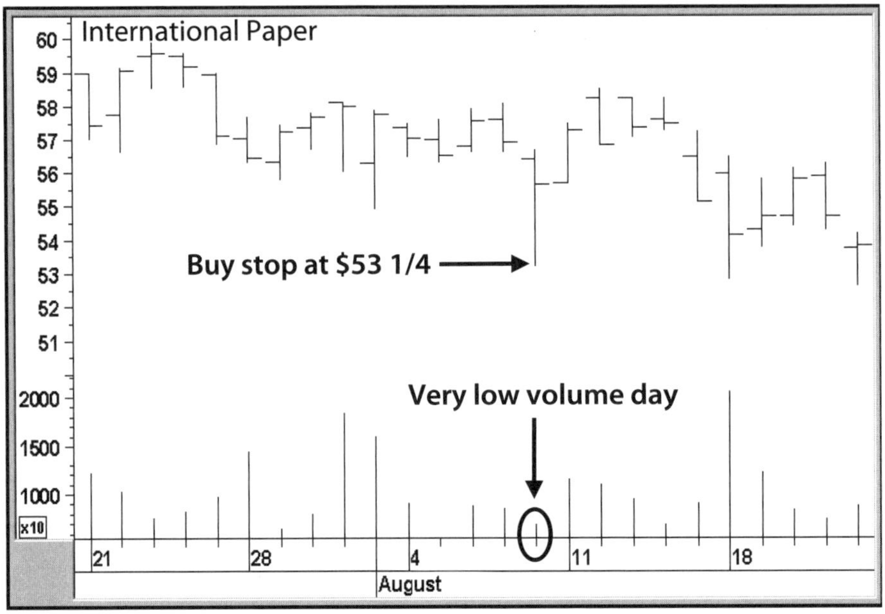

(Source: pring.com)

market order since this ensures that your order should be filled fairly closely to the price.

Buy-stop limit orders and *sell-stop limit orders* in Chart 10-4 are orders to close out an existing position by buying or selling when a price reaches a designated level. Prices, though, may move well beyond the designated price. This is where the limit comes in. Let us say I want to buy the Japanese yen when it breaks above the trendline. The breakout occurs with a rally above 71.8¢. Instead of placing a stop at 71.8¢, which would be executed at the market, I place a *stop limit* at 72.5¢. This means if the price opens higher than 71.8¢, or if the price trades too quickly through the 71.8¢ to 72.5¢ zone, then I do not get filled. There is a good chance that my order may not get filled since the yen trades around the world and is especially liquid in Asia. That is exactly what happened in this case because the price opened at 74.3¢ with a low of 72.75¢ (Chart 10-5). If you research and test a system using limit orders this is definitely a problem for which an allowance has to be made. In this instance, if I had come into the day short and the price had traded through my limit, it would have been quite painful. This is why I would never place a limit order when trying to get out of a position since the risk can be substantial, especially where a large amount of the trading takes place outside of my time zone.

Chart 10-4 September 1998 Japanese Yen

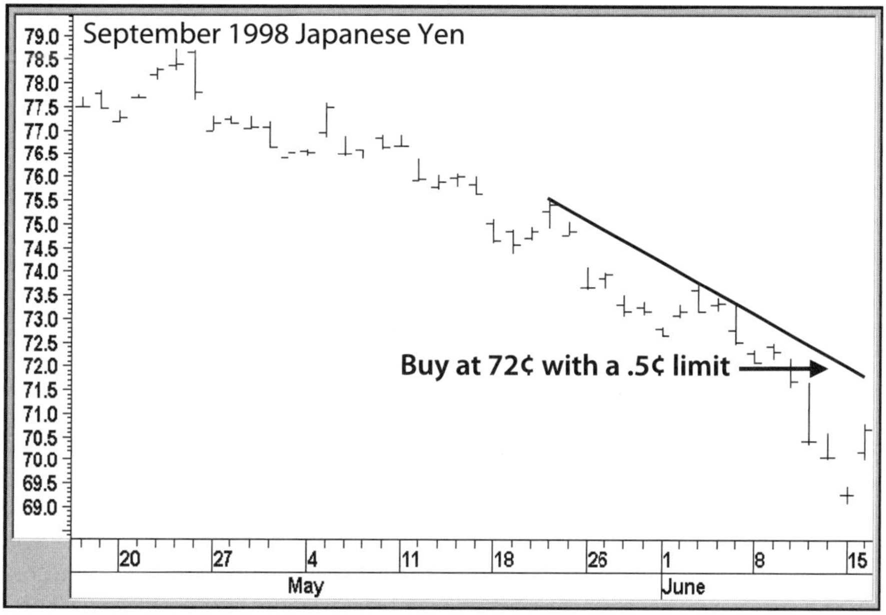

(Source: pring.com)

Chart 10-5 September 1998 Japanese Yen

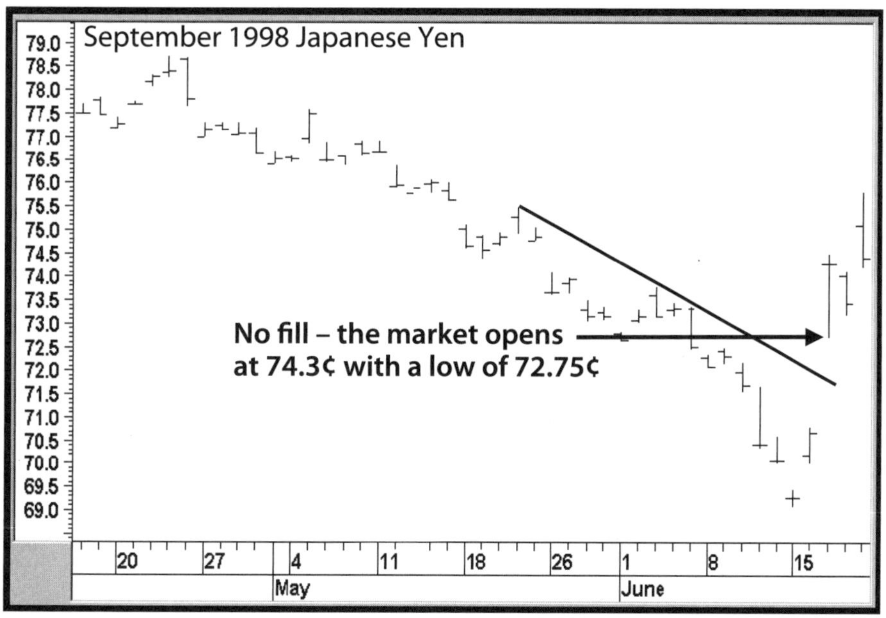

(Source: pring.com)

MORE ON SLIPPAGE

Whereas commissions are a transaction expense paid to a broker, *slippage* is a transaction expense paid to the trading floor. Commissions are easy to factor into a system since they are known ahead of time. Slippage, alternately, being the difference between the price you set and the one you get, is not. It should now be apparent that the amount of slippage will depend on liquidity conditions at the time the trade is executed. Often, a signal triggered by a system will develop at the same time as some important news is breaking. This means that everyone wants to buy, or head for the exits at the same time. It is then more or less impossible to satisfy your order at the requested price. Since extreme slippage will not occur very often and can vary a great deal from transaction to transaction, it is a good idea to add on a small cost to each trade as compensation, somewhat like an actuarial calculation in an insurance policy. Remember, it is better to err on the conservative side and lose out on a couple of opportunities than to trade with rose-colored spectacles and blow your account.

All markets are subject to *opening gaps.* These must be taken into consideration when setting up a system, particularly one with a time horizon of a few days. In such cases, it is of paramount importance to simulate the test incorporating opening prices. For example, if my buy stop is at 100 and the market opens at 101, this needs to be taken into consideration, but if the price opens at 99.5 and then trades through 100 this is not a problem. Consequently, some form of condition, allowing for either the triggered sell price or the opening price (whichever is higher) should be made for new longs or covering shorts and vice versa for sales and new short positions. Note that not all exchanges will accept these types of orders.

A final reality check for simulating real-time market conditions concerns *limit moves.* Many futures markets have trading limits. A *locked limit day* develops when the open, high, low and close for the day are the same and volume is low. When simulating historical trading activity an allowance must be made for the fact that it is extremely unlikely a buy or sell signal could be executed under such conditions, unless it is in the opposite direction to the trend at that time. Moreover, even if a stop is entered just close to a limit move, it is quite likely the market will move so quickly the trace could not be executed prior to the price trading at the limit.

Chart 10-6 features little horizontal bars that represent locked limit days. The whole rally during March encompassed a pretty sizeable gain that should have been taken into consideration in any simulation. Some markets, particularly agricultural ones, are very prone to limit moves. Crop

Chart 10-6 Lumber

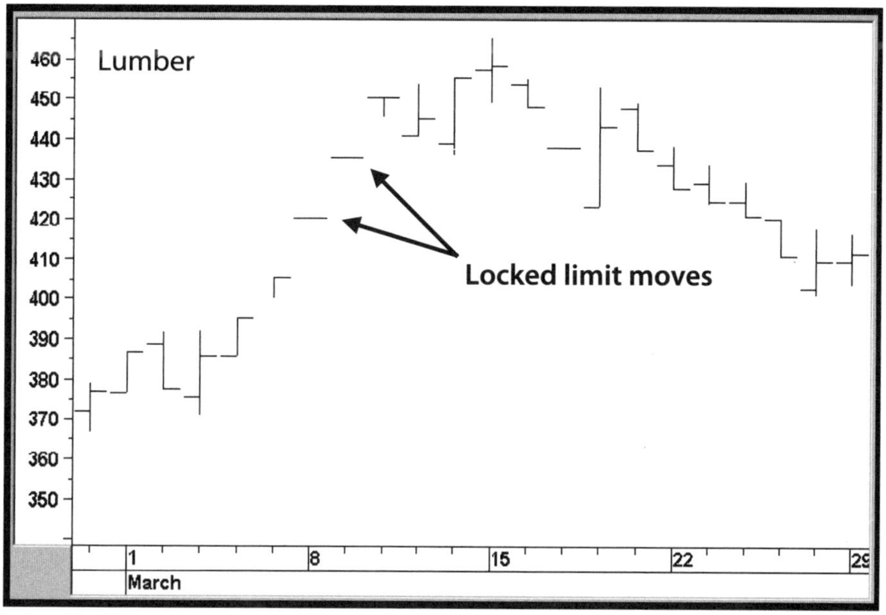

(Source: pring.com)

reports and extreme weather changes can easily affect their outlook. It is mandatory for any test period to be examined for the appearance of limit moves or a series of limit moves over a very long period of time, say, ten years or so. If your system cannot stand up to this type of scrutiny you run the risk of having it wipe out your account should you be caught on the wrong side of the market at the wrong time.

OVERFITTING

Overfitting involves the establishment of a profitable set of parameters for a specific sample of test data that has little or no forecasting value. This could be achieved by introducing specific rules or by overoptimization, and so forth. Any time your objective is to make the test period appear to be more profitable than it actually is counts as overfitting. Such a process totally ignores the fact that traders are interested in real-time trading in the future, not the past. The past is only useful in that it can be a guide to future performance. If an overfitted system looks fantastic on paper but does not bear any resemblance to the future, it is worse than useless.

Let us take an example. Look at Chart 10-7. Here is a nice uptrend for Heinz Foods. The system only trades from the long side and uses 25-day MA crossovers as buy and sell signals. As you can see, there are several whipsaws as indicated by the ellipses. I can easily get around this problem by finding out what filter would be required to eliminate them. In this case, I could say, buy on a positive crossover instead of selling on a negative crossover and wait until the price slips 5 percent below the moving average. In Chart 10-8, you can see that the 5 percent rule eliminates all of the whipsaws. Based on this sample of data, the system looks pretty good. However, if I move to a different period, you can see in Chart 10-9 that crossovers not only give late signals, but result in numerous whipsaws. By introducing this special rule, I may have made the test data as close to perfect as possible. In most instances this fantasyland cannot happen because the results cannot be extrapolated into the future with any degree of reliability.

Chart 10-7 Heinz

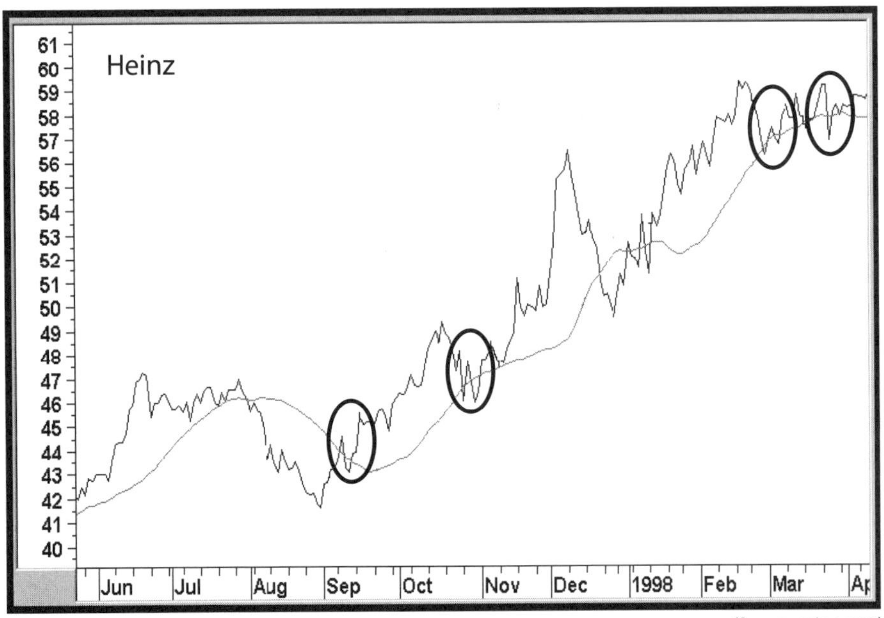

(Source: pring.com)

Chart 10-8 Heinz

(Source: pring.com)

Chart 10-9 Heinz

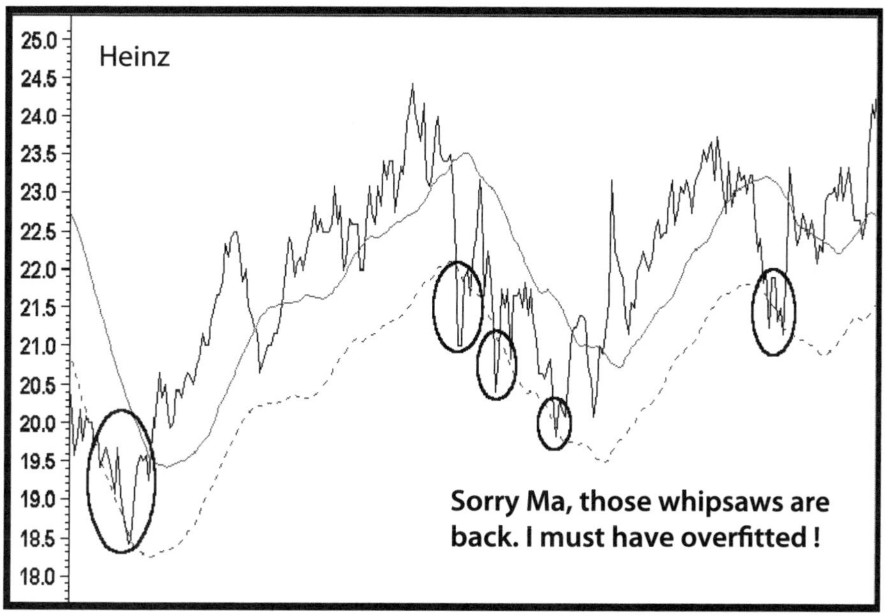

(Source: pring.com)

A more subtle form of overfitting comes when you *optimize for too many variables.* For example, I could optimize for a number of different MA timespans and instead of using simple crossovers I could use filters based on percentage crossovers. In addition, if the system only buys when the average is above a second optimized longer-term moving average, I am almost certain to come up with a pretty profitable combination. However, if I did a walk-through test using this set of optimized parameters, the odds of success would be very low. This is because optimizing three parameters in the test period is likely to have given me a good curve fit for that particular data sample but would not extrapolate to the future.

Chapter 11
The (Almost) Perfect System

MAKE SURE THE SYSTEM FITS YOUR PERSONALITY

If anyone says they have "The Perfect System" it is a bit of a misnomer since there is no such thing. I use "The (Almost) Perfect System" as the title of this section as a guideline to help you tailor-make the kind of system that can work for you. This is a very important part of the process. Remember, to be successful you need to act on every signal without question and without second-guessing what might happen. In order to arrive at this point, you must be psychologically tuned-in to the system and have total confidence in the outcome. The following are a few guidelines to steer you in that direction.

First, the system should be one that trades with your personality. If you are an intraday trader who likes the excitement of the moment, there is no sense in adopting a system that will trigger signals every six months or so. Chart 11-1 shows the Nikkei and the buy and sell signals that resulted from a 2-day MA crossover with no margin. This just happened to be the best-optimized timespan from a test ranging from 2 to 65 days as shown in Table 11-1. You will also notice a 17 percent drawdown in 1997. While we can say the system is successful based on these limited results, it is not for everybody. Many people just do not have time to devote to such trading, nor do they relish the constant excitement and emotional drain that its execution might involve. In this test, 222 signals, or one every 4 days, were triggered just based on going long. You also have to take your lifestyle into account.

Chart 11-1 Nikkei and a 2-Day MA Crossover

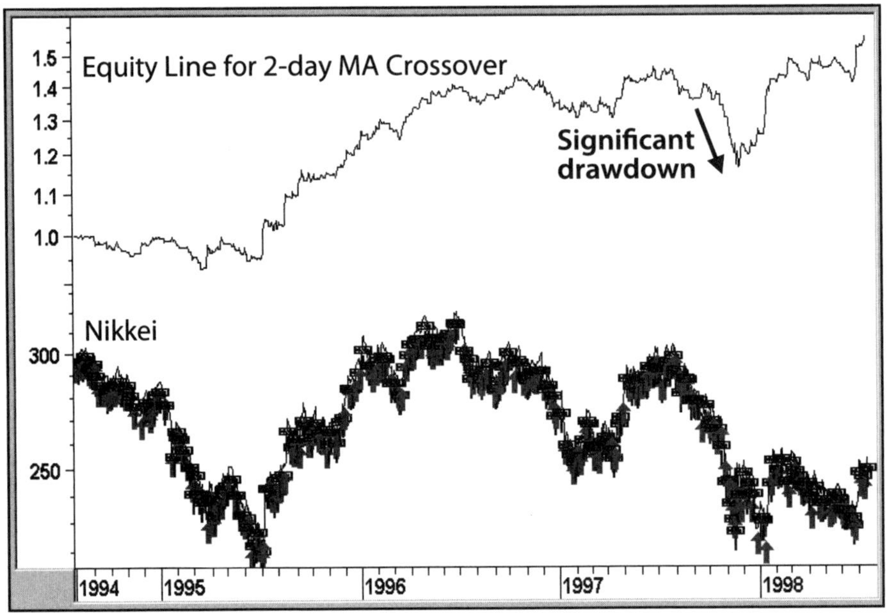

(Source: pring.com)

Table 11-1 Nikkei Optimized Results 1994–1998

NIKKEI							
Lots of signals							
Status	Net Profit	Percent	Total Trades	Winning Trades	Losing Trades	Average Win	Optimization
OK	0.5522	55.22	222	80	142	2.2965	2
OK	0.4223	42.23	36	13	23	2.8006	33
OK	0.4007	40.07	24	6	18	5.6867	48
OK	0.4000	40.00	27	7	20	4.7727	45
OK	0.3991	39.91	27	7	20	4.7250	44
OK	0.3977	39.77	29	7	22	5.2218	43
OK	0.3946	39.46	23	7	16	4.4967	53
OK	0.3901	39.01	23	7	16	4.4351	54
OK	0.3850	38.50	32	9	23	3.9149	38

Those with a full time job should not be trading on a day-to-day basis. Do your homework in the evenings, or better still, the weekends, and plan your trades using systems based on daily or weekly closes. This way you can do a good day's work without the distraction of entering new positions or being stopped out. It is impossible to concentrate on your job and the market at the same time. If you try to do both, one or both will slip.

Chart 11-2 features the Bank Commerciale with a 15-month MA crossover. You can see this is a great equity line, with a steep profit trend, but with very little in the way of drawdowns (Table 11-2). This timespan tested the best in our range of 2 to 65 months over nearly a half century of data. The consistently profitable equity line would have returned generous rewards, but how many people have the patience and discipline to act on a system that generates a signal once every 2 1/4 years?

BE COMFORTABLE WITH THE MARKETS YOU TRADE

Understand which markets you are comfortable with. If you are really interested in a particular market, group of stocks, currencies, and so forth,

Chart 11-2 Bank Commerciale and a 15-Month MA Crossover

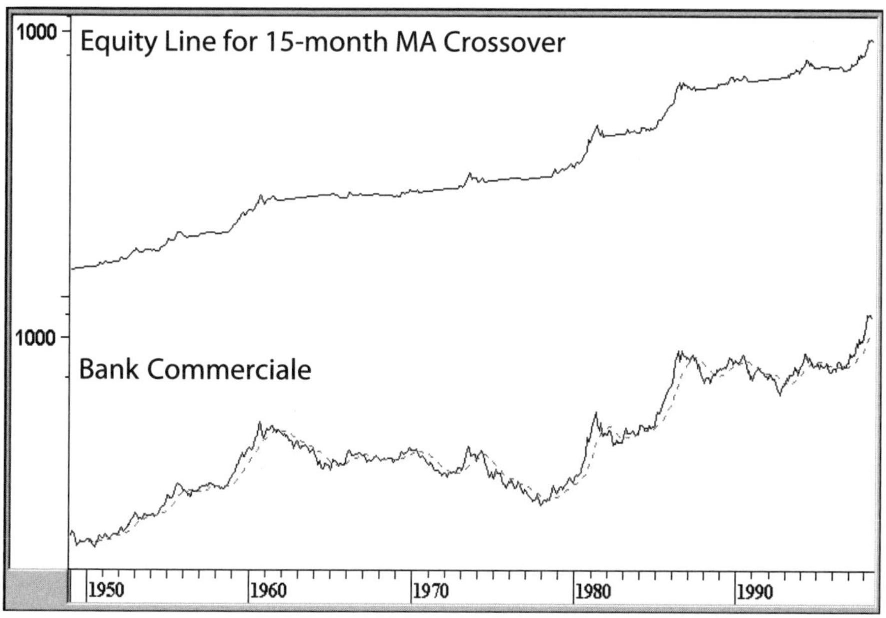

(Source: pring.com)

Table 11-2 Bank Commerciale and a 15-Month MA Crossover

BCI MONTHLY

tatus	Net Profit	Percent ...	Tot...	Win...	Losi...	Avg Wi...	OP...
	758.2115	75821.15	22	11	11	4.6954	15
	675.8333	67583.33	25	12	13	5.0447	14
	633.0059	63300.59	21	11	10	4.8712	17
	621.4258	62142.58	21	11	10	3.4659	16
	610.0525	61005.25	19	11	8	3.8798	18
	576.2650	57626.50	126	64	62	2.8769	2
	570.1052	57010.52	32	14	18	4.7324	13
	533.2081	53320.81	18	12	6	2.7340	19
	469.3175	46931.75	20	11	9	4.2485	20
	446.7277	44672.77	75	29	26	4.0119	4

you will find that you will quickly pick up on their idiosyncrasies. It will be much easier to design a better system armed with this knowledge and experience. If you are not interested in a particular security, or get involved because everyone else is, then you are unlikely to do well. Generally speaking, the more you feel at home with a particular sector, the more fun you will have and the easier the learning process will be.

Many investors have grown to like no load mutual funds and there is probably a good reason why, apart from the lack of commissions. Look at Chart 11-3 comparing American Barrick (now Barrick Gold Corporation) with the American Century Gold Fund. The fund is designed to mimic the performance of the Philadelphia Gold and Silver Share Index, and American Barrick is one of its components. I optimized for MA crossovers, just on the long side, for three other components. I found that Barrick offered the best returns of any of these gold shares. Then I compared this to the American Century Gold Fund. The equity lines for both are shown in Chart 11-3. See how Barrick moves from $1 to $2, but the fund increases by 50 percent more to $3. These equity lines reflect a 7-day MA crossover, which was the best timespan for Barrick, but not the best for the American Century Fund. For American Century, it came in as the sixth best with the four-day span as the actual winner. My point here is funds tend to trend better than individual

Chart 11-3 American Barrick versus American Century Gold

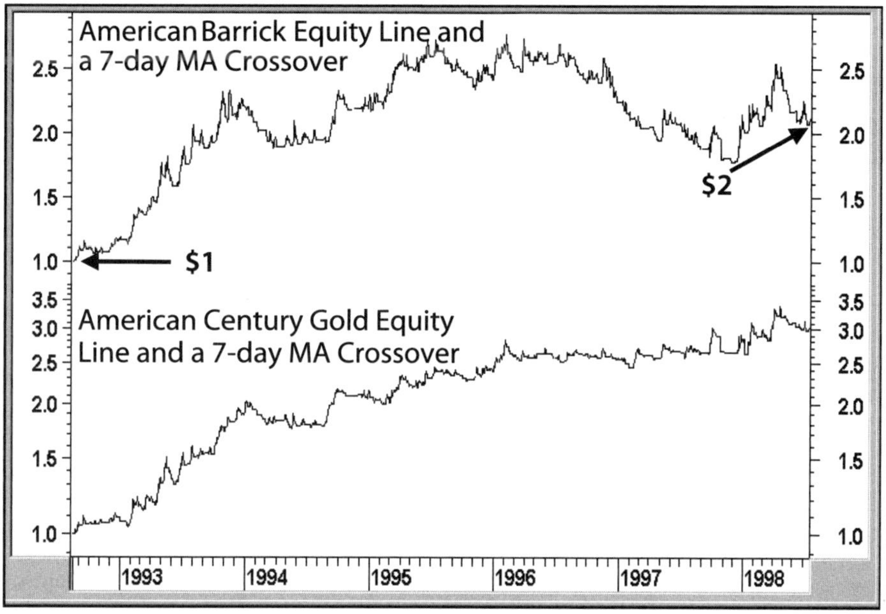

(Source: pring.com)

stocks and make better subjects for mechanical systems. If you personally have an affinity to the fund type investments, then use them as your vehicle rather than individual stocks. The main problem you will run into is not knowing the daily value of the fund until after the close has taken place. Therefore, your transaction will be based on the closing price of the subsequent day. This is not such a problem if the fund truly reflects an index. You can then use the index to approximate for the fund's close. If this is not possible, a major allowance must be made in the system for this type of slippage. Even so, the closing time for switching most funds is set 30 minutes or more below the market close so this also presents a problem.

HAVE CONFIDENCE IN THE SYSTEM

Make sure you have confidence in the system and fully understand it. This is very important. It may be one you or someone else developed, but it is mandatory that you have confidence in it and understand how it works. If you lack the confidence, then as soon as times get bad and the market goes against you, you will likely have to give up on it. Ironically, that is also the time when the system is most likely to go into a profitable mode.

Chart 11-4 A Discouraging System

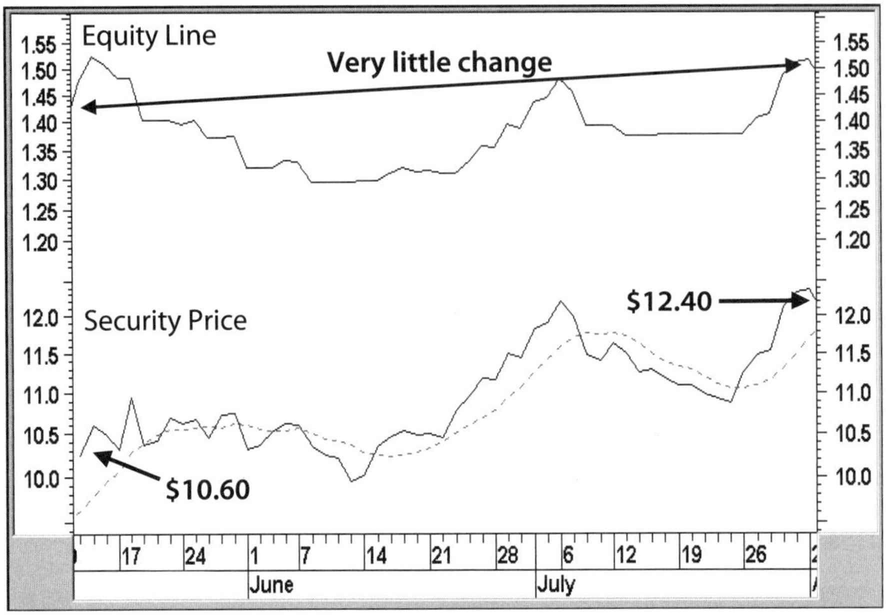

(Source: pring.com)

Look at the security price and equity line in Chart 11-4. The price increases from about $10.60 to $12.40 in this period, yet the equity line is basically unchanged. It starts off with a small drop and then regains lost ground. If you have not tested, have not understood, and have no confidence in the system, you might give up on it. This was one of the worst trading periods I could find for the 7-day MA crossover for the American Century Gold Fund. Remember, that system turned in a performance of 300 percent over a 6-year period.

Another proviso is that the system has been tested and retested over a huge number of periods and securities. This is the only way you can have real confidence that it stands a good chance of working in the marketplace.

It is amazing how many people think they can design a system, then, when it does not work as expected, use hindsight to introduce a rule that depends on judgment of the situation at the time. Then they rationalize why the system didn't perform. Including such a rule defeats the whole objective of a mechanical system because it allows emotion and judgment to influence a decision. The only place for judgment in the whole process is in the construction of the system, *not* in its application.

Lastly, it is great to have confidence in trading a particular system and be willing to persevere when it goes against you. However, it is equally important to keep an open mind at all times. If conditions change and the relationship on which the system is based breaks down, you can make the judgment call to stop using it until you have been able to fix the problem. This is because it is highly likely that your system will fade over time. Never be afraid to make an evaluation, and then be prepared to update it.

PART II
Systems Based on One Security

Chapter 12
Optimizing for the U.S. Equity Market

SAMPLE TESTING AND WALK THROUGH

In their book, *Encyclopedia of Market Indicators*, Robert Colby and Thomas Meyers looked at many different indicators used by technicians and optimized them for the U.S. stock market. One of the most useful studies they did was to test for the best moving average over a period of almost 80 years between 1910 and 1987. I cite this particular study because it is instructive in the testing process.

Look at Chart 12-1. Colby and Meyers split the period into segments of about a decade and optimized for each one. The optimization tested for timespans between 2 and 20 months. They started off with the 1910–1926 span and found that 2 months was the best average. That means buy signals were generated as the S&P Composite crossed above its 2-month MA, and sell signals when it crossed below it. Short signals were generated when the Index slipped below its average and covered when it rallied back above it again. Thus, there was always a position, either long or short. No allowance was made for transaction costs, interest, or slippage. Table 12-1 displays the results projected blindly forward for the next 10 years by testing December 1926 to December 1936. Again, the 2-month period was profitable, although when I tested, I found the 4-month span came out on top with the 2-month a close second. However, re-optimizing for the whole period of 1910–1936 continued to produce an excellent return from the 2-month average, as you can see in Table 12-2. Chart 12-2 shows the equity line and the S&P for the 1915–1937 period using the 2-month average.

Chart 12-1 S&P Composite and a 2-Month MA Crossover System

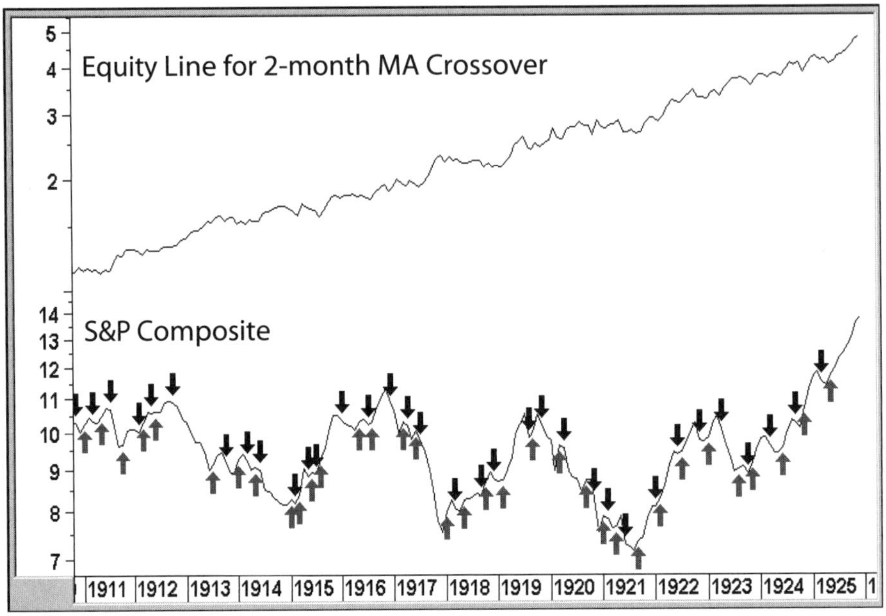

(Source: pring.com)

Table 12-1 S&P Composite 1926–1936 Optimization Summary

S&P Composite 1926-1936							
Status	Net Profit	Percent	Total Trades	Winning Trades	Losing Trades	Average Win	Optimization
OK	5.7336	573.36	19	11	8	2.9825	4
OK	5.0653	506.53	39	20	19	2.0495	2
OK	4.0507	405.07	27	15	12	2.0541	3
OK	3.2670	326.70	17	8	9	2.9844	5
OK	2.9604	296.04	7	3	4	4.5699	12
OK	2.9604	296.04	7	2	5	8.9143	10
OK	2.6044	260.44	3	2	1	9.6450	14
OK	2.0644	260.44	3	2	1	9.6450	15
OK	2.4442	244.42	7	2	5	6.0721	11

Table 12-2 S&P Composite 1910–1936 Optimization Summary

S&P Composite 1910-1936							
Status	Net Profit	Percent	Total Trades	Winning Trades	Losing Trades	Average Win	Optimization
OK	34.8442	3484.42	115	64	51	2.0284	2
OK	19.6430	1964.30	72	36	36	3.8130	4
OK	18.5378	1853.78	89	46	43	2.4748	3
OK	17.6982	1769.82	26	13	13	5.0391	10
OK	15.2410	1524.10	22	13	9	3.3478	12
OK	13.9175	1391.75	56	25	31	3.4040	5
OK	13.4826	1348.26	22	12	10	3.1036	11
OK	12.3464	1234.64	17	11	6	7.9972	14
OK	12.0358	1203.58	16	10	6	10.9394	15

Chart 12-2 S&P Composite and a 2-Month MA Crossover System

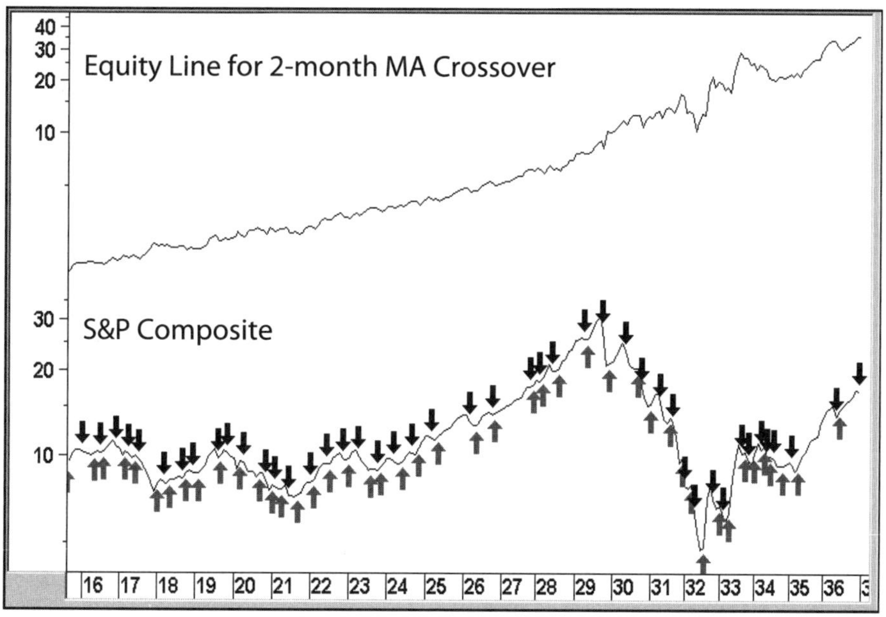

(Source: pring.com)

The study shown in Table 12-3 ran between 1926–1986. The 2-month average was best between 1926–1946. The 6-month timespan was the overall winner over the next two 10-year segments. Only in the 1976–1986 period did the parameter once again change, and this time it was an 11-month period that came out on top. This shows how important it is to understand that market conditions can and do change. What is a good parameter for one period may not be for another, and vice versa.

OPTIMIZE FOR THE WHOLE PERIOD

Since the software they were using could only test for a maximum of 42 years, they were unable to come up with an optimized result for the 1910–1987 period. I was able to, though, and the result is shown in Chart 12-3, of a 10-month average crossover. It may look as if there are a lot of signals, but it is important to remember there are almost 100 years of data here. This chart also includes the 1900–1910 and 1987–1998 periods that were not included in the original test. The initial 1900 $1 investment grew to over $7,500 using this approach. Part of the success was due to the very

Table 12-3 S&P Results

Period	Best Time Span
1926-36	2
1936-46	2
1946-56	6
1956-66	6
1966-76	6
1976-86	11

Chart 12-3 S&P Composite and a 10-Month MA Crossover System

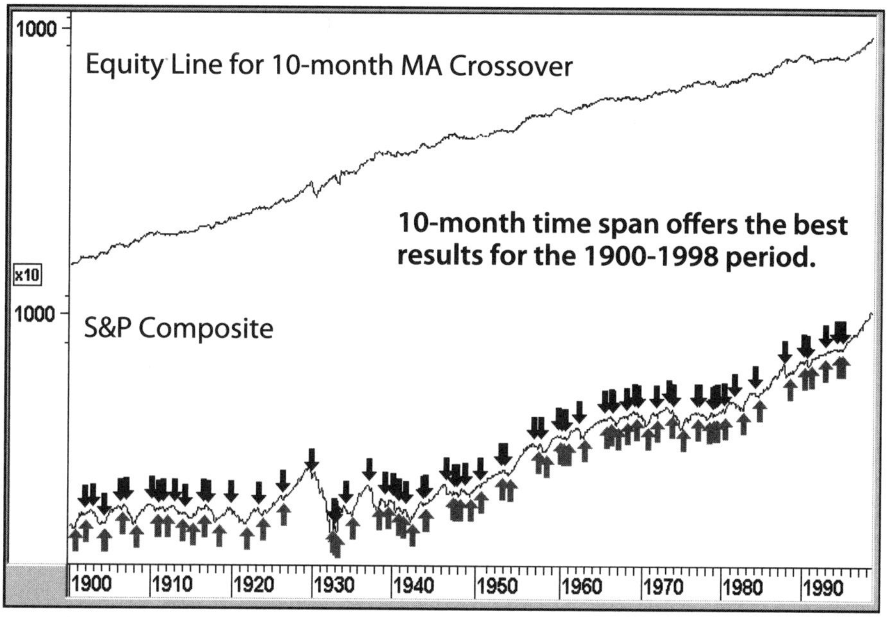

(Source: pring.com)

timely sell signal in 1929. How well would the system have worked in the bull market of the 1980s and 1990s?

The answer is shown in Chart 12-4. A $1 investment in 1980 increased to $2.60 by mid 1998, which is a very impressive performance. Actually, the 10-month period was well down on the list when I optimized it. The important point is not that the 10-month average fails to be the best one in a specific period, but that it is, in fact, profitable during that space of time. The summary of the 1900–1998 optimization is shown in Table 12-4. You can see that it experienced more losing than winning trades, but returned no less than 7,500 percent on the initial investment. It is important to recognize this test did not make any provision for commissions, and that is, perhaps, not very fair.

Table 12-5 did by using the assumption of a 1 percent round trip commission. The results are less impressive, since the best parameter of 10-months returns is just over 2,000 percent. In this day and age, when it is possible to trade no load index funds, it is probably too conservative to assume a 1 percent commission. Even so, this example clearly shows that commissions can really put a dent on even the best system. This means if the trades are sufficiently numerous, the system is likely to *become profitable for the broker, not the trader.*

Chart 12-4 S&P Composite and a 10-Month MA Crossover System

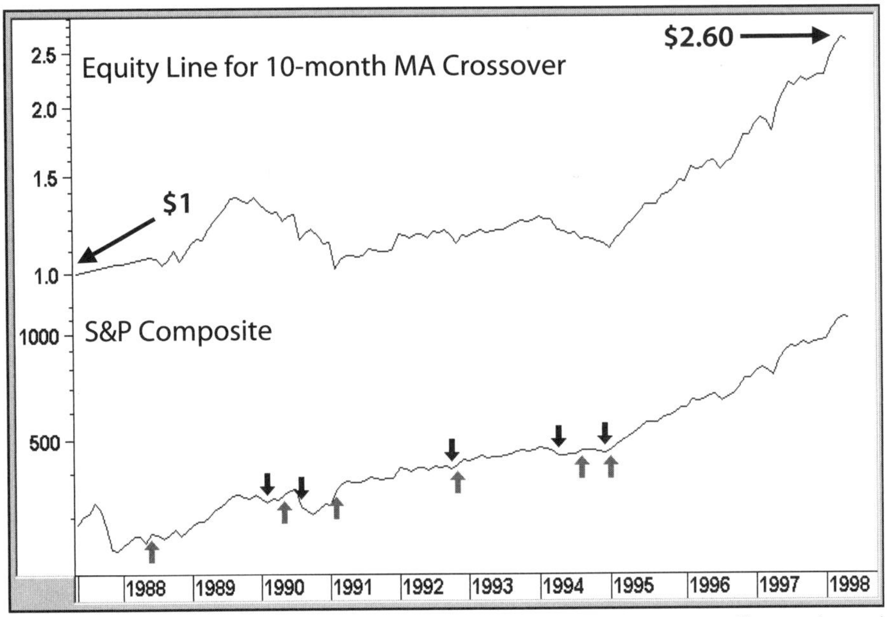

(Source: pring.com)

Table 12-4 S&P Composite 1900–1998 Optimization Summary

S&P Composite Close MONTHLY							
Status	Net Profit	Percent	Total Trades	Winning Trades	Losing Trades	Average Win	Optimization
OK	7642.5244	764252.44	124	57	67	3.1020	10
OK	4827.4741	482747.41	107	50	57	3.4589	11
OK	4393.9077	439390.77	283	134	149	2.1920	4
OK	3709.9014	370990.14	184	85	99	2.3690	6
OK	3557.0786	355707.86	101	48	53	3.7391	12
OK	3344.2605	334426.05	166	73	93	2.9070	7
OK	2787.8215	278782.15	477	208	269	2.0347	2
OK	2670.2119	267021.19	140	61	79	2.8466	9
OK	2315.4241	231542.41	232	102	130	2.3566	5

Table 12-5 S&P Composite 1900–1998 Optimization Summary (1% commission; long and short)

S&P Composite Close MONTHLY							
Status	Net Profit	Percent	Total Trades	Winning Trades	Losing Trades	Average Win	Optimization
OK	2202.5452	220254.52	124	55	69	2.6300	10
OK	1647.5488	164754.88	107	49	58	2.8113	11
OK	1288.5420	128854.20	101	47	54	3.0894	12
OK	655.7424	655774.24	140	59	81	2.3940	9
OK	633.9806	63398.06	166	68	98	2.5180	7
OK	587.8772	58787.72	184	80	104	2.0562	6
OK	409.3787	40937.87	95	44	51	2.9824	13
OK	409.0733	40907.33	95	43	52	2.9279	14
OK	329.2522	32925.22	158	61	97	2.3238	8

OPTIMIZE FOR JUST LONG POSITIONS

I would now like to turn to the possibility of just taking long positions and investing the cash during periods when the price is below the moving average. In this exercise, I assumed an annual rate of interest of 4 percent, which is a little bit below the post-war average of about 5 percent. Using these parameters, the 10-month span still optimized out the best. Interestingly, when we take out the short sales (Table 12-6), we find that the 9-, 11-, and 12-month timespans are all in the top five. This indicates the results are less likely to be a fluke, than if the 10-month span alone were in the top periods. This parameter, even when allowing for a 1 percent round trip commission, returned close to $4,000 in profit from an initial $1 investment. Unfortunately, few people would have lived the 98 years to be able to make and then spend the profits. However, it would have beaten the buy-hold approach quite handsomely as you can see from the summary in Table 12-7. The average win lasted 20 months compared to the average loss of 4 months. The largest drawdown in points was 123. However, the largest drop from an equity peak occurred between 1929 and 1932 when the system with two signals lost 37 percent. Look at Chart 12-5. This was a

Chart 12-5 S&P Composite and a 10-Month MA Crossover System

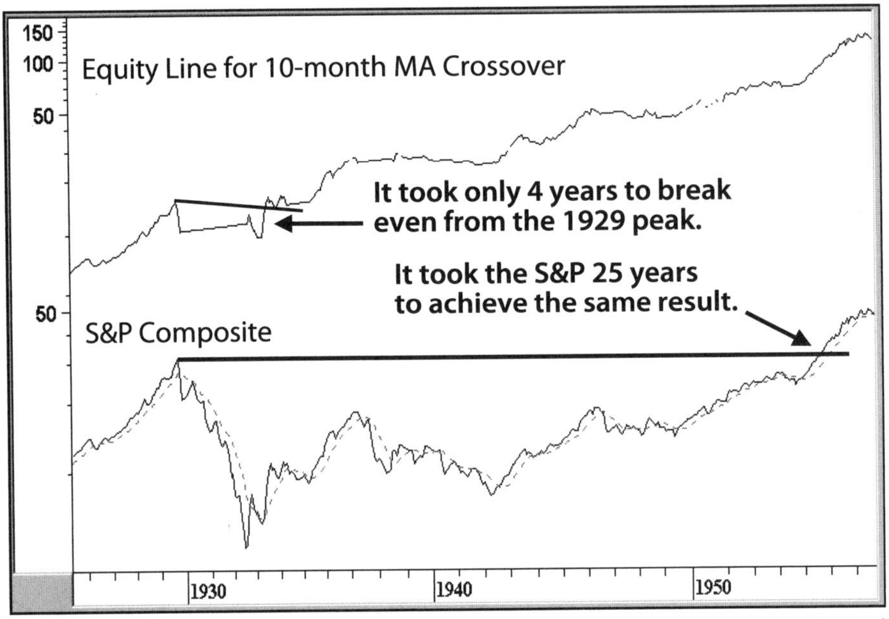

(Source: pring.com)

Table 12-6 S&P Composite 1900–1998 Optimization Summary (1% commission; 4% interest long only)

S&P Composite Close MONTHLY						
Net Profit	Percent	Total Trades	Winning Trades	Losing Trades	Average Win	Optimization
3791.6929	379169.29	62	33	29	4.6341	10
3037.6116	303761.16	53	29	24	5.0930	11
2696.3867	269638.67	83	43	40	5.0360	7
2648.5291	264852.91	50	28	22	5.8176	12
2491.5649	249156.49	70	36	34	3.7959	9
2401.9429	240194.29	92	49	43	3.8867	6
1780.6423	178064.23	79	37	42	3.4894	8
1680.6288	168062.88	141	73	68	3.3588	4
1456.4221	145642.21	116	57	59	3.6669	5

Table 12-7 S&P Composite 1900–1998 Optimization Summary (1% commission; 4% interest long only)

Winning long trades	33	Winning short trades	0
Total winning trades	33	Total losing trades	29
Amount of winning trades	1662.77	Amount of losing trades	-315.32
Average win	50.39	Average loss	-10.87
Largest win	479.82	Largest loss	-123.66
Average length of win	20.15	Average length of loss	4.10
Longest winning trade	41	Longest losing trade	10
Most consecutive wins	5	Most consecutive losses	4
Total bars out	487	Average length out	7.73
Longest out period	33		
System close drawdown	0.00	Profit/Loss index	92.32
System open drawdown	0.00	Reward/Risk index	100.00
Max open trade drawdown	-123.66	Buy/Hold index	3596.45

pretty big decline, but was less than half of what would have developed in the overall bear market buy-hold approach. It only took until 1933 for the equity line to return to its 1929 peak. The buy-hold approach—that is the S&P Composite itself—did not return to the 1929 peak until 25 years later in 1954. This also underscores the point that controlling losses is extremely crucial. For example, if the equity of a system declines by 50 percent, it requires a 100 percent increase in price to return to the level prior to the loss. Alternately, a decline of 25 percent only requires about a 33 percent advance from the low to get back to the same position.

I also closely examined the performance of the 10-month span in other difficult periods. While it was not the best-performing timespan in every segment, it was usually pretty well near the top. The 1966–1983 period was a particularly difficult one, since it was a huge trading range. The best result came from a 12-month span, as you can see in Table 12-8, but the 10-month was not too far behind. Look at Table 12-9. You can see from this summary that the 10-month span beat the buy-hold approach. Chart 12-6 shows the actual signals together with the equity line. As you can see, there were no serious drawdowns in this period at all.

Chart 12-6 S&P Composite and a 10-Month MA Crossover System

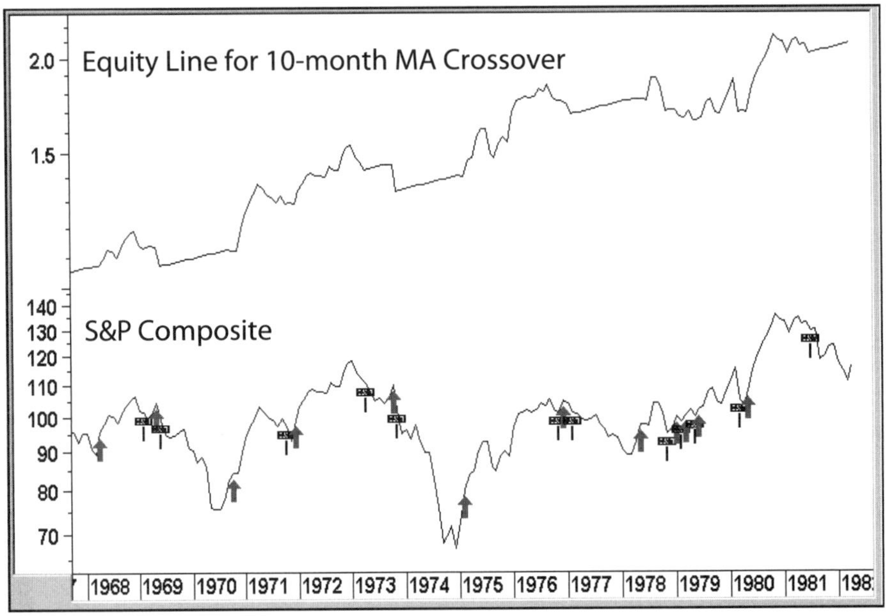

(Source: pring.com)

Table 12-8 S&P Composite 1966–1983 Optimization Summary

S&P Composite 1966-1983 MONTHLY							
Status	Net Profit	Percent	Total Trades	Winning Trades	Losing Trades	Average Win	Optimization
OK	1.3861	138.61	8	6	2	2.6655	12
OK	1.2737	127.37	10	6	4	2.7296	11
OK	1.2235	122.35	8	6	2	3.0925	14
OK	1.2223	122.23	8	6	2	3.0644	13
OK	1.1885	118.85	17	9	8	2.1285	7
OK	1.0996	109.96	25	10	15	2.6483	4
OK	1.0829	108.29	12	6	6	2.6284	10
OK	1.0526	105.26	6	5	1	2.1983	17
OK	1.0526	105.26	6	5	1	2.1983	18

Table 12-9 S&P Composite and a 10-Month MA Crossover System

Winning long trades	6	Winning short trades	0
Total winning trades	6	Total losing trades	6
Amount of winning trades	1.05	Amount of losing trades	-.040
Average win	0.17	Average loss	-0.07
Largest win	0.35	Largest loss	-0.12
Average length of win	14.67	Average length of loss	3.17
Longest winning trade	22	Longest losing trade	7
Most consecutive wins	2	Most consecutive losses	4
Total bars out	109	Average length out	8.38
Longest out period	24		
System close drawdown	0.00	Profit/Loss index	73.10
System open drawdown	0.00	Reward/Risk index	100.00
Max open trade drawdown	-0.11	Buy/Hold index	224.58

You might think with this amount of data and differing market conditions other stock markets would also test well with a 10-month span, and they did. I tested for ten different markets including the Morgan Stanley Capital International World Stock Index. They all made money, which is what should be expected given the fact that all data covered the bullish post-World War II era. However, we also find *half* of them beat the buy-hold approach which, I think, is pretty good.

From this study we should conclude:

1. *The 10-month timespan has tested profitably over a 98-year period including trending and trading environments;*
2. *Other timespans in close proximity, particularly the 11- and 12-month parameters, also test consistently well;*
3. *The 10-month span can also be successfully extended to other equity markets around the world;*
4. *The 10-month timespan is not the Holy Grail but has stood the test of time, and offers no reason why it should not continue to operate in a profitable way.*

Chapter 13
Combining a Moving Average and an Oscillator

RATIONALE FOR THE SYSTEM

This chapter explains a method where performance can be enhanced using the integration of two indicators. A technique that allows investors to take advantage of both trending and trading range markets is to combine a moving average with an oscillator. Moving-average crossovers are used to generate buy and sell signals, and the oscillator to take partial profits. Look at Chart 13-1. The rationale behind this technique is that moving average signals are often followed by a profitable move, but by the time the countervailing signal comes, the profit either turns to a loss or is greatly eroded. On the one hand, the February crossover is pretty good because the price rises then retreats back to the moving average, without a negative crossover. The price then goes on to make a new high so the crossover results in a profitable signal. On the other hand, a very sharp rally and an equally precipitous decline follow the April buy signal. All of the profits are given up by the time a negative crossover develops.

The combination of an oscillator with a moving average is a technique that tries to capture some of the profit resulting from the sharp rally with part of the position, while allowing the rest of the position to ride with the trend in the hope that it continues. The system may limit profits a bit, but, more important, it is limiting losses as well. It will also make it possible to capitalize on the potential of a trending market, but some profits will be

Chart 13-1 JP Morgan

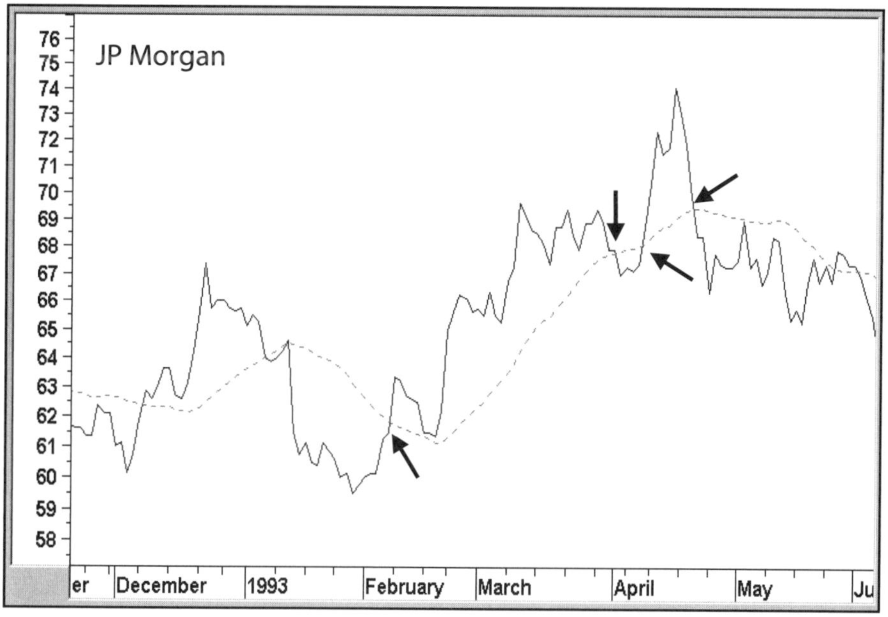

(Source: pring.com)

taken in case subsequent market action turns out to be part of a volatile trading range. If we knew ahead of time the trend was going to perpetuate, we would not need to worry about taking profits along the way. Unfortunately, there is no known method of forecasting the magnitude of a move, so this technique is a compromise. If partial profits are taken and the price moves even more in our favor, this is a mistake. Alternatively, if the price does not move in our favor, this is also a problem, because hindsight will tell us we should have liquidated everything as a result of the oscillator signal. The object of the game is not to maximize profits, because that is impossible, but to gain a respectable return on our capital with a consistent and realistic level of profit.

THE SYSTEM IN A NEUTRAL TREND

Chart 13-2 features international paper together with two momentum indicators, an RSI and a CMO. I have chosen the CMO because it accentuates overbought and oversold conditions and generally experiences smoother swings than the RSI. It is actually a derivative of the RSI. The timespans are

Chart 13-2 International Paper and Two Indicators

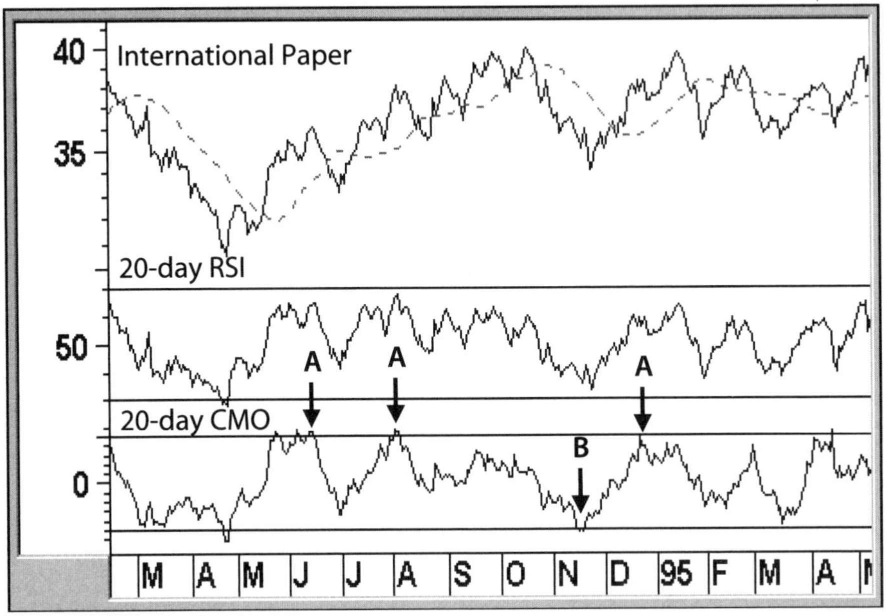

(Source: pring.com)

20 days for both series. The arrows marked A point to the periods when the CMO reaches an overbought condition, but the RSI does not. The B arrow shows the same thing for oversold readings. Since we want an oscillator that is more likely to move to overbought and oversold extremes, the CMO fits the bill quite nicely. (For those wishing to learn more about the CMO, please see the glossary on our Web site at http://www.pring.com.)

Chart 13-3 just features the 20-day CMO together with a 25-day simple moving average advanced by 5 days. Look at the MA crossover in July 1989 (A). That was the signal to buy. The sell signal came in early September, as the price crossed back below the average again. Partial profits would have been taken in August (B) because that is when the CMO crosses back below its overbought zone. As it turned out, this was roughly the same level as the MA crossover. Notice that I use the re-crossing of the overbought zones as my signaling point, rather than the initial touching of the overbought line. This is because the re-crossing acts as a kind of trend reversal signal for momentum. After all, how do I know at the initial overbought contact point that the indicator is not going to go higher and remain in an overbought condition for an extended period? I do not. However, on most occasions when the CMO crosses back below the +50 overbought zone, this confirms a momentum peak has been seen and the trend of the oscillator is now down. Also, the price is *usually* higher at this return crossover point than at the initial overbought reading. This, of course, is not the same thing as saying the price trend itself has also reversed. That will not be confirmed until the price crosses below its moving average. All we know is once the oscillator begins its descent towards zero from above the overbought zone, the odds of the rally extending are far less than when the price initially crossed above the moving average. If the odds are lower, so too should be our exposure.

Take another look at Chart 13-3. As the final long position was liquidated, at point C, a short position was initiated. Part of it was covered when the CMO rallied above its −50 (D) oversold zone. As it happened, this was a whipsaw crossover and the price went lower, but at the time this was not known. Since the whole idea of this oscillator technique is to protect part of the profits while they are there, and thus offset losses from the inevitable whipsaw signals, it makes no sense to fool around waiting to see if it is a whipsaw or not. In this instance, the second part of the trade would have

Chart 13-3 International Paper and a CMO 20

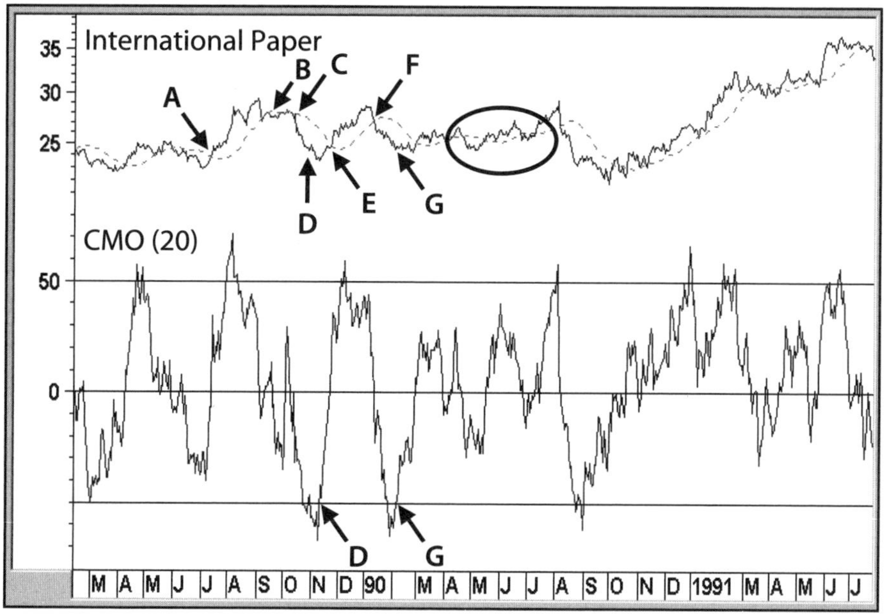

(Source: pring.com)

been covered at a slightly higher price, since the price crosses above the average again (E).

The next short sale (F) would have worked quite well since the oscillator position would have been covered almost at the actual low for the move (G). This was just as well, since the next signals, which are contained in the ellipse, were basically breakeven and we would have needed some reserves to offset commission and slippage expenses. The period just covered was, for all intents and purposes, a neutral trading range, but what if the conditions were different? What if it was a bull or bear market?

THE SYSTEM IN A BULL MARKET

I mentioned earlier that it is always best to trade with the trend. Let us consider a bull and bear primary trend to see how this might work out. Chart 13-4 shows American Barrick, a gold stock, during the 1993–1994 mini bull market. The actual bottom occurred in April 1992, prior to the period displayed on this chart, but it is extremely unlikely we would have known that at the time. However, it would have been fairly evident in early 1993 since the price experienced a series of rising peaks and troughs. These were confirmed in February as the price rallied above the horizontal trendline marking the peak of the previous rally. Consequently, I have assumed the bull trend was self-evident in early April at the MA crossover indicated by the arrow. This is because Barrick had already experienced a series of rising intermediate peaks and troughs and was also above its 40-week MA. This moving average is not shown on the chart. Since the system rule only permits trades from the long side in a confirmed bull market, the initial position was entered in early April at point A. Some profit would have been taken at the first dip below the overbought level in mid April (B). This was not a classic profit-taking signal, but was, nevertheless, worthwhile. The final liquidation occurred higher up in May (C) from a whipsaw signal. A new position would have quickly been entered as the price rallied above its average again (D). This time, the oscillator-generated sell signal would have developed fairly close to the short-term rally high (E). This was just a tad above the MA crossover, which developed a couple of months later (F). Note the oscillator sell (H) resulting from the buy signal at point G was not an actual overbought crossover, but a reversal in direction from a quick touch of the dashed +50 line. You can see we did not maximize profits by selling at the exact top or even close to it on most occasions. However, by trading with the trend, all, except the August 1993 signal, were profitable.

Chart 13-4 American Barrick and a CMO 20

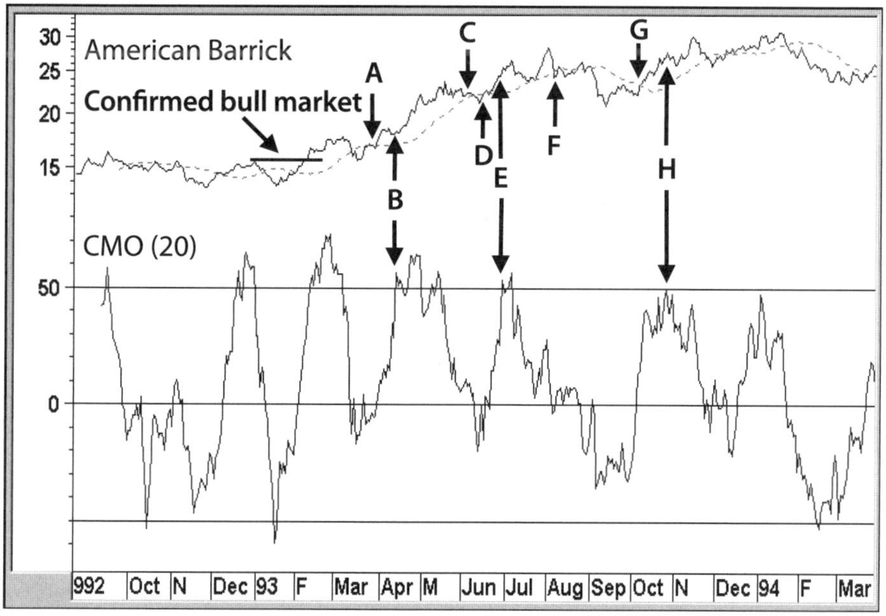

(Source: pring.com)

THE SYSTEM IN A BEAR MARKET

Now let us take a look at a bear market environment, as shown in Chart 13-5. For this I have chosen the Argentina Fund, a closed-end investment fund on the NYSE. The bull market peak developed in February 1994. Although there were some signs of a top early on, in all fairness, we must work on the assumption this trend was not officially confirmed until May or June. This means the first short signal occurred in late June (A). The oscillator position would have been covered fairly close to the bottom (B) and the MA crossover signal slightly higher in July (C). The next signal, in the ellipse, was a whipsaw and lost a little money.

However, the next signal (D) really shows how this approach comes into its own. It was triggered about halfway down the decline, but the oscillator signal (E), to cover half the position, developed just off the low. This was just as well, since the price rallied and the moving average part of the position was closed out with a small loss (F). The net overall gain, though, was positive. The next shoring opportunity developed soon after (G), and

Chart 13-5 Argentina Fund and a CMO 20

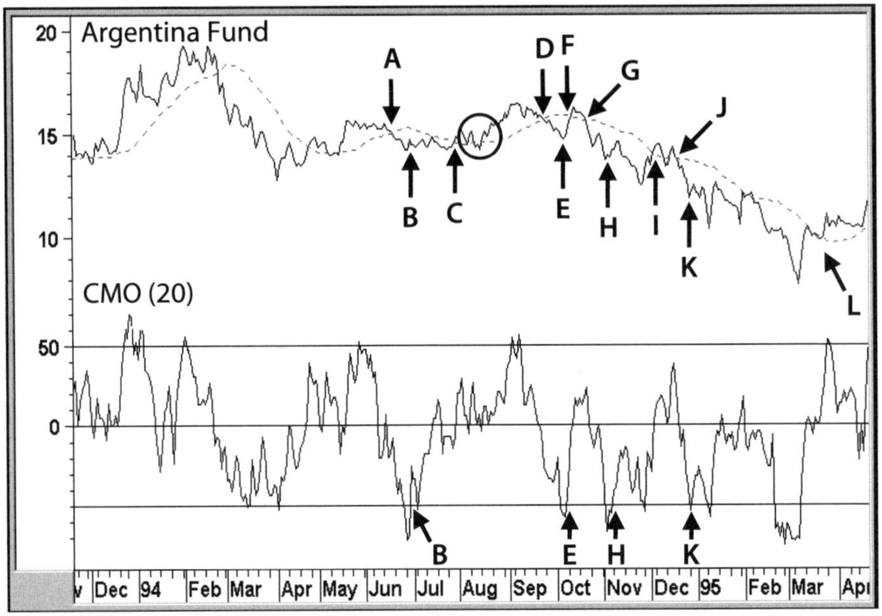

(Source: pring.com)

the oscillator would have taken us out relatively early (H). The price continued to decline, but by the time it recrossed the moving average (I), it was at approximately the same level. Another small whipsaw followed in December, with a nice profitable signal (J) for both positions, as the oscillator crossover developed in late December (K) and the trend signal confirmed with a signal in February (L). Finally, another quick whipsaw occurred just after L, and a covering of both positions at around the same price in early March resulted in a small profit.

You can see from these examples that a lot of profit was given up, both in terms of the price continuing to trend after the oscillator liquidation, and because we had to wait for an MA crossover. However, it is also quite clear that if you trade with the trend, it is possible to harvest small but consistent profits, and that is the principal objective of mechanical trading systems.

Chapter 14

Testing a Moving Average and an Oscillator

THE APPROACH

Earlier we saw how it is possible to set up a system that anticipates both a trending and trading range price environment. Now it is time to take an actual system by combining two techniques. In this test, I will be using a continuous contract for U.S. T-Bonds, a moving average, and a price oscillator (Chart 14-1). A price oscillator is calculated by dividing a short-term moving average by a longer term one. In this case, I used a one period moving average; that is, the close as the shorter average and the 10-day simple moving average as the longer-term one. The 10-day average is plotted in the upper panel with the oscillator underneath. The negative MA crossovers are reflected in the oscillator moving below zero as at point A, for example. Similarly, point B represents the positive crossovers.

Chart 14-2 shows the way the system works. It is really very simple: Buy when the price crosses above a moving average (as it does in late July at point A). Then sell either when it crosses below the average, or the price oscillator reaches a specific pre-determined level. As you can see, the oscillator reaches the designated overbought level a few days later (B). In this case, I selected the $+2^1/_2$ percent and $-2^1/_2$ percent. This means the overbought and oversold lines are the equivalent of the price being $2^1/_2$ percent above and below the 10-day moving average. Then, in early August, the price crosses below the average and this initiates a short signal (C).

Chart 14-1 Treasury Bonds and a 1/10 Price Oscillator

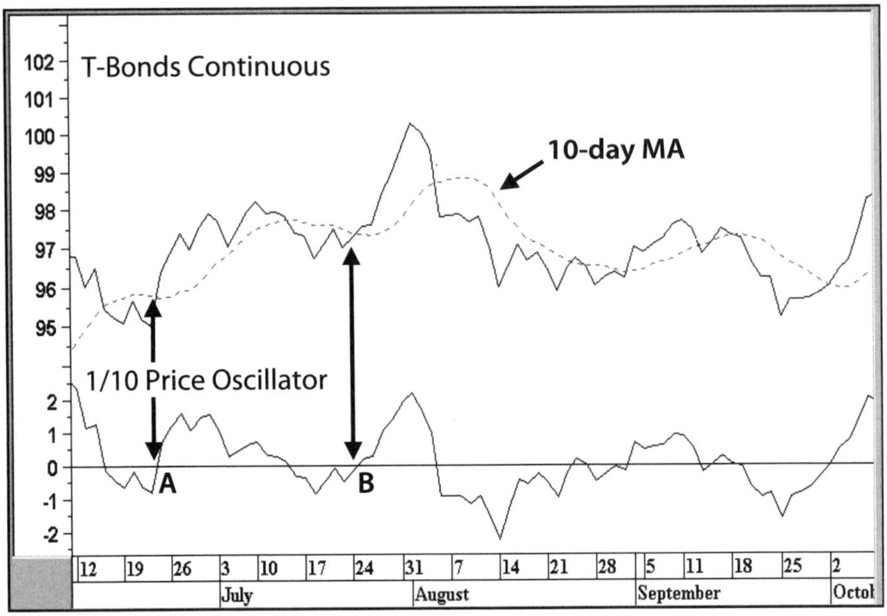

(Source: pring.com)

Chart 14-2 Treasury Bonds and a 1/10 Price Oscillator

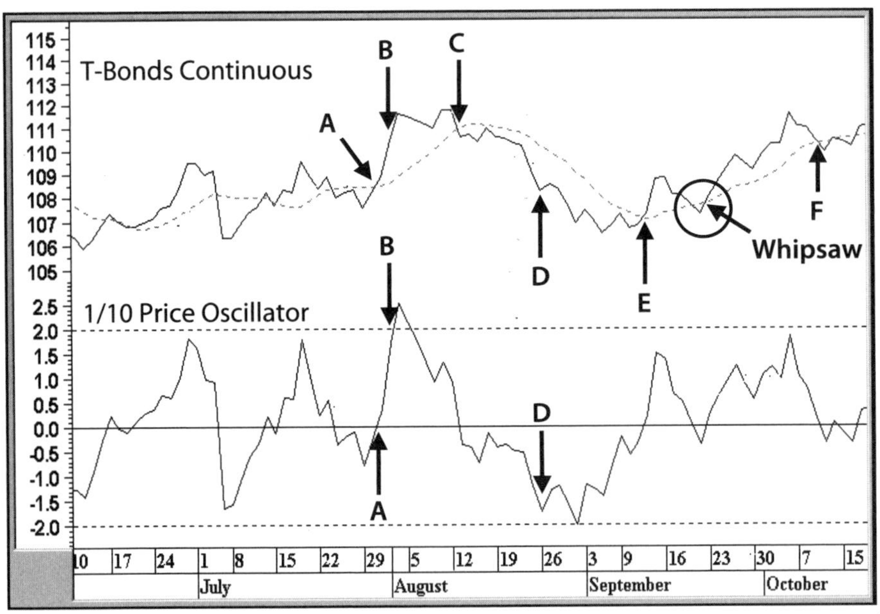

(Source: pring.com)

The position is covered at the end of the month fairly close to the actual low as the oscillator touches its oversold zone (D). The next buy signal comes on a MA crossover in early September (E). The oscillator never has a chance to move to the $+2^1/_2$ level because the MA crossover comes first. The next short signal is a whipsaw, followed by the final buy that resulted in a small profit (F).

I optimized this system by using one variable for the moving average and the oscillator, and another for each of the overbought and oversold conditions. After the walk-through analysis, the best overall returns were given by the 26/2/−4 combination, as you can see in Table 14-1. This was not the one I finally chose, because I like to see the overbought and oversold triggering points the same distance from the equilibrium line. The rationale for this arises from the fact that oscillator sensitivity to overbought and oversold conditions depends on the direction of the primary trend. In a bull market, oscillators move to higher overbought levels and rallies are generated from moderate oversold levels. If you know you are in a bull market you could skew the triggering points to the upside, and vice versa. Unfortunately, we never learn the primary trend has reversed until sometime later. Also, if we go with numbers skewed to a bull market environment, the system is definitely going to be under pressure when a bear market begins. It makes sense to evenly balance the overboughts and oversolds. That is why I chose

Table 14-1 Treasury Bonds

CBOT US Treasury Bonds 2000-2003 Continuous							
Percent	Total Trades	Winning Trades	Losing Trades	Average Win	Optimization 1	Optimization 2	Optimization 3
160.39	387	126	261	2.6001	26	2	-4
156.80	388	137	251	2.2558	26	2	-2
155.73	365	131	234	2.2056	28	2	-2
153.62	425	133	292	2.7005	24	2	-4
149.68	426	145	281	2.3202	24	2	-2
144.52	365	119	246	2.6470	28	5	-2
143.89	365	119	246	2.6598	28	6	-2
130.52	387	127	260	2.4372	26	2	-3
129.80	353	110	243	2.7424	30	5	-2

the 28/2/−2 combination. I could have chosen the 26/2/−2 combo, but the profit was only slightly better. The 28-day moving average generated fewer signals, and fewer signals mean fewer chances for mistakes.

On the face of it, the number of losing signals of 234 to 131 winners looks pretty grim. However, when you look at the more detailed report of Table 14-2, the average win was 2.2 times greater than the average loss, which shows this system does a reasonable job of cutting losses short. The top panel of Chart 14-3 shows the equity line where we can see the starting amount of $1 was increased to $2.55. Even though the system trailed the buy-hold approach, there were no major drawdowns in terms of peak-to-trough equity. The one in 1994 of 10 percent was the worst. Not bad, considering the 150 percent gain was achieved at a 9.4 percent annualized rate.

APPLIED TO SOYBEANS AND THE CRB

I tried this approach on many markets and found it to work quite well. Since the characteristics of one security to another can differ considerably, this is also true of the parameters. The 28/5/−5 combination appeared to

Table 14-2 Treasury Bonds

Total closed trades	365	Commissions paid	0.20
Average profit per trade	0.00	Average Win/Average loss ratio	2.21
Total long trades	183	Total short trades	182
Winning long trades	70	Winning short trades	61
Total winning trades	131	Total losing trades	234
Amount of winning trades	4.15	Amount of losing trades	-3.36
Average win	0.03	Average loss	-0.01
Largest win	0.10	Largest loss	-0.06
Average length of win	8.06	Average length of loss	4.52

Chart 14-3 Treasury Bonds

(Source: pring.com)

Table 14-3 Soybeans continuous

Total net profit	1.15	Open position value	N/A
Percent gain/loss	114.61	Annual percent gain/loss	14.67
Initial investment	1.00	Interest earned	0.28
Current position	Out	Date position entered	10/9/98
Buy/Hold profit	-0.01	Days in test	2852
Buy/Hold percent gain/loss	-0.98	Annual Buy/Hold percent gain/loss	-0.13
Total closed trades	158	Commissions paid	0.06
Average profit per trade	0.01	Average Win/Average loss ratio	2.27
Total long trades	79	Total short trades	79
Winning long trades	36	Winning short trades	32
Total winning trades	68	Total losing trades	90
Amount of winning trades	2.07	Amount of losing trades	-1.21

offer satisfactory profits on everything I tried, but with differing degrees of success. It was never the best, but often quite high on the list. The following are offered as starting points. Let's begin with soybeans.

Chart 14-4 shows the best equally weighted, overbought/oversold dollar parameters with a 36-day moving average and price oscillator with +/−14 triggering levels. In this case, the best results came when I substituted dollar or point amounts for percentage amounts. In effect, the 14 and −14 mean the price is 14¢ above the 36-day moving average. This is because percentages represent proportions. The five points on a $10 stock are obviously more significant than $5 on a $100 stock. This means that systems based on points or dollar-based amounts, as opposed to percentages, should be refined more often, especially after substantial price moves have taken place. This is why I always prefer to use the percentage calculation wherever possible. In this case, though, the results were consistently better using the dollar or points approach, so I decided to compromise.

The results, as shown by the equity line in Chart 14-4, were acceptable but not spectacular. The total return was 146 percent at an annualized rate of 14 percent (Table 14-3). The win/loss ratio was just over 2 to 1. Remember though, in all these tests with futures markets, I am using continuous contracts and not making allowances for slippage. Actual results will not be as

Chart 14-4 Soybeans Continuous

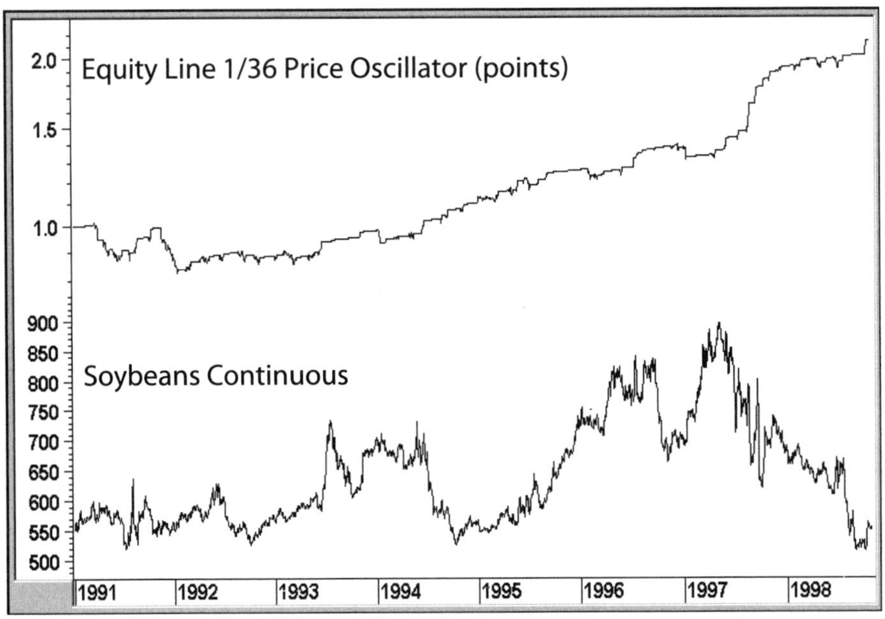

(Source: pring.com)

preferable. However, this approach definitely beats the straight MA crossover without the oscillator, which is displayed in Chart 14-5. I mentioned before the 18/5/−5 combination seems to work successfully on many markets. It is shown in Chart 14-6 for soybeans. The rate of return was certainly better than the buy-hold approach, but at 40 percent, lagged behind our best testing system based on a 36-day moving average, which we saw had earlier generated a return of 146 percent.

Chart 14-7 is an example of the CRB Composite using the 28/5/−5 combo. It barely makes money during this 18-year period. Even if I run a 1,000-day moving average through the equity line, it is fraught with whipsaws. When I studied the chart more closely for buy and sell signals, I found the price oscillator rarely moved to the plus and minus 5 percent areas. You can see in Chart 14-8, for instance, the oscillator never crosses these levels between 1988 and 1998. For 10 years it was literally a simple 28-day MA crossover system. Consequently, I tested for smaller variations and came up with a 12/2/−2 combination (Chart 14-9). It worked very well during this same period assuming a $35 round trip commission. The return was 275 percent earned with 683 trades, 225 of which were profitable. Table 14-4 shows the average win/loss ratio was close to 3. The largest losing trade was .07 points or $350 per contract, and the largest string of losses was 9. The

Chart 14-5 Soybeans Continuous

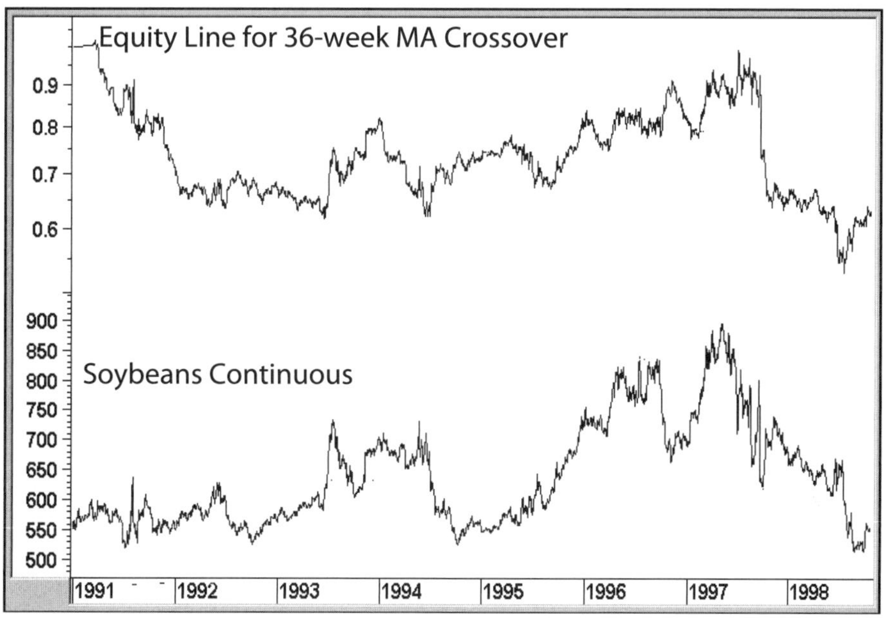

(Source: pring.com)

Chart 14-6 Soybeans Continuous

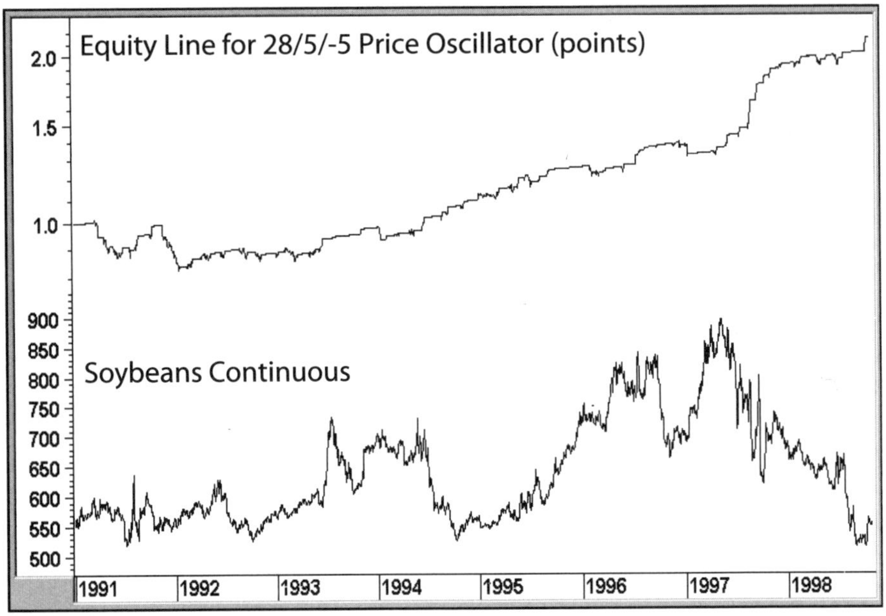

(Source: pring.com)

Chart 14-7 CRB Composite

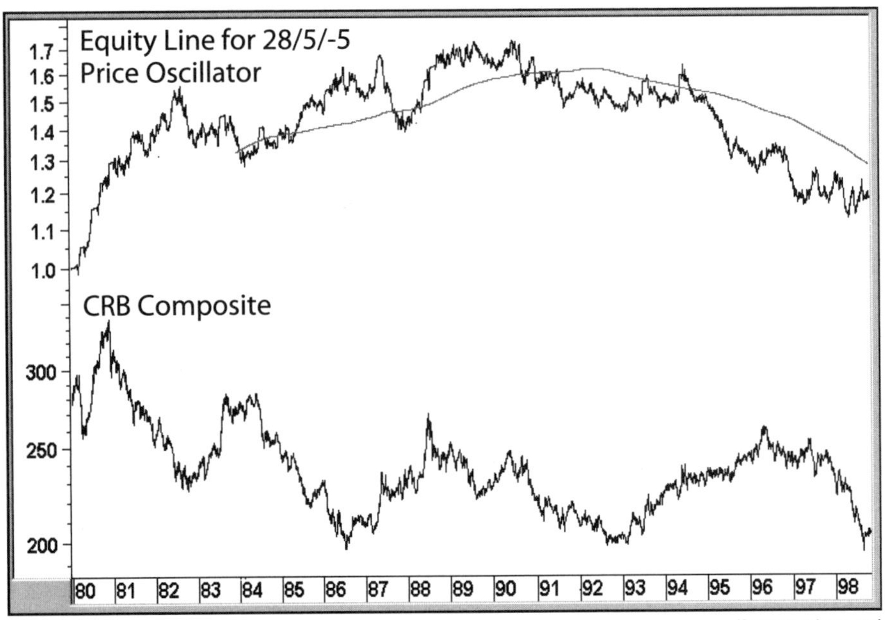

(Source: pring.com)

Chart 14-8 CRB Composite and a 1/28 Price Oscillator

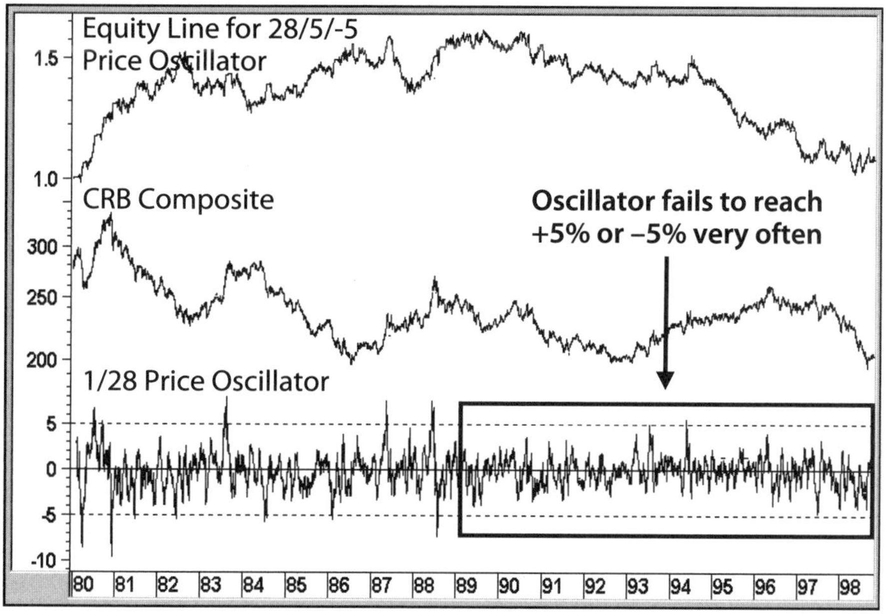

(Source: pring.com)

Chart 14-9 CRB Composite

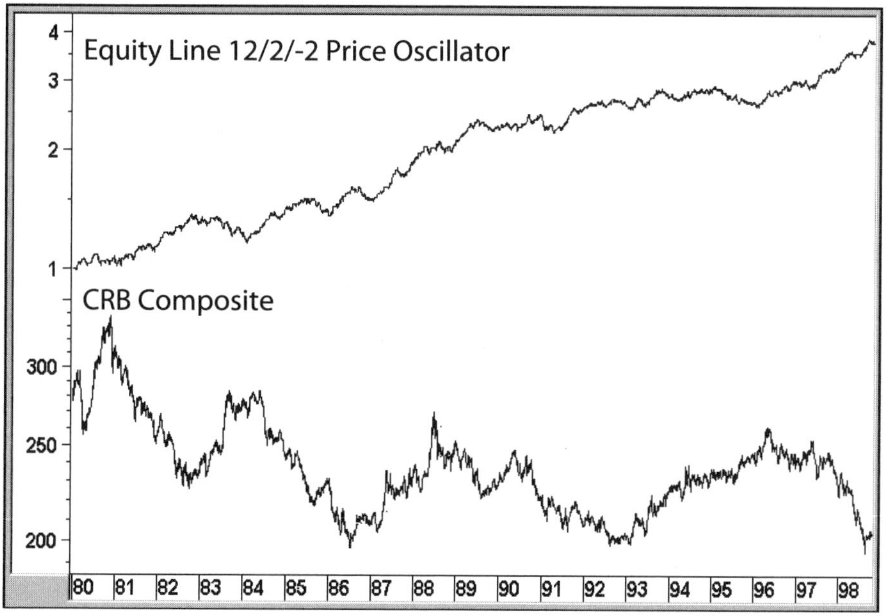

(Source: pring.com)

Table 14-4 CRB Composite

Buy/Hold profit	-0.28	Days in test	6873
Buy/Hold percent gain/loss	-27.87	Annual B/H percent gain/loss	-1.48
Total closed trades	68.3	Commissions paid	0.43
Average profit per trade	0.00	Average Win/Average loss ratio	2.98
Total long trades	341	Total short trades	342
Winning long trades	111	Winning short trades	114
Total winning trades	225	Total losing trades	458
Amount of winning trades	7.77	Amount of losing trades	-5.31
Average win	0.03	Average loss	-0.01
Largest win	0.22	Largest loss	-0.07
Average length of win	11.70	Average length of loss	3.95
Longest winning trade	37	Longest losing trade	14
Most consecutive wins	6	Most consecutive losses	9

equity line shows the peak-to-trough drawdowns were not that great though. The 1983–1984 period peaked at $1.36 and fell to about $1.17. In 1995, the equity fell from $2.91 to $2.61, but these declines were certainly manageable. The system beat the buy-hold approach by a very wide margin while the reward/risk at under 99 percent-plus was about as close to the maximum 100 percent reading as it could be.

APPLIED TO CLOSED-END MUTUAL FUNDS

This type of approach appears to work extremely well on most no load mutual funds. This is because the funds contain a portfolio of stocks that, taken together, have far better trending characteristics than their individual components. I ran some tests for a variety of funds reflecting different markets and I would like to share some of the results. I will start off by showing some parameters that appear to operate relatively successfully in a number of markets. Chart 14-10 is the 28/5/−5 combo. The oscillator is based on a percentage calculation. For the Scudder Japan the results came in at a very impressive 500 percent return over the approximate decade being tested.

Chart 14-10 Scudder Japan Fund

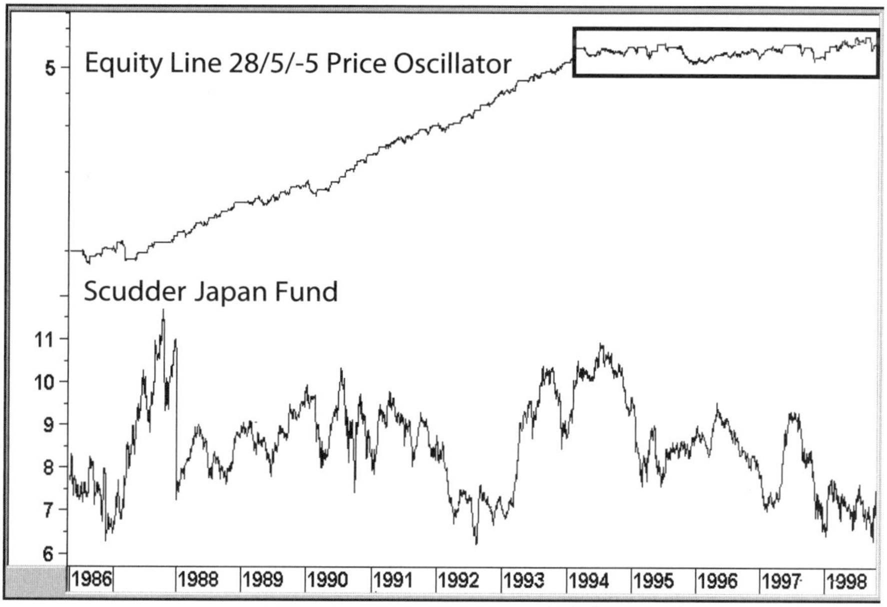

(Source: pring.com)

However, if you look carefully, you can see the results were basically flat between 1995 and 1998. This was not an easy market environment because of the ups and downs, but certainly fit the profile of this system.

If you want the Holy Grail, look no further than Chart 14-11 that returned over 1,000 percent (over 8,000 with 50 percent margin). The win/loss ratio was nearly over 4 to 1. Look at the equity line. There were virtually no significant drawdowns, with the exception of the 1995 decline from \$8.8 to \$7.7. The consistency of this approach is amazing considering the extremely choppy action of the fund itself.

Chart 14-12 of the Scudder Greater Europe, alternately, offered a much more bullish picture in terms of its own price performance, but the system was only able to turn in a performance of 63 percent for an average annual gain of 16 percent. The win/loss ratio for trades was 18 to 42, but the average winner outdid the average loser by nearly 5 to 1. Obviously the system was doing a great job of cutting losses. Even so, its performance was barely one-third of the buy-hold. Again, remember this was not the best system tested.

Chart 14-13 came from a 20/10/−10 combination, which gave a 103 percent—including a 5.4 to 1 win/loss ratio. It even beat the buy-hold approach by 40 percent. However, I need to explain a couple of caveats.

Chart 14-11 Scudder Japan Fund

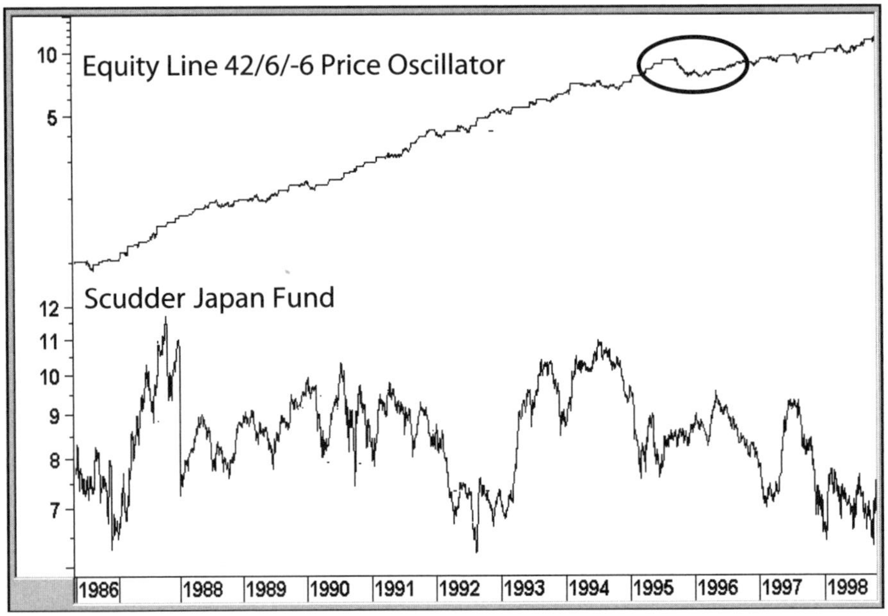

(Source: pring.com)

Chart 14-12 Scudder Greater Europe

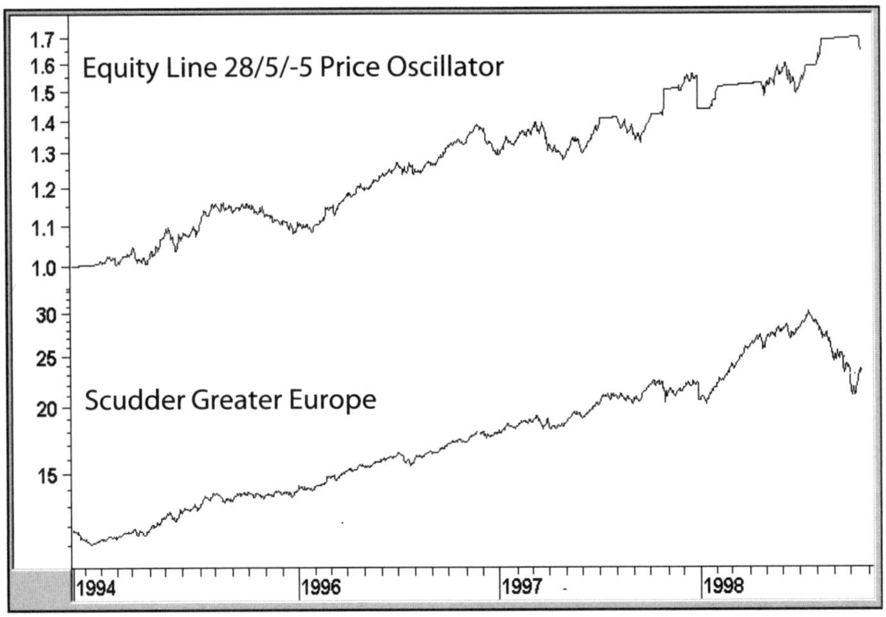

(Source: pring.com)

Chart 14-13 Scudder Greater Europe

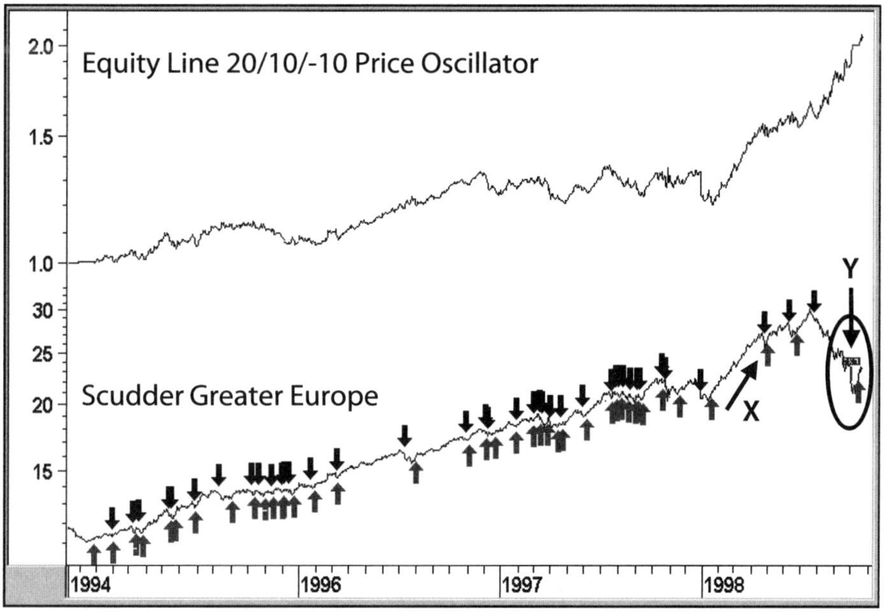

(Source: pring.com)

First, there is only one profit-taking signal (in the ellipse), which shows the rest of the test was conducted basically on an MA crossover approach. There is nothing wrong with that, of course, as long as it makes consistent profits. Second, a substantial amount of profit came from two signals—the one marked X at the start of 1998, and the other marked Y short sale in summer 1998. Take out 1998 and you will still have a good system, but certainly not as good as the overall return would have us believe.

Chart 14-14 is the Montgomery Growth Fund. Here again, the 28/5/−5 combination gives a respectable near 60 percent return, but not without its problems. The opening years, for instance, were not particularly inspiring. In fact, with the peak-to-trough drawdown between 1995 and 1996 of 16 percent, the system went underwater in early 1996. The reason was due to the moving average whipsaws, even though this was a strong trending market. Clearly, this would have been a very frustrating time. It represents a strong reason why it is necessary to apply systems such as this to several securities simultaneously. Chart 14-15 shows the 1997–1998 period in greater detail. This is where the fund itself actually lost ground. However, in this difficult environment, the system allowed the equity line to steadily rise from \$1.30 to \$1.57. These declining phases should be borne in mind when making comparisons to the buy-hold approach because the 1990s spoiled

Chart 14-14 Montgomery Growth

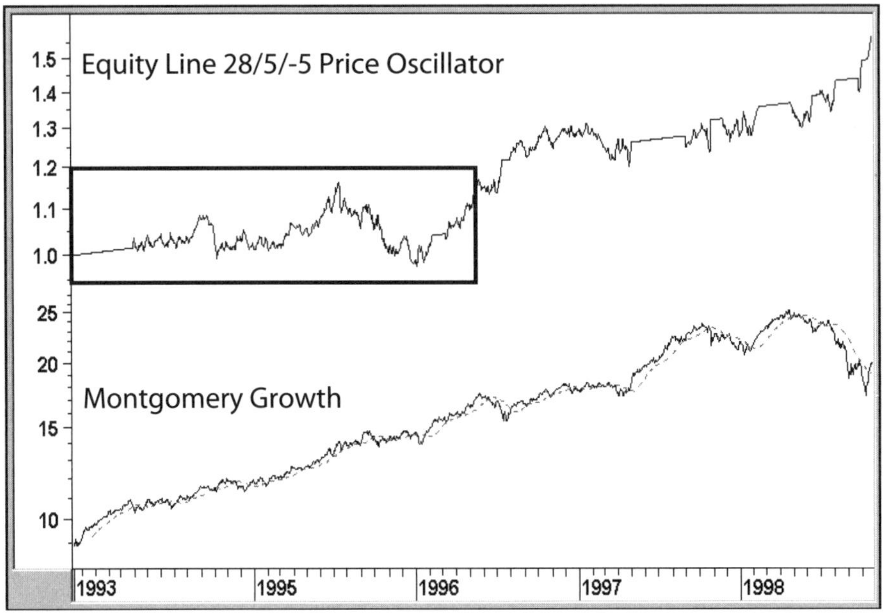

(Source: pring.com)

Chart 14-15 Montgomery Growth

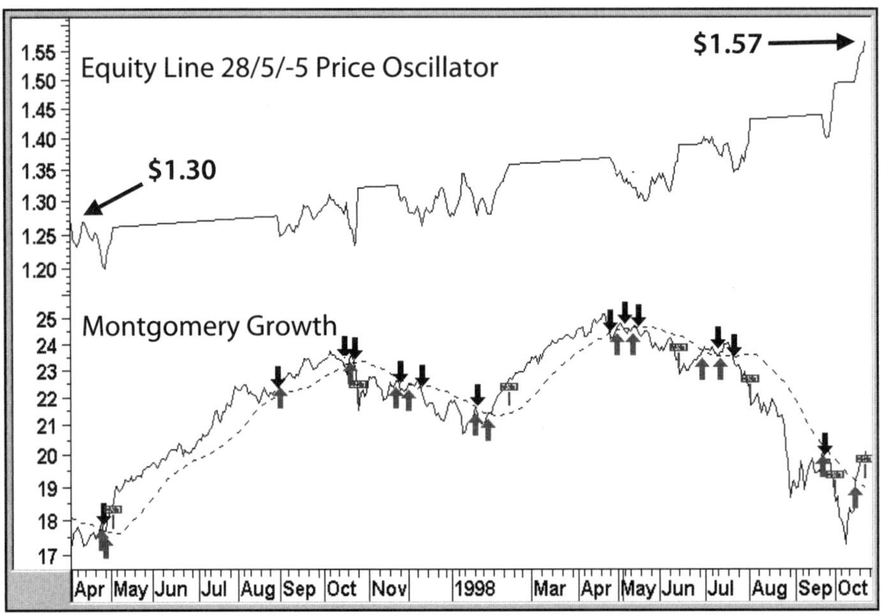

(Source: pring.com)

many investors with many funds barely pausing for breath. Those times are unlikely to return, so do not forget what goes up can also go down. I do not want to leave you with the impression that everything works well with this 28/5/−5 combo, and that it can be blindly applied to any market. Nothing could be further from the truth.

APPLIED TO THE STOCK MARKET

I have saved the best tests for last, starting with the Russell 2000® (Chart 14-16), a measurement of low cap U.S. stocks. First, the standard 28/5/−5 combination works fairly well, offering a 374 percent return, or 33 percent on an annualized basis. The win/loss ratio at 4.79 to 1 is excellent and, as you can see, there were no significant drawdowns. After optimizing using the percentage approach, a large number of combinations were found to offer truly great results. The best combination was a 10/10/−10. As shown in the summary in Table 14-5, the system returned a staggering 2,687 percent. Losses outnumbered gains by 188 to 145. Table 14-6 shows the average gain outstripped the average loss by a staggering factor of over 8 to 1. The

Chart 14-16 Russell 2000®

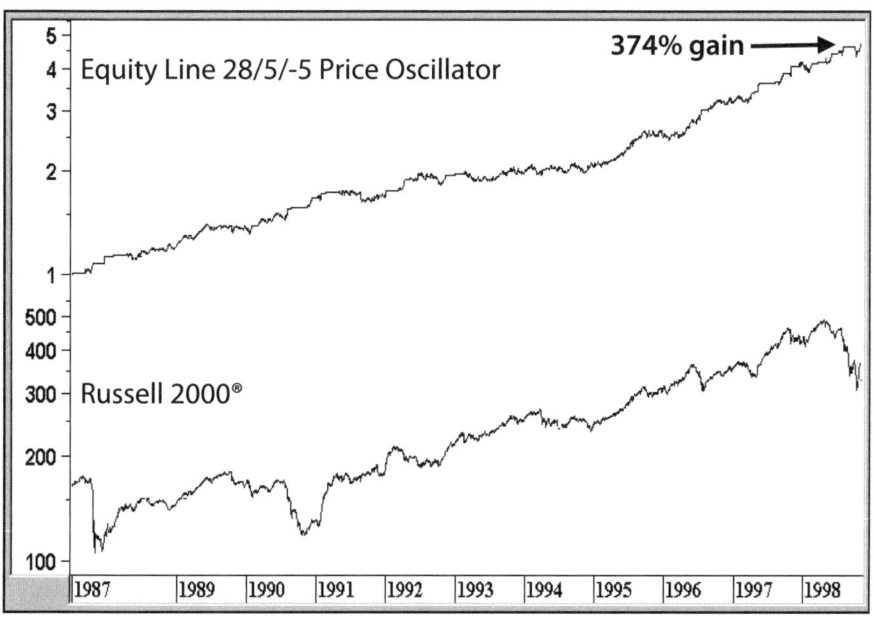

(Source: pring.com)

Table 14-5 Russell 2000®

RUSSELL 2000®							
Percent	Total Trades	Winning Trades	Losing Trades	Average Win	Optimization 1	Optimization 2	Optimization 3
2687.45	333	145	188	4.4554	10	10	-10
2687.45	333	145	188	4.4554	10	12	-10
2687.45	333	145	188	4.4554	10	14	-10
2687.45	333	145	188	4.4554	10	16	-10
2621.98	334	146	188	4.6542	10	8	-10
2581.21	333	145	188	4.2403	10	10	-8
2581.21	333	145	188	4.2403	10	12	-8
2581.21	333	145	188	4.2403	10	16	-8
2581.21	333	145	188	4.2403	10	14	-8

Table 14-6 Russell 2000®

Total closed trades	135	Commissions paid	0.04
Average profit per trade	0.06	Average Win/Average loss ratio	8.33
Total long trades	67	Total short trades	68
Winning long trades	27	Winning short trades	19
Total winning trades	46	Total losing trades	89
Amount of winning trades	9.70	Amount of losing trades	-2.25
Average win	0.21	Average loss	-0.03
Largest win	1.50	Largest loss	-0.15
Average length of win	46.41	Average length of loss	6.99
Longest winning trade	191	Longest losing trade	28
Most consecutive wins	3	Most consecutive losses	8
Total bars out	242	Average length out	48.40
Longest out period	72		

maximum number of consecutive losses was eight, but we could certainly live with this in view of the tremendously profitable performance. It beat the buy-hold approach by 575 percent.

The equity line in Chart 14-17 is one of the best I have ever seen for profit and consistency. With a system as consistent as this, it sometimes pays to play the margin game. In that spirit, the system with a 50 percent margin gained over 50,000 percent! Ironically, the number of times the oscillator reached the 10 percent and −10 percent overbought/oversold extremes were few in number and, in this case, a simple 10-day MA crossover would have produced a return of 2,400 percent with no margin—not far from the oscillator approach of 2,600 percent. The record of this system is excellent over a relatively long period. I would again caution that there is no guarantee it will continue to perform as well in the future.

You may be wondering how this system worked on other market averages such as the S&P Composite. Chart 14-18, for example, shows the system using the 28/5/−5 combination. It certainly makes money, turning $1 into $1.84. However, there is a substantial decline in the equity line in the early 1980s and between 1991 and 1994 when the peak equity of $2.59 falls to $1.60. Even the best-tested combination, using equal overbought/oversold

Chart 14-17 Russell 2000®

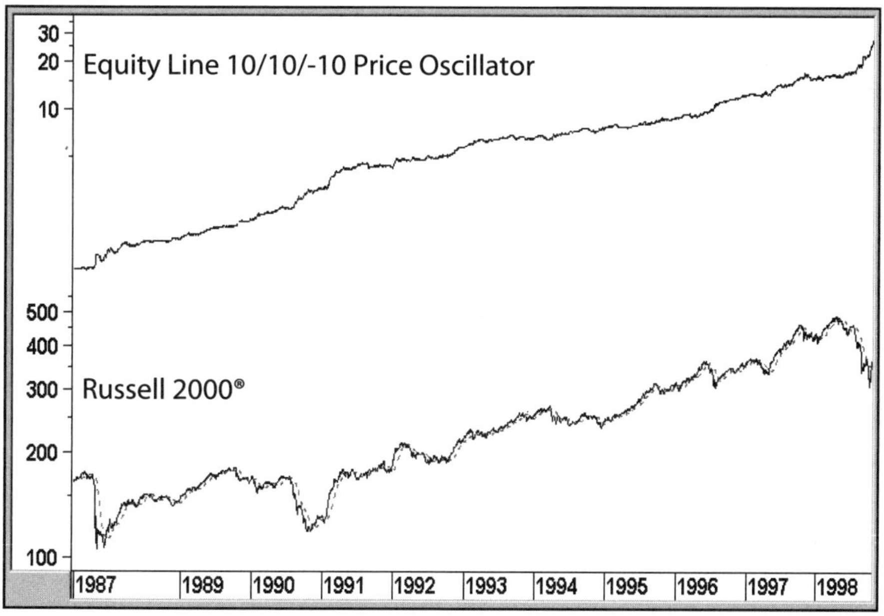

(Source: pring.com)

Chart 14-18 S&P Composite

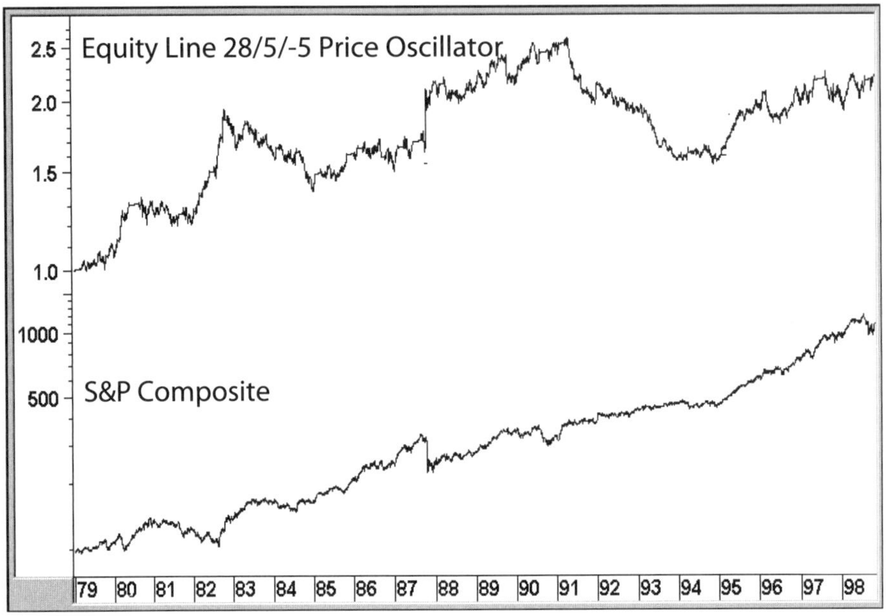

(Source: pring.com)

parameters of 28/4/−4, really under performs. It turned $1 into $2.34 and was still unable to avoid the two major drawdowns in the early 1980s and 1990s.

However, when we turn our guns to the NASDAQ, we get a completely different story. The experience was very similar to the Russell 2,000 only more so. Virtually every combination I tested came away with tremendous results. Look at Chart 14-19. One of the best combinations was 10/10/−10. It gave a total return of over 30,000 percent. The 556 signals averaged about one every 10 days with 228 winners and 328 losers. The win/loss ratio was a comfortable 3.19 percent and the system beat the buy-hold approach by nearly 3,000 percent. Chart 14-19 shows the equity line to be a consistent profit maker with very little in the way of drawdowns. Chart 14-20 shows the progress of the system in 1997 and 1998. This was a relatively troubled period but the equity line, nevertheless, continued to rise. The largest peak-to-trough drawdown in the entire test appeared in 1997 when it sank from $183 to $161, and then, again, in 1998 when it sank from $252 to $231, as shown in the ellipses. When consideration is given to the fact that the starting equity was only $1, these 10 percent declines are a very small price to pay. While there is no reason why this system will not continue to operate

Chart 14-19 NASDAQ Composite

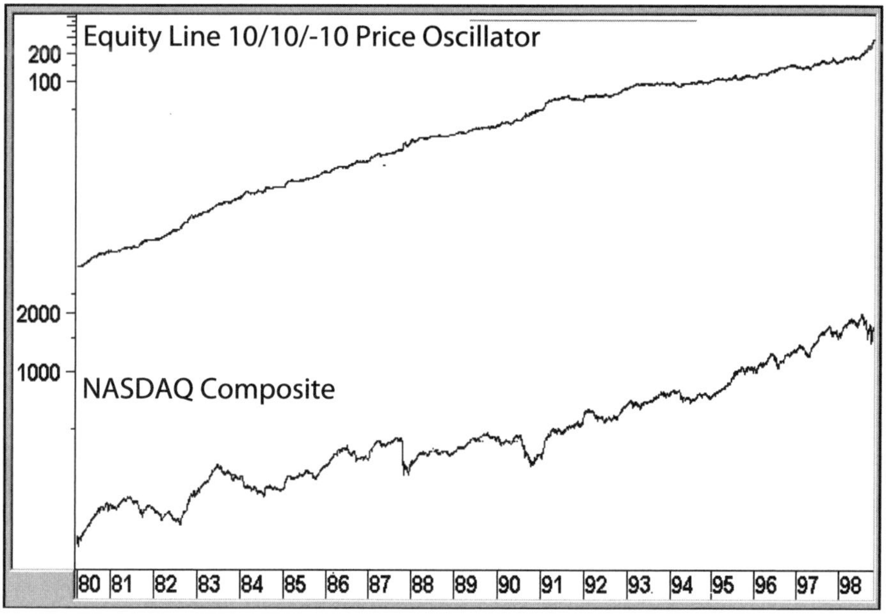

(Source: pring.com)

Chart 14-20 NASDAQ Composite

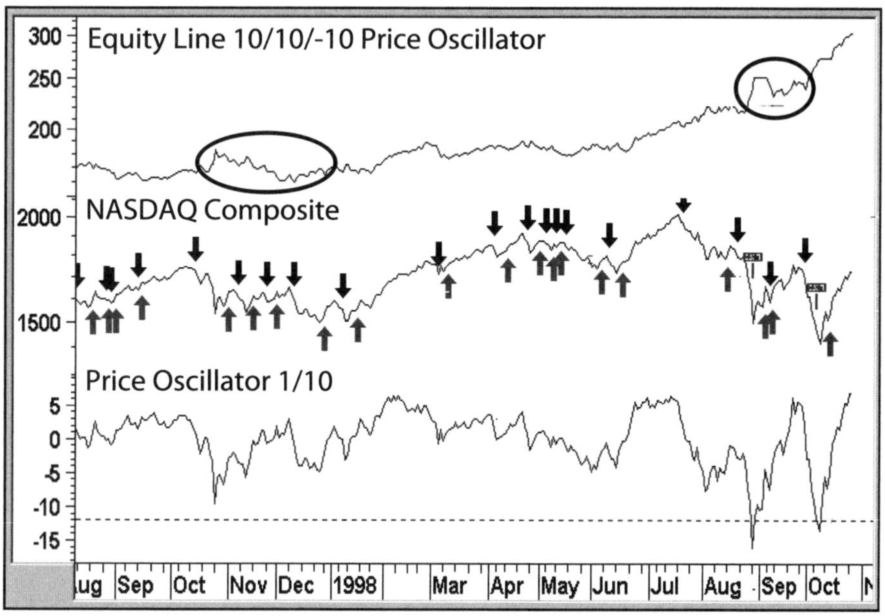

(Source: pring.com)

in the future, it is important to remember that virtually all systems break down at some point. Also, the data tested here were in a strong, secular bull market. True, there were some trading ranges and important declines, but I have seen enough of the results in other markets to suggest that a diversified approach is still the best. Then, if one market breaks down, it has a far smaller adverse effect than if we put all our eggs in one basket.

Chapter 15 The Triple Indicator System

THE RATIONALE

One important principle that should be followed when designing a system incorporating several triggering mechanisms is to make sure it incorporates different indicators based on different timeframes. The contrasted timeframes are important because prices at any one time are determined by the interaction of many different time cycles. We cannot make provisions for all of them, of course. If we can ensure there is a good time difference that separates the indicator construction, we will at least have made an attempt to monitor more than one cycle.

A system I devised in the late 1970s combines an MA crossover with a signal from two ROC indicators. These are 10-week simple MAs, a 6-week ROC and a 13-week ROC. Thus, we have two different types of indicators: a trend-following moving average, and two oscillator types. The system also consists of three different timeframes. The buy and sell rules are very simple. Buy when the price is above the 10-week MA *and* both ROCs are above zero. Sell when *all three* go negative, that is, the ROCs cross below zero and the price crosses its moving average. *Signals cannot be generated unless all three agree.* This is because we want to make sure the various cycles reflected in the three different timeframes are all in gear. Originally, when I introduced this system, it was applied to the pound/dollar relationship because it was one that trended very consistently. Let us take a close look at Chart 15-1 to see how it works by starting off with a simple 10-week MA crossover between mid 1974 and 1976. Buy signals are once again indicated by the upward pointing arrows and short positions by the downward pointing ones. There were 13 signals for a total profit of 19¢ on an initial $1 investment, from both the long and the short side. This compares to the buy-hold approach, with a loss of almost 70¢. Taken on its own, this was a fairly commendable performance, but let us remember that for a significant portion of the time, that is, most of 1975 and 1976, the British pound was in a sustained downtrend. It is true there were a number of whipsaws in late 1975 and early 1976. These are shown in the two ellipses, but were of minor consequence as it turned out.

The next step is to introduce a 13-week ROC. Buy and sell signals are triggered when the 13-week ROC crosses above and below its zero reference line. This approach, shown in Chart 15-2, nets a gain of 23¢, with six signals. This was better than the results with the MA crossover, especially since fewer signals dramatically reduced the potential for whipsaws. Even so, there were a couple of nasty whipsaws in 1976.

The next step is to introduce a second ROC indicator to filter out some of the whipsaws. A 6-week ROC was chosen mainly because it spans approximately half the timespan of the 13-week series. The result, as shown in Chart 15-3, was an improved 35¢, but the number of signals also increased.

Chart 15-1 British Pound System (Source: *pring.com*)

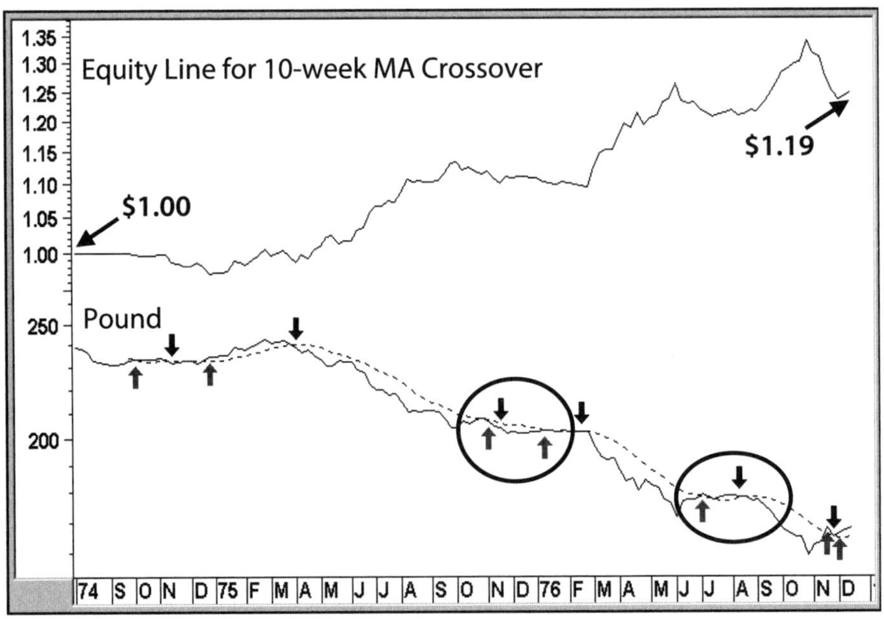

(Source: pring.com)

Chart 15-2 British Pound System (Source: *pring.com*)

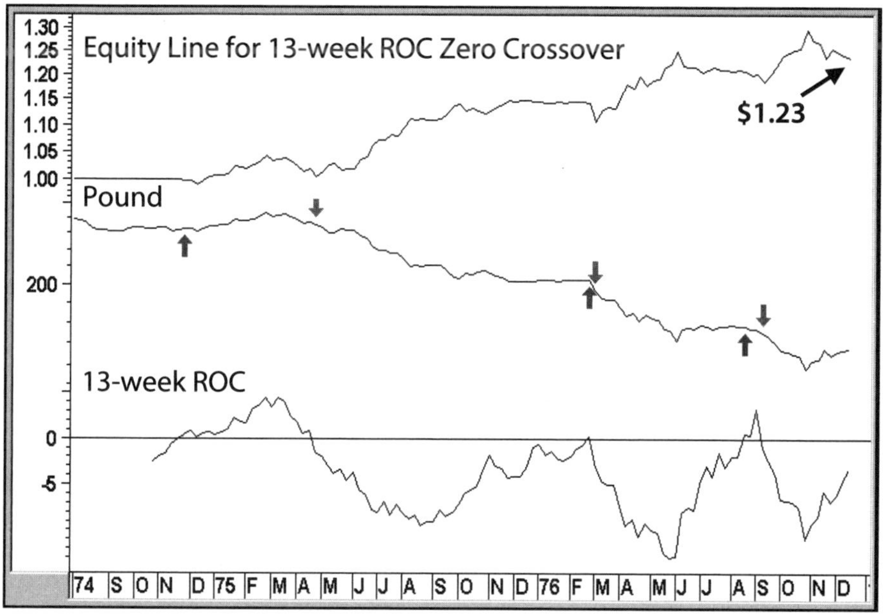

(Source: pring.com)

Chart 15-3 British Pound System (Source: *pring.com*)

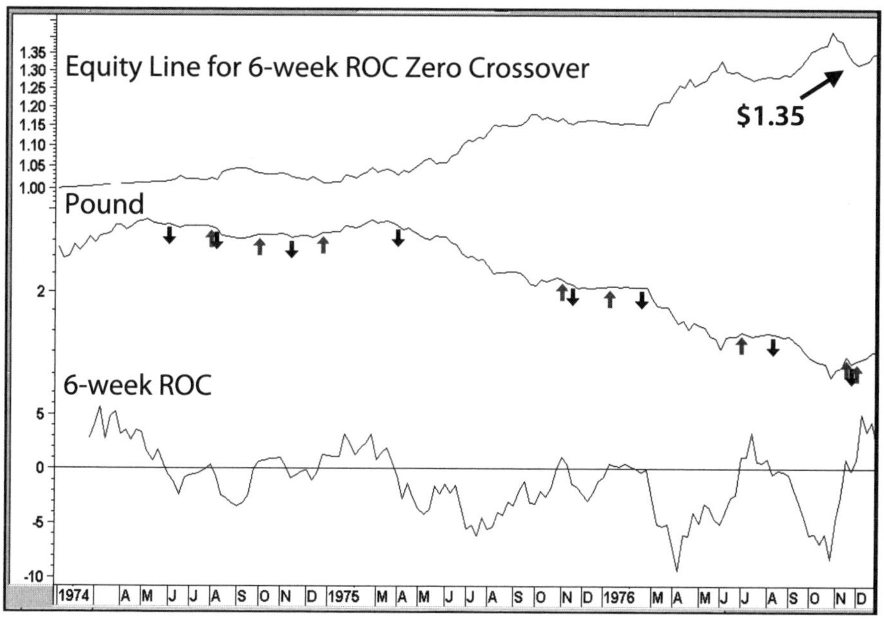

(Source: pring.com)

PUTTING THE INDICATORS TOGETHER

I put all three indicators together in Chart 15-4 so you can see how their integration improves things. The actual result was a slight increase in profit over the previous 6-week ROC test. However, the important thing was that the signals were reduced to only three. Note the equity line at the top of Chart 15-5 shows a good, steady increase. A closer look at Chart 15-4 shows that the first sell comes in October 1974, as the 6-week ROC follows the others into negative territory. Then, in December, the 13-week ROC crosses above zero, which is closely followed by an MA crossover. Finally, the 6-week series moves above zero for a buy signal. All three then move into negative territory in April 1975. The moving average and 6-week ROC go bearish simultaneously, and this is then followed by the 13-week series. The system stays bearish all the way through late 1976. It almost goes bullish when the price crosses its average and the 6-week ROC goes positive in February 1976. However, the 13-week series, which had been bearish, now goes bullish, but by this time, the currency had slipped below its moving average and the 6-week series fell below zero. As a result, all three indicators were never in agreement. The same is true in the July–August period of 1976 when the two ROC indicators take turns in being bullish and bearish.

Chart 15-4 British Pound System

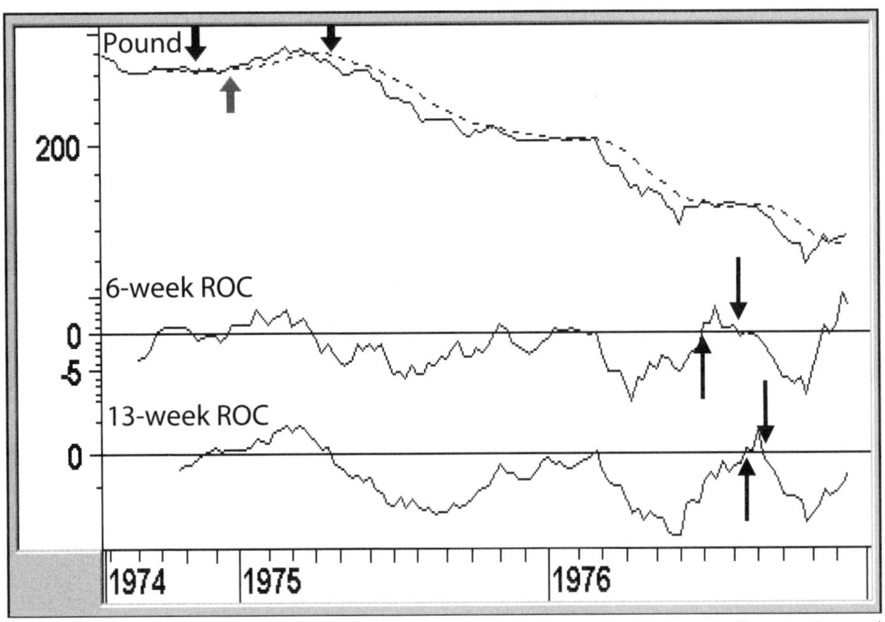

(Source: pring.com)

Students of my momentum course will recognize this as a form of a negative complex divergence. The combination of all three indicators works extremely well in this environment. This is about as good as it gets.

APPRAISING THE SYSTEM

I introduced this approach in my book *International Investing Made Easy* in 1981 with some hesitancy because there was obviously no guarantee it would continue to operate profitably. It was subsequently reintroduced in the third edition of *Technical Analysis Explained* in 1992 with the same proviso. What I said was, "It is important to understand this approach will not necessarily offer such large rewards in the future. The example of the British pound must be treated as the exception rather than the rule, but it is introduced to give you an incentive to *experiment* along these lines."

The system continued to work extremely well, as you can see by looking back at the equity line in the upper portion of Chart 15-5. However, I am glad I used the cautionary statement, because once we move past 1993, the system falls apart. Just look at the declining equity line between 1993 and

Chart 15-5 British Pound System

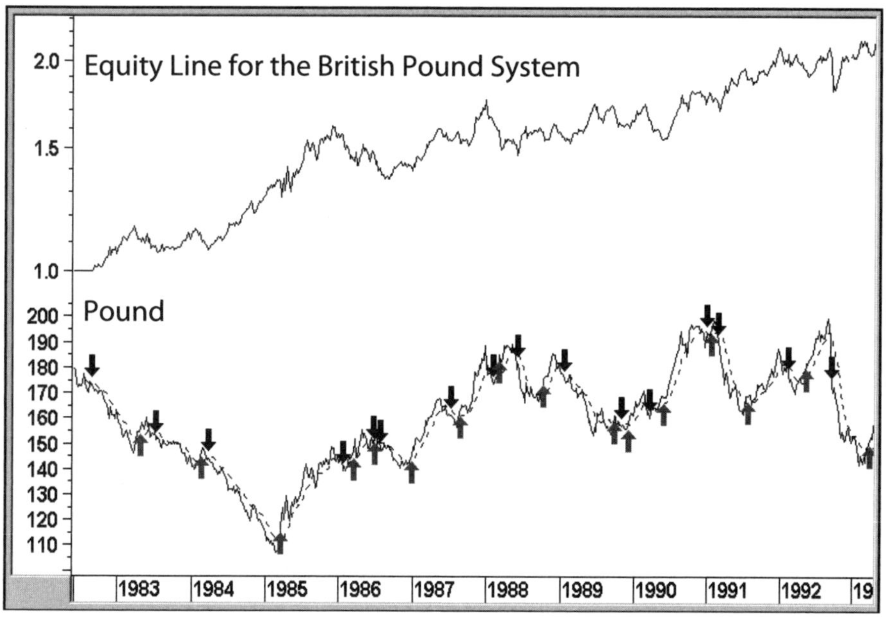

(Source: pring.com)

1998 in Chart 15-6. This was due to the many whipsaws arising from the trading range that followed the drop from $2.00 in 1993. This goes to show that even if a system works well for 20 years, as this one had, market conditions can and do change, so you must be prepared for such instances. Obviously, we do not know until some time after the fact that the market environment has changed. Is there anything we can do to avoid such situations? One possibility is to run a very long-term MA or trendline through the equity line. In Chart 15-7, I have plotted a 300-week simple MA. I used 300 weeks because I felt it necessary for the system to undergo a fairly long period before it can be considered out of touch. After all, with the pound system, the history goes back to the early 1970s, so 6 years is not a particularly long time. The idea is when the equity line crosses below the moving average something is seriously wrong with the system, and it should at least be temporarily abandoned. At this point, it would make sense to reappraise it and see if it could be improved, and I do not mean by introducing special rules to block out a bad period. You could also wait until the equity line crosses back above the moving average again.

Chart 15-6 British Pound System

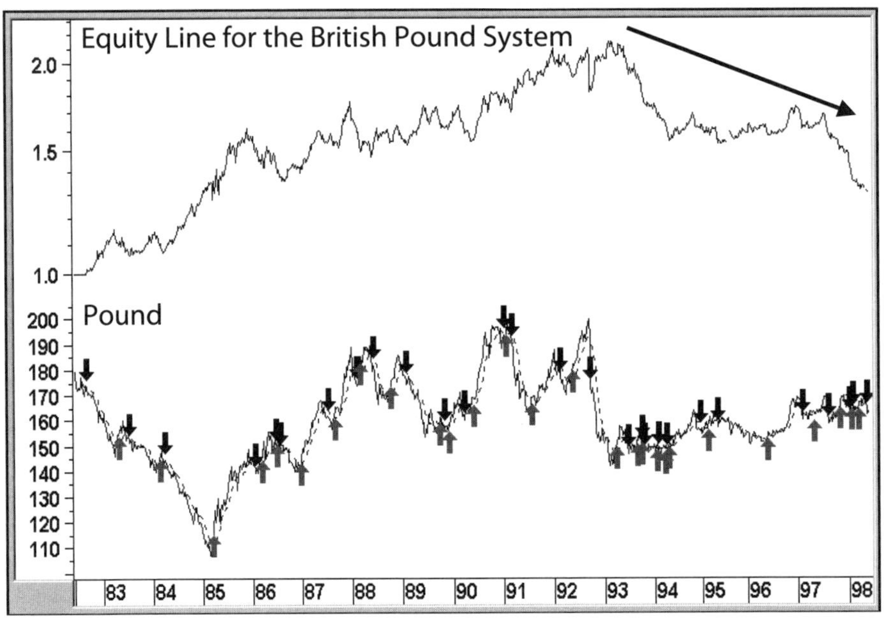

(Source: pring.com)

Chart 15-7 British Pound System

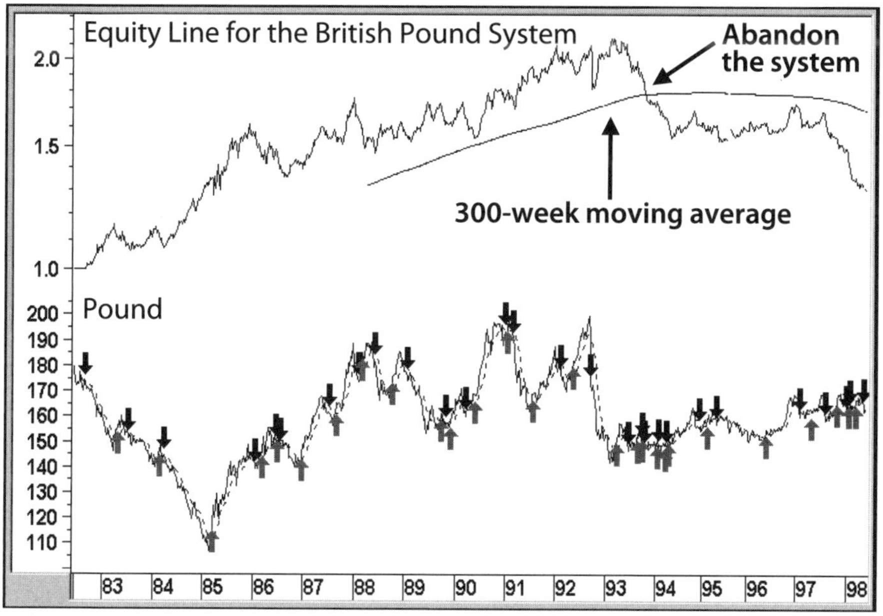

(Source: pring.com)

THE ADVANTAGES OF DIVERSIFICATION

The second possibility is to use the same system on different markets; that is, diversify. Once again, we need to make sure the system tests well on any of the markets that are to be traded. Chart 15-8 features the same system for the Nikkei. It has a very profitable, but more consistent, feel to it. There are a few drawdowns in the early 1990s. The initial one in 1992 was just over 20 percent, but, by and large, it operated very successfully over this 12-year period.

Chart 15-9 shows the system as applied to the S&P Composite. It doubles the initial $1 investment, but nothing like the 10 times return from the buy-hold approach. Also, look at the volatility in the swings in the equity line. Even the 300-day moving average does not act that well since the equity line gives a sell signal for the system in 1992 after a nasty loss. Then, in 1995, the equity line moved back above the 300-week MA, telling us it was OK to trade the stock again. The stock continued to make money, but the drawdowns indicated by the declines in the equity line, though not that large, were too frequent to give confidence that the system was truly robust.

Chart 15-8 British Pound System Applied to the Nikkei

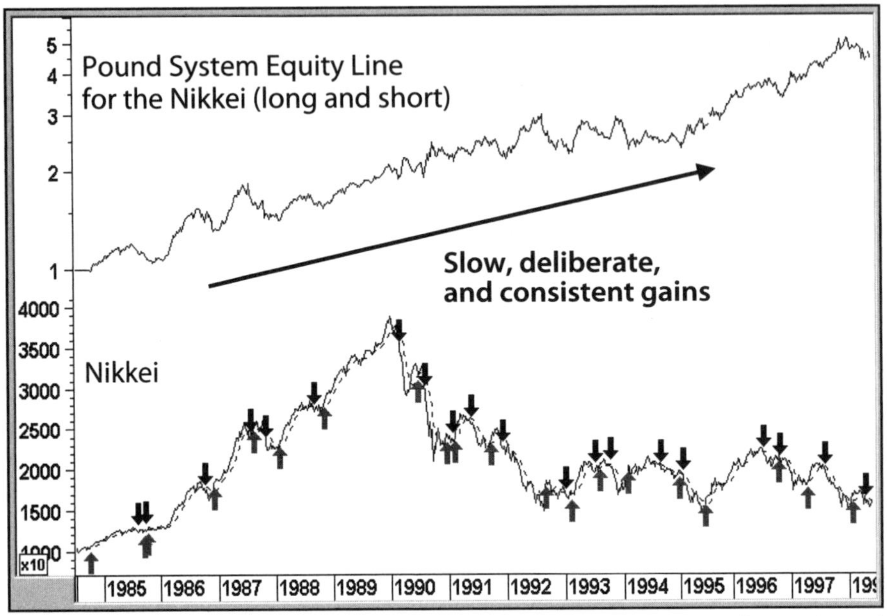

(Source: pring.com)

Chart 15-9 British Pound System Applied to the S&P Composite

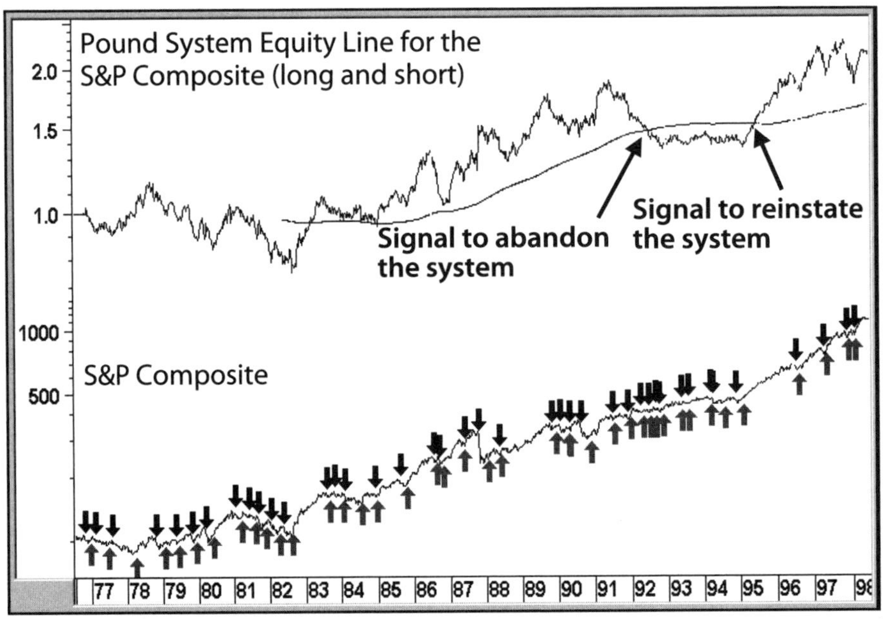

(Source: pring.com)

Chart 15-10 shows the system worked extremely well for the gold price until 1980. After that, the enormous trading range provided huge commissions for the brokers, but virtually no profits for the trader. Here again, running a 300-week moving average on the equity line can be very helpful. True, there was a whipsaw sell signal in the mid-1980s, but the sell signal in early 1991 would have more than compensated because it would have avoided several years of frustrated trading.

One sector that appears to trend very well is the bond market. We can see this in Chart 15-11 of Moody's Corporate AAA Yield. The equity line is in a very consistent uptrend throughout the period. This is because the bond market is very much driven by economic events that tend to be slow and deliberate as they unfold. Gold, on the other hand, is driven at the margin by investment and speculative demand—that is, psychological factors—and is more subject to schizophrenic whipsaws. Good, consistent results such as those shown in Chart 15-11 of the AAA Yield are often improved by introducing some leverage. In this case, using a 50 percent margin, the initial investment grows to around $10. This compares to the nonmargined result of $3. However, with greater reward comes greater risk. In this case (Chart 15-12), the drawdowns are not that much, but neverthe-

Chart 15-10 British Pound System Applied to the Spot Gold

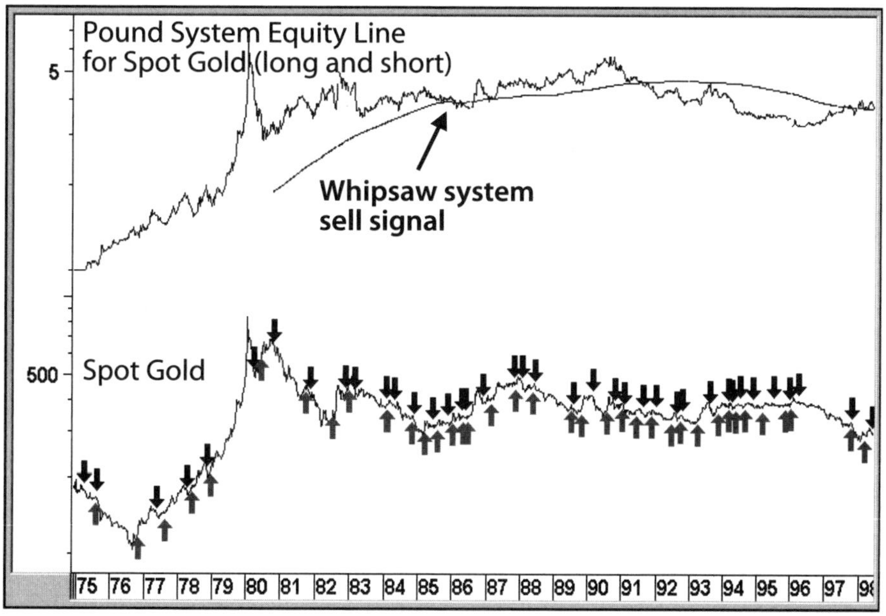

(Source: pring.com)

Chart 15-11 British Pound System Applied to the AAA Yield

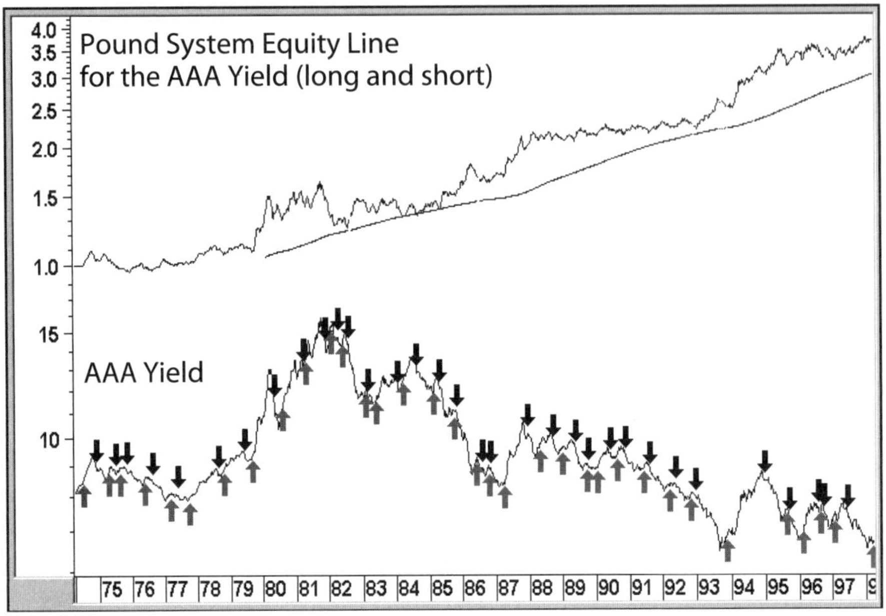

(Source: pring.com)

Chart 15-12 British Pound System Applied to the AAA Yield

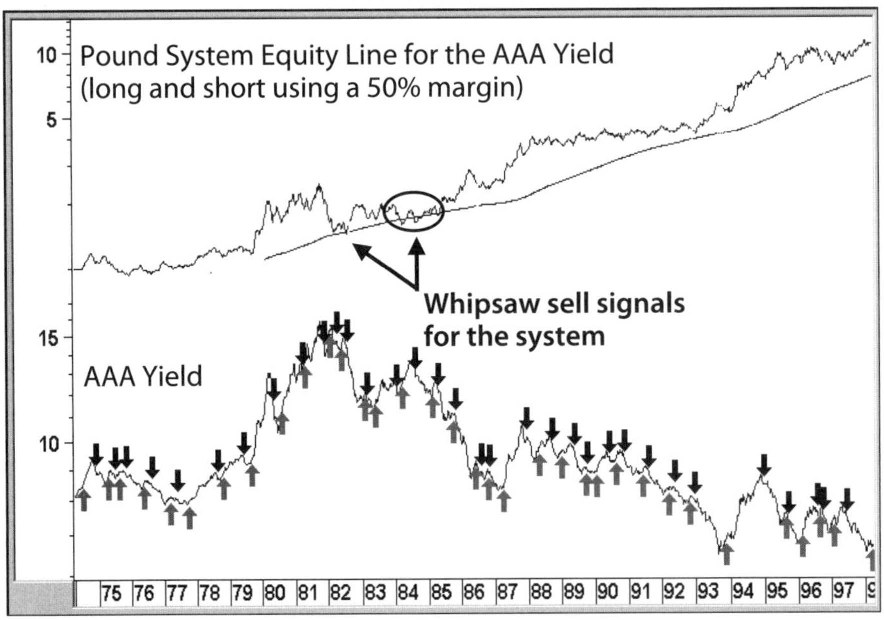

(Source: pring.com)

Chart 15-13 British Pound System Applied to the German Mark

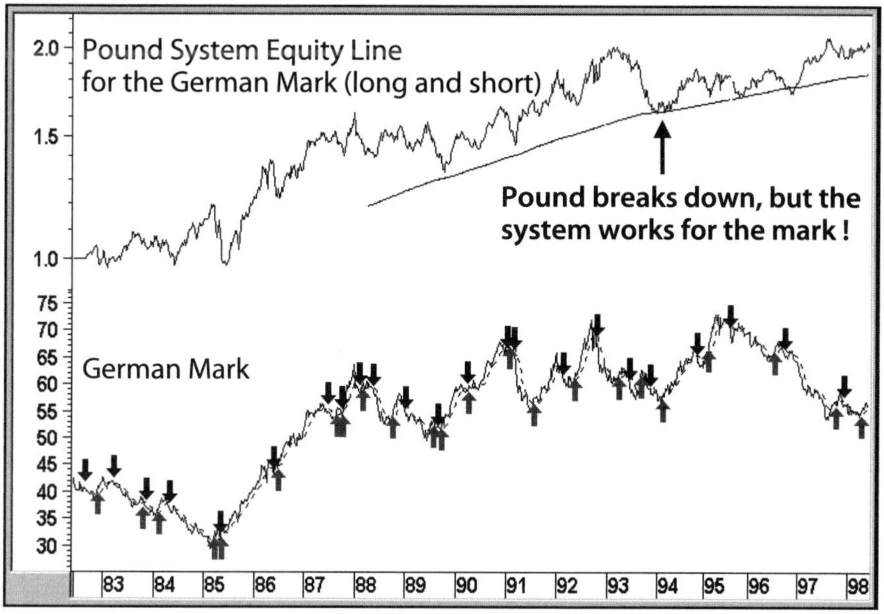

(Source: pring.com)

less, they cause a couple of negative whipsaw signals with the 300-week MA. I have some more comments to make on the uses and abuses of margin in the next chapter.

Finally, you will recall I said that the pound system worked best on the pound, as compared to the other currencies, during its initial testing period. Ironically, while the pound system was breaking down against the pound itself in 1993, it was starting to work very well for the German deutsche mark, as we can see from Chart 15-13. How do we know when to switch from the pound to the mark? Use of a long-term MA can help, but this, again, underscores the importance of diversifying a system into several different, but well-tested markets. Had we been trading the pound, the mark, gold, the Nikkei and bonds through the AAA Yield, the hits taken from the pound breakdown in 1993 and the mid-1990s problem with gold would have been far less spectacular than if we had limited our trading solely to the pound.

Chapter 16
A Word Regarding Leverage

USING LEVERAGE

We saw in Part 2 of the pound system that leverage, when applied to a consistent system, not only increases the volatility, but also can really enhance the results. Just because a system tests well using 100 percent cash does not necessarily mean you can multiply the results by the amount of leverage. That will depend greatly on where the good and bad signals develop and how significant they are. Chart 16-1 features the American Century Gold Fund. The lower portion is the fund, and the upper one shows the equity line for a system using a simple 10-day MA crossover, from both the long and short side. It starts off with $1 in 1989 and ends with just over $9 in mid 1998. I also assumed a small commission to approximate a futures contract even though this is a no load fund. This is not a bad return, but what happens if I work on a 5 percent margin, thereby gaining a 20 times gearing effect? Will my profits be 20 or more times greater?

The answer is in Chart 16-2. Things start out very well and my money would triple in a matter of a few weeks. However, as time passes, all my money would have been frittered away with losing trades in the first couple of years. I certainly do not have to worry about paying commissions now! The initial losing trades were exaggerated by a factor of 20, that is, the 5 percent margin, and before I could establish a profitable run, my capital was totally wiped out. One of our trading rules was to make sure you have enough capital to survive the worst losing streak. Well, if you test without a margin and then apply a margin in the marketplace, your results are

Chart 16-1 American Century Gold Fund

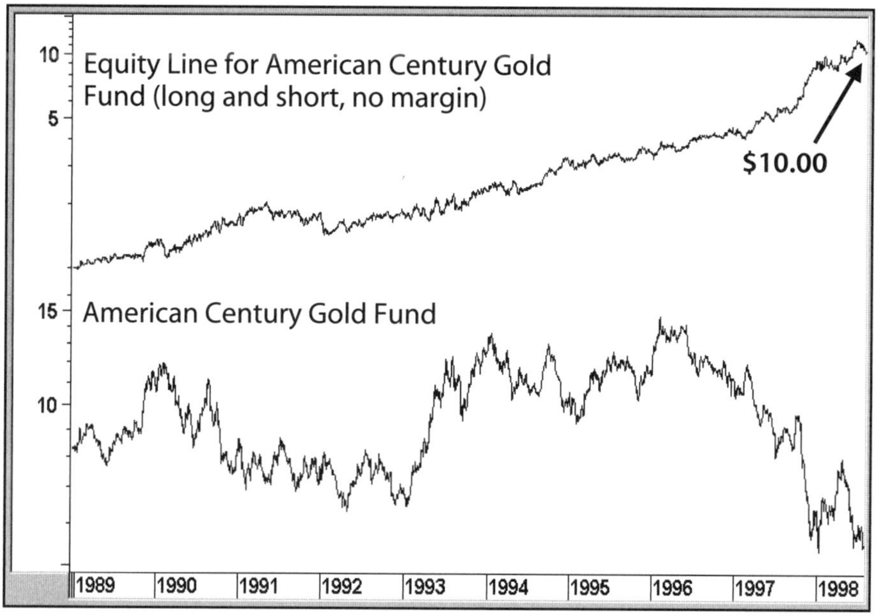

(Source: pring.com)

Chart 16-2 American Century Gold Fund

(Source: pring.com)

Chart 16-3 American Century Gold Fund

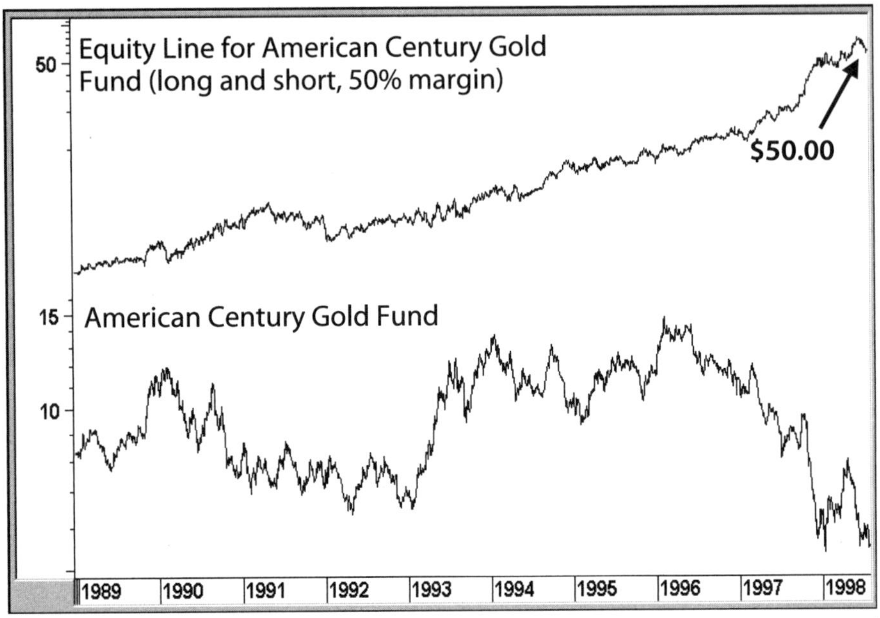

(Source: pring.com)

incorrect because margin means greater volatility, and that, in turn, means far greater drawdowns.

Sometimes a little gearing works better than either cash or a substantial leverage. Chart 16-3 shows the American Century Gold Fund again, but this time with an equity line based on a 50 percent margin. You can see the initial $1 investment grew to almost $50 during this period because the initial losing trades were not sufficiently leveraged to wipe out the position. The account still declined in those initial trades, but nevertheless, lived to take advantage of the profitable signals down the road. These examples show the high-risk nature of leveraging. If things go wrong it is terrible, but if they go right it is great. Remember, it is vitally important to maintain consistency and cut losses quickly. Over-leveraging is a simple way to break these rules in spades.

Keep in mind, the results of leveraging will depend on three things: the consistency and resiliency of the system, the amount of leverage, and finally, the position and amount of losing trades relative to the starting point. The closer the losses develop to the initial trades, the greater the loss will be.

PART III

Systems Based on Intermarket Relationships

Chapter 17
Equities Versus Short-Term Interest Rates

THE RELATIONSHIP

So far, we have just considered particular securities or markets in isolation using statistically derived data from that security alone. An alternative approach is to adopt a tried and tested intermarket relationship as a cross-reference to obtain better results. An intermarket relationship develops when one market consistently influences another. The first step is to rationalize why such a relationship exists in the first place. Perhaps the most basic is between equity prices and short-term interest rates. There are several reasons why this relationship works, but the most important is related to the economy. When rates rise, this adversely affects business activity sooner or later, and since stock prices discount corporate profits, equity market participants sell stock in anticipation of such news. From a forecasting point of view, the problem is the leads and lags vary in each cycle. Also, each economic recovery requires a different "dose" of rising rates to trip it up. Consequently, it is not possible to use interest rates only as a trading system for the stock market.

In Chart 17-1, I have plotted the 3-month commercial paper yield inversely so it corresponds with movements in the stock market. A falling series in the lower panel is, therefore, bearish for equities since it means yields are rising, and so forth. The period covered is quite long. As you can see, there is not much of a relationship between the two series. Money

Chart 17-1 S&P Composite Versus 3-Month Commercial Paper Yield

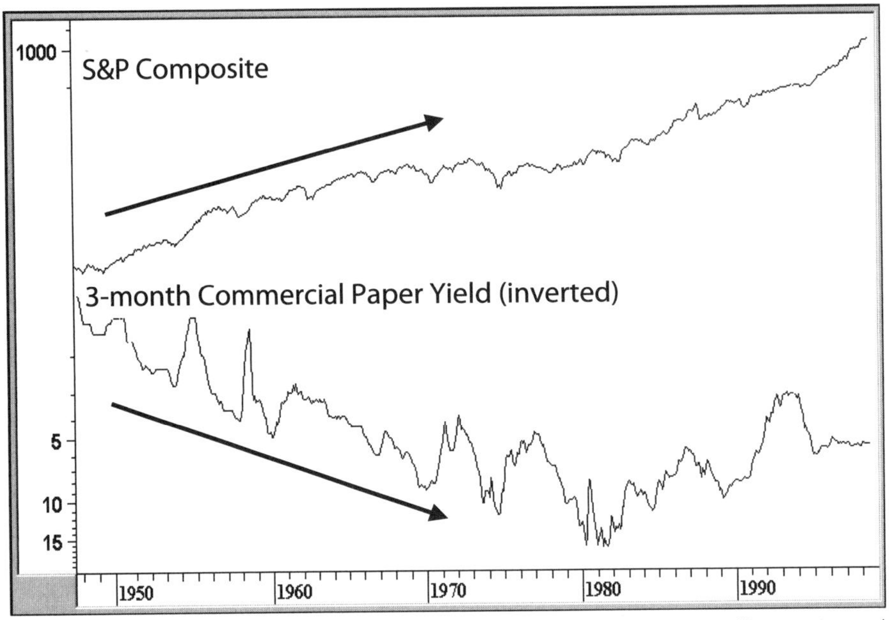

(Source: pring.com)

market prices were falling between 1950 and 1966, yet stock prices rose. It is the relationship within each individual business cycle that is important.

Chart 17-2 shows the two series between 1950 and 1964. The arrows join the peaks in money market prices to bull market highs in the stock market. You can see from their angle that the lead-time between the peaks differs quite considerably from cycle to cycle. Look at the long lead-time between 1950 and 1953, compared to the relatively short period on the extreme right between 1961 and 1962. The level of decline in money market prices does not appear to have an influence on the proportionate decline in stock prices. Here you can see a very sharp drop in the commercial paper series between 1958 and 1959, yet the stock market correction was relatively mild. Whereas, the decline that started in 1961 was a lot more shallow, but eventually resulted in the sharp 25 percent drop of 1962.

THE SYSTEM

Chart 17-3 shows a later period between 1970 and 1984. In this case, the lead was about average. However, in 1976, stocks actually led money market prices down. Finally, the commercial paper series also leads at market bot-

Chart 17-2 S&P Composite Versus 3-Month Commercial Paper Yield

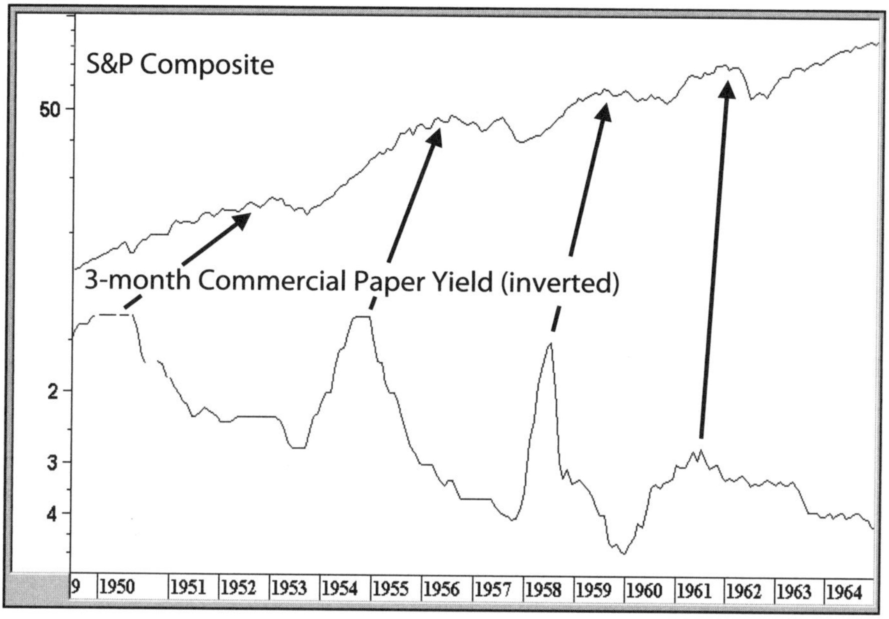

(Source: pring.com)

Chart 17-3 S&P Composite Versus 3-Month Commercial Paper Yield

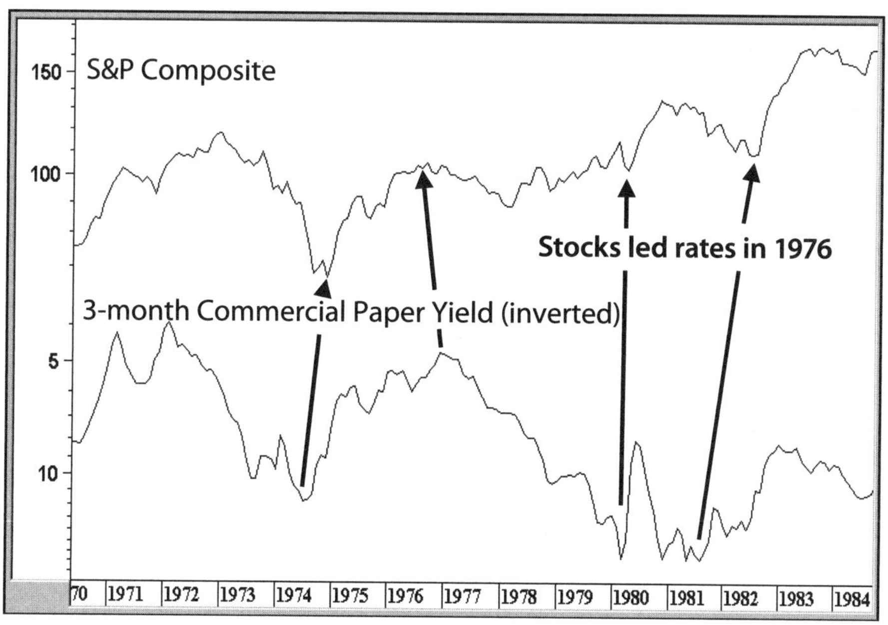

(Source: pring.com)

toms, but here again the leads and lags vary. In 1980 the two series bottom simultaneously. In 1981, though, the difference was much greater with a lead time of about a year. Generally speaking, the lead between short-term interest rates is usually far longer at market tops than at bottoms.

Okay, we know that rises and falls in short-term rates eventually affect stock prices, but we do not know the lead time or the magnitude of the ensuing stock rally. What do we do? Well, the answer is to classify the trend of money market prices, which is what the inverted short rate actually is, with an MA crossover. When a rising trend of money market prices has been established, it is then time to look at the trend of equities to see when they respond. The rationale is a rising trend of money market prices setting the scene for an equity bull market. This is not confirmed until the S&P Composite crosses above its moving average. Just think of this as something akin to an unconscious swimmer receiving mouth-to-mouth resuscitation. You know the treatment is good for the patient, just as falling rates are good for equity prices. However, we do not know how much treatment is required and whether the patient will recover until he is able to breathe by himself. In our analogy, the stock market is shown to respond to the interest rate treatment when it crosses its moving average.

Here is how it works. Look at Chart 17-4. In October 1981, the inverted commercial paper yield crosses above its 12-month MA (shown in the ellipse), indicating the environment is now bullish for equities. However, the equity market does not respond and does not bottom out until August 1982. When the S&P rallies above its 12-month MA (A), it indicates the market is responding to the positive interest rate environment. In this case, the crossover comes in August 1982. At that time, both trends are bullish and so is the system. It remains positive until *either* series moves back below its average, which, in this case, developed in June 1983 (B). It then goes bullish again in September of 1984 (C). This is one of the few instances when the stock market buy signal actually leads the buy signal for the commercial paper yield.

Finally, the yield rallies above its average in early 1987 (D). The market continues to rally, but the system is no longer bullish. In most instances, it would be better to generate the sell signals after the S&P crosses below its average. In this instance, though, the 1987 crash was over before the average was penetrated. Since the risk increases as the money market series crosses below its average, it is probably best to act on the signal in two parts. This would involve taking off half the position as the money market series goes negative and then liquidating the rest when the S&P crosses its average.

I developed this approach before system-testing software was widely available and 12-month MA spans represented a good round number that eliminated seasonality. I recently had the opportunity to optimize for a

Chart 17-4 S&P Composite Versus 3-Month Commercial Paper Yield

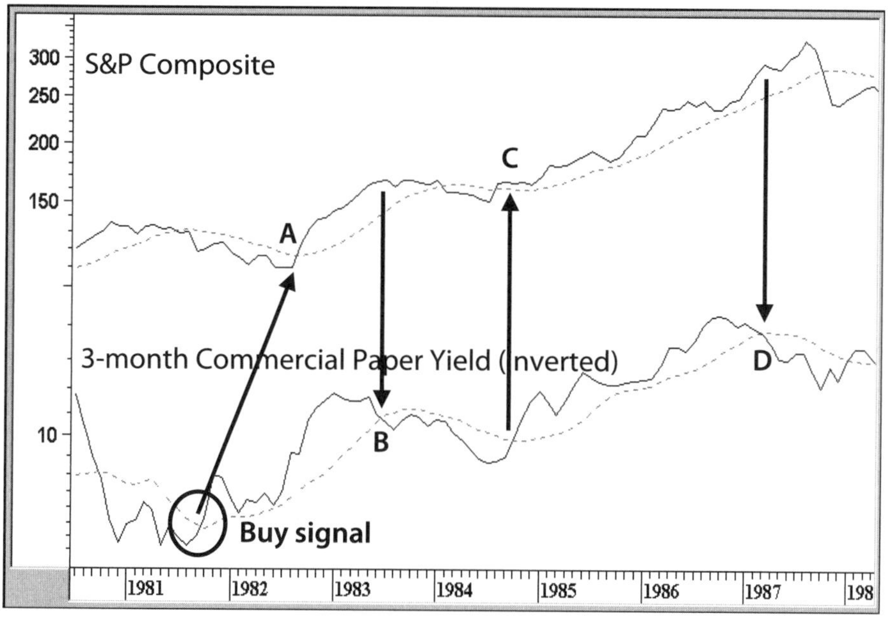

(Source: pring.com)

better combination, which I will talk about later. However, I would first like to run through some of the results using a 12/12 combination.

Fig. 17-1 shows the risk/reward for the system between 1948 and 1991. The vertical axis measures the reward on an annualized basis and the risk is measured on the horizontal axis. In this sense, risk is measured as volatility. The best place for any system to be is in the top left hand corner, often referred to as the northwest quadrant. This is where the reward is high and the risk, or volatility, is low. In the case of this system, the star labeled "positive environment" reflects the risk/reward of our stock-interest rate system. At close to 25 percent annualized return, with about 5 percent volatility, it is clearly a superior system. The star labeled "entire period" reflects the buy-hold approach where the return is just under 10 percent with a bit over 12 percent volatility. Finally, the "negative environment" represents those periods when the system is not positive. It could be a bear market or there could be times when the interest rate side of the equation is negative but the S&P is still above its average. At any rate, you can certainly appreciate the difference of a 25 percent low-risk return when the system is bullish and the high-risk/low-reward period when it is not. In conclusion, not only was the reward from the system excellent but the way in which it was earned, with low risk, was tremendous too.

Figure 17-1 Risk/Reward Ratio for the S&P Composite Versus 3-Month Commercial Paper Yield (inverted)

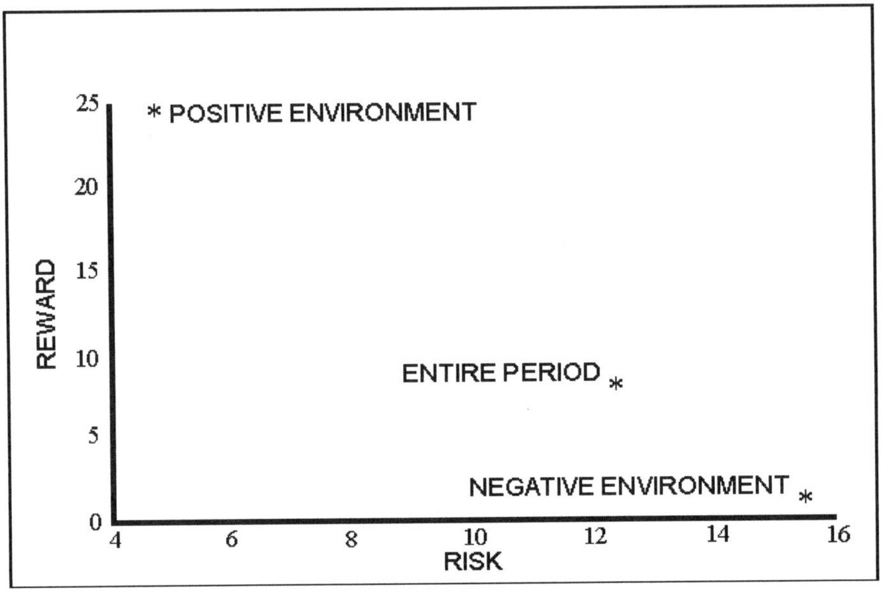

The system says nothing about periods when the market is above its average and rates are not, since those are obviously bullish periods as well. However, once rates move above their 12-month MA, there is a real danger that the next correction could be the first down leg in a bear market. It is true that sooner or later the S&P Composite will cross below its moving average, thereby stopping us out—but why run the risk when good returns and little volatility can be had under more favorable conditions?

If you are a short-term trader you probably feel this approach is worse than useless. However, it can be put to very good use if you realize that when the system is bullish, short sell signals are likely to result in losses. They are not just going against the main trend but are occurring in one of the most bullish equity environments you can get. By the same token, you can use this knowledge to position yourself from the long side when a short-term buy signal is triggered. I am not going to say that sharp corrections will never happen when this system is positive, because there have been periods such as 1971 when a fairly large retracing move did materialize. It is merely when the system is positive that the odds favor strong short-term rallies and whipsaw reactions.

USING DIFFERENT BUY AND SELL SIGNALS

I mentioned earlier that I optimized the results using timespans from 2 to 36 in one-step increments. Interestingly, the 12/12 combination tested the best, with 7 months a close second. As you can see in Table 17-1, there were 17 winning trades since 1960 and only eight losses for the 12-month combos. Not shown in this particular table is the fact that the average win was about four times that of the average loss. Wins last on average 12 months with losing trades averaging 2 months in duration. The 7-month span produced 47 signals, nearly twice as many. There were 31 wins and 16 losses, so the win/loss ratio was about the same. Both results indicate consistent profits and an acceptable system.

I also tested using different moving averages for a buy signal than for a sell, the idea being that bear market bottoms are usually quick affairs, whereas tops generally take longer to develop. Therefore, the system should have different variables to compensate for this. As you can see from Table

Table 17-1 S&P Composite Versus 3-Month Commercial Paper Yield (inverted)

S&P Composite MONTHLY							
Status	Net Profit	Percent	Total Trades	Winning Trades	Losing Trades	Average Win	Optimization
OK	19.4610	1946.10	25	17	8	4.6982	12
OK	19.4225	1942.25	47	31	16	4.4120	7
OK	18.4204	1842.04	26	18	8	6.3283	13
OK	18.1311	1813.11	38	25	13	6.1765	9
OK	17.9133	1791.33	34	23	11	5.7033	10
OK	17.2100	1721.00	21	15	6	5.5737	17
OK	16.8828	1688.28	15	13	2	4.2922	21
OK	16.7584	1675.84	26	17	9	6.7125	14
OK	16.7439	1674.39	30	20	10	5.0778	11

Table 17-2 S&P Composite Versus 3-Month Commercial Paper Yield (inverted)

S&P COMPOSITE MONTHLY							
Net Profit	Percent	Total Trades	Winning Trades	Losing Trades	Average Win	Optimization 1	Optimization 2
78.6625	7866.25	29	22	7	7.3534	2	33
76.5619	7656.19	29	21	8	8.7595	2	32
74.0049	7400.49	27	20	7	7.8397	2	34
71.9410	7194.10	27	19	8	7.6777	2	35
69.3173	6931.73	19	17	2	63.0637	8	34
68.6222	6862.22	20	16	4	11.0223	7	34
67.3824	6738.24	19	16	3	74.5288	8	35
66.7064	6670.64	20	16	4	9.3011	7	35
66.4066	6640.66	22	18	4	9.2364	7	33

17-2, the 2/33 combination worked the best; that is, buy when both series are positive vis-à-vis their averages, and sell when either crosses below its 33-month average. There were 22 wins and only seven losses for a 3 to 1 win/loss ratio. The average win was more than seven times the average loss. That sounds pretty good, does it not?

Let us take a closer look though, to make sure the system is as good as it promises. In Chart 17-5 I took the 1969–1979 trading range to see how this would have worked out. Unfortunately, the distance between the 2-month average and the price is very small, so you cannot see the crossovers. These are indicated by the arrows and flags. You can appreciate that there were some quite large drawdowns, as flagged by the two lines labeled Y. Even worse is the drawdown in 1969 in the rectangle. Notice how a buy signal is triggered just prior to a major collapse in prices. How could that come about? Well, the answer is very instructive because it undermines the point I made earlier about keeping things simple and being precise about the rules.

Chart 17-6 magnifies the 1969–1970 bear market so you can see what was actually happening. A buy signal (A) was triggered in late 1968 and the market rallied. Shortly after, the commercial paper rate moved above its 2-month MA (B). This still kept the system bullish, because the sell signal came when either series crosses below its 33-month average and that

Chart 17-5 S&P Composite Versus 3-Month Commercial Paper Yield

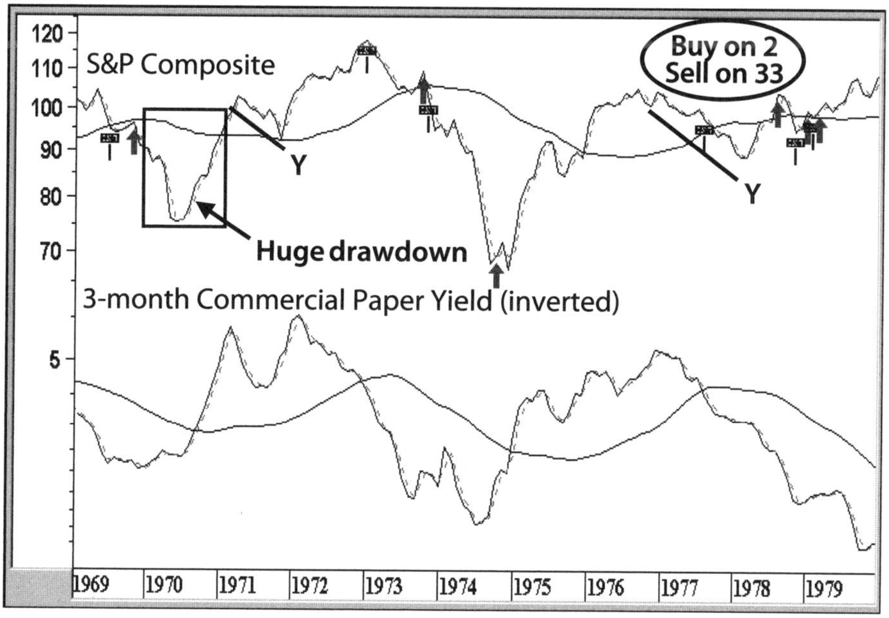

(Source: pring.com)

did not occur until mid 1969 (X). The next buy signal is triggered as the S&P slipped above its 2-month average (C), and this is confirmed by the money market price rising above its average as well. Both series quickly move back below these averages, but a sell signal is not triggered because both series are already below their 33-month MAs. In effect, the conditions for a sell signal are in force but it cannot be generated. As a result, what looks on paper to be a great system, based on the statistical results, keeps you in for most of the 1969–1970 bear market. Now let us see what happened in the case of the 12/12 combination that did not return as much profit and did not have such a good win/loss ratio.

In Chart 17-7, you can see that going into the 1969–1970 bear market, the system was flat. Then a buy signal is triggered in mid 1970, and this is followed by a very worthwhile move. Some whipsaw signals are triggered and these are again repeated in the mid-1970s but that, I believe, is a price worth paying. After all, the system certainly kept us out of the other really bad declines in 1973–1976 and 1977. Remember that the number one rule in trading is managing losses first, then letting the profits take care of themselves. This sometimes means foregoing a good move to the upside, an example developed between 1978 and 1980. Rising rates kept the system in a non-bullish mode but the market rallied about 25 percent. As a matter

Chart 17-6 S&P Composite Versus 3-Month Commercial Paper Yield

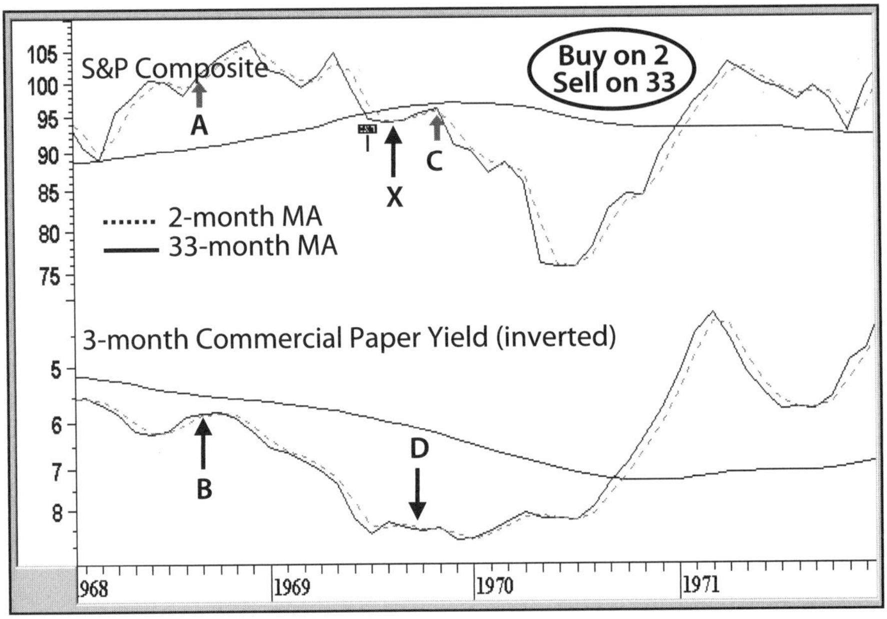

(Source: pring.com)

Chart 17-7 S&P Composite Versus 3-Month Commercial Paper Yield

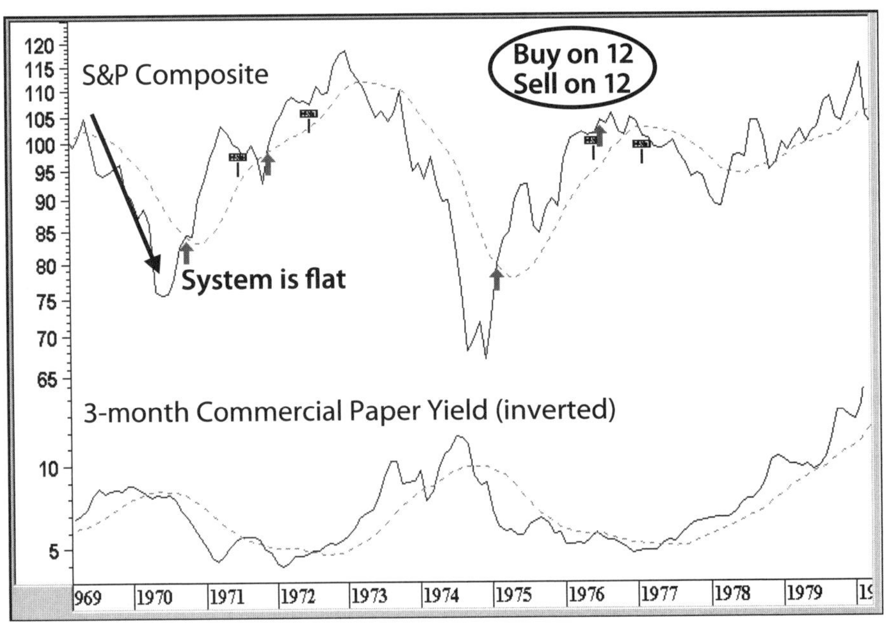

(Source: pring.com)

of fact, this was not terribly serious because the return on high yielding money market instruments was almost as good, with far less risk.

For those who are willing to take a long-term view, the intermarket system using the stock-bond relationship has proven to be very rewarding. Even short-term traders can take advantage of this approach because when the system is in a bullish mode, it increases the odds that signals triggered from long positions will be profitable.

Chapter 18
CRB Versus Gold

THE RELATIONSHIP

Another great intermarket relationship is between the CRB Composite and the gold price. Chart 18-1 shows the gold price consistently leads the CRB at major bottoms. As with all intermarket relationships, the lead times vary from cycle to cycle but there is no mistaking the fact that the arrows are all pointing in a northeasterly direction. Chart 18-2 shows the same relationship but now the tops are being connected. The same principle; that is, gold leading the CRB is in force. We can therefore conclude the price of gold discounts future commodity inflation in a similar way to stocks discounting trends in the economy and corporate profits. Since the leads and lags vary from cycle to cycle, it is necessary to create a moving average system relating the two series in a similar manner to the Stock Interest Rate model discussed earlier. When gold is above its moving average it indicates the environment for commodities might be about to improve. Whether it does or not can be determined by the CRB moving above its MA—that is the confirmation signal. The sell signal develops when either of the moving averages is crossed in a negative way.

I ran a test over a 25-year period to see what kind of result I could achieve. It would have been possible to use four optimized variables: one for the buy side of gold, one for the buy side of the CRB, and one each for the respective sell signals. However, I believe in keeping things as simple as possible. Consequently, I kept the rules the same as the Stock Commercial Paper Yield model—buy when both averages are positive and sell when either goes negative. The range of moving averages selected was 6 to 36 in one-step increments. There was no margin, trades were from the long side only, and .01 percent was allowed for a round trip commission. Also, both series are calculated as 4-week moving averages for the last Friday of the

Chart 18-1 CRB Versus Gold

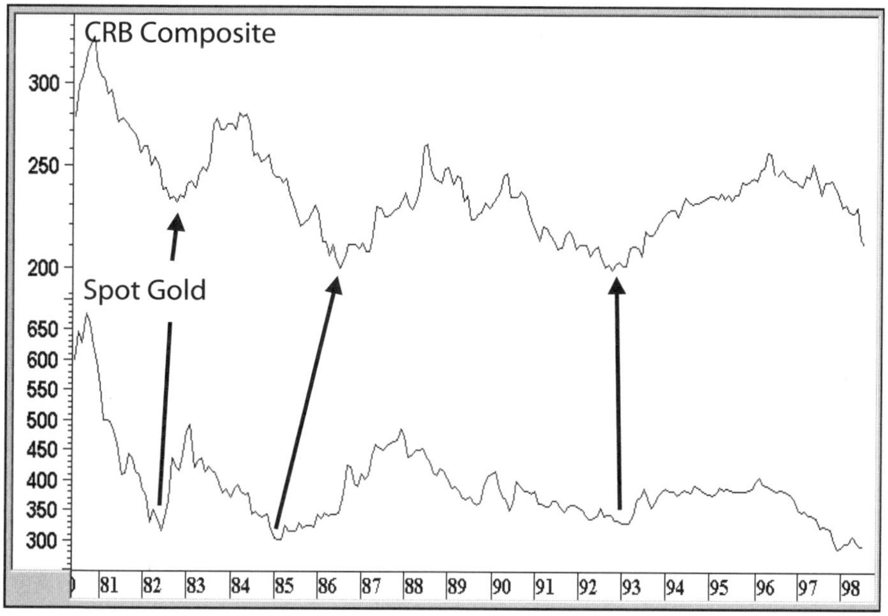

(Source: pring.com)

Chart 18-2 CRB Versus Gold

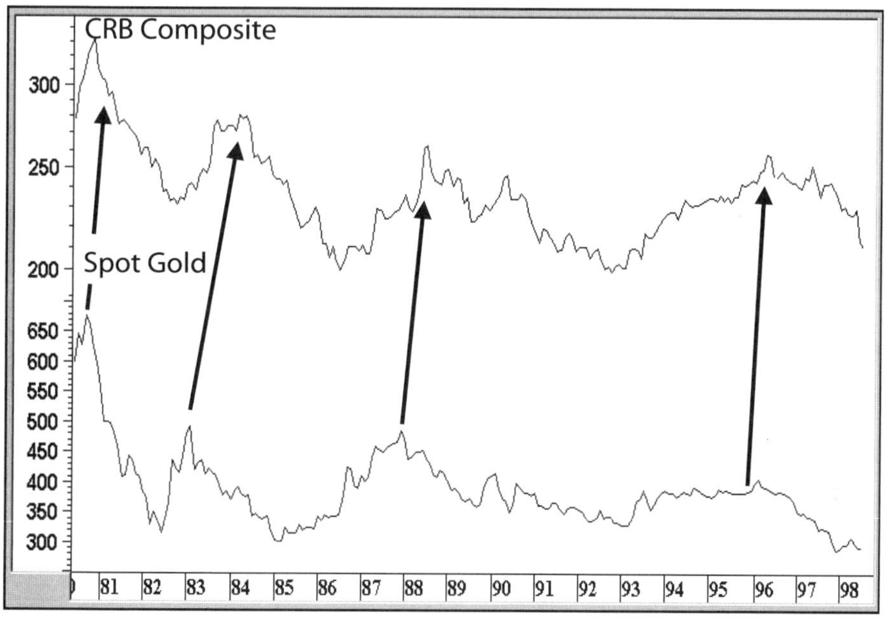

(Source: pring.com)

month as opposed to a month-end close. The monthly average tends to have fewer whipsaws and offers more consistent returns than a month-end close. The results of this test were very promising since *all* the combinations returned a profit.

Also, you can see from Table 18-1 the top six tests reflected very similar moving average combinations: 8/21, 8/25, 8/22, 8/24, 8/29, and 8/26. There was not much difference in the performance of any of these combinations, so I decided to take the 8/24 combination since 24 months is, of course, equivalent to two calendar years of data, and I prefer to deal with round numbers, if possible. The win/loss ratio was a very respectable 12 to 5, although, had I selected the 8/29 combination, this would have improved to a 1:2 ratio in favor of the winners. The rules for this system are buy when both gold is above its 24-month average and the CRB is above its 8-month MA and sell when either falls below its respective MA.

THE SYSTEM

Here is how it works. In Chart 18-3, the CRB is plotted with its 8-month average, and the gold price with its 24-month average. In spring 1980, the gold price is already above its MA and is then joined by the CRB. Now that

Table 18-1 CRB Versus Gold

CRB COMPOSITE MONTHLY							
Net Profit	Percent	Total Trades	Winning Trades	Losing Trades	Average Win	Optimization 1	Optimization 2
3.3334	333.34	17	13	4	5.5981	8	21
3.2425	324.25	17	13	4	5.2030	8	25
3.1815	318.15	17	12	5	6.1431	8	22
3.1635	316.35	17	12	5	6.7585	8	24
3.1556	315.56	17	15	2	4.6580	8	29
3.1515	315.15	17	13	4	5.1177	8	26
3.1159	311.59	19	14	5	4.2295	7	25
3.0810	308.10	11	7	4	11.1551	21	17
3.0670	306.70	18	12	6	7.2974	8	23

Chart 18-3 CRB Versus Gold

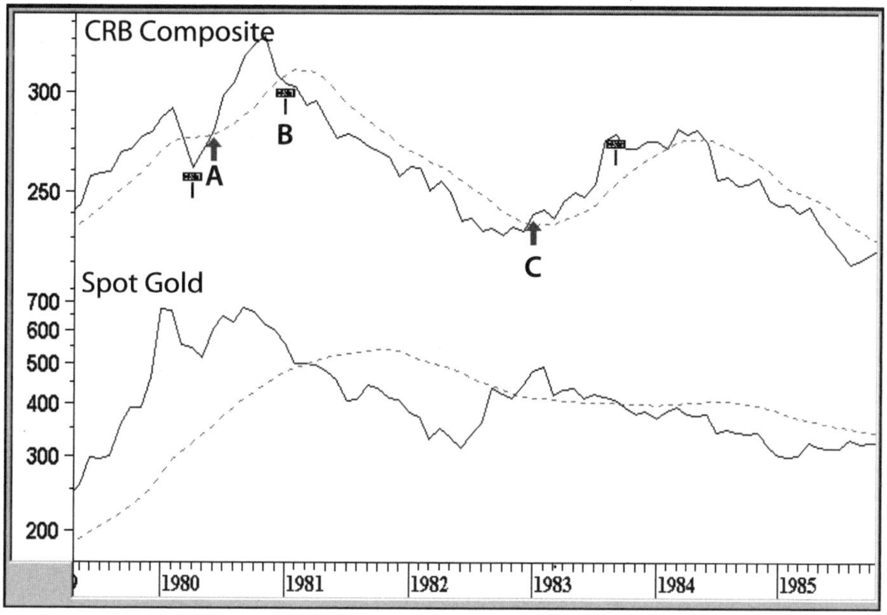

(Source: pring.com)

each series is positive, a buy arrow (A) signals the all clear. Then in late 1980 (B), the CRB slips below its average and we are in a cash position. It is not until late 1982 that the gold price goes bullish again. A positive crossover in the CRB (C) then confirms this in early 1983.

You can see from the equity line in Chart 18-4 that this intermarket system consistently made profits with very small dips. The overall gain was 307 percent. The line indicates in graphic perspective there was very little in the way of drawdowns. The worst period developed in the early 1970s when the system experienced a peak-to-trough equity drawdown of about 30 percent. The actual trade though, when closed out, was very profitable. The largest loss was seven points. What is most impressive about this system is that none of the combinations lost money. It is true there was a large amount of time where the system was flat, as indicated by the horizontal patches in the equity line.

Chart 18-5 shows what would have happened if I had allowed for an annual interest rate of 4 percent from a cash position during these idle periods. The end profit would have improved from 30 percent to 698 percent, a pretty healthy increase. The number of winning and losing trades would have remained the same, of course. The results merely reflect the improvements due to the compounding effect of the interest on an already profitable system.

Chart 18-4 CRB Versus Gold

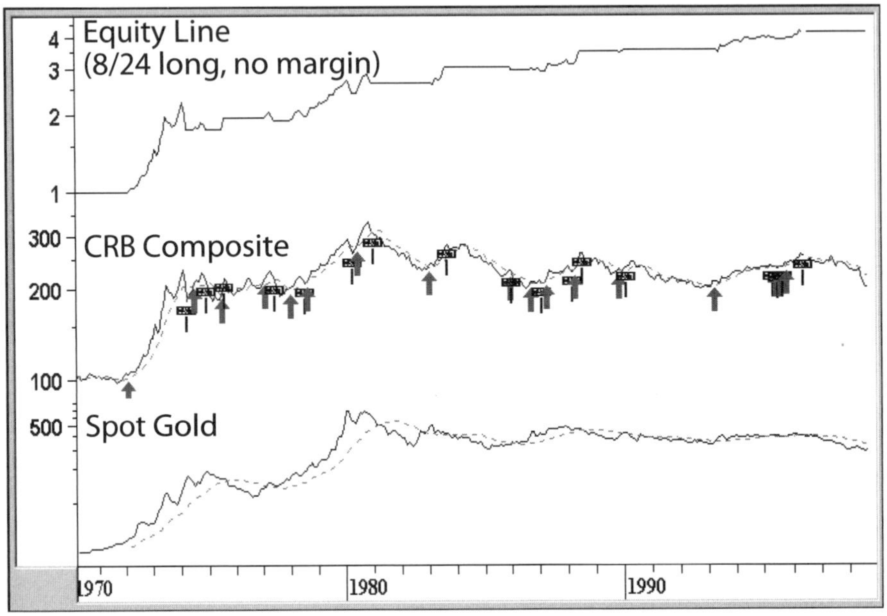

(Source: pring.com)

Chart 18-5 CRB Versus Gold

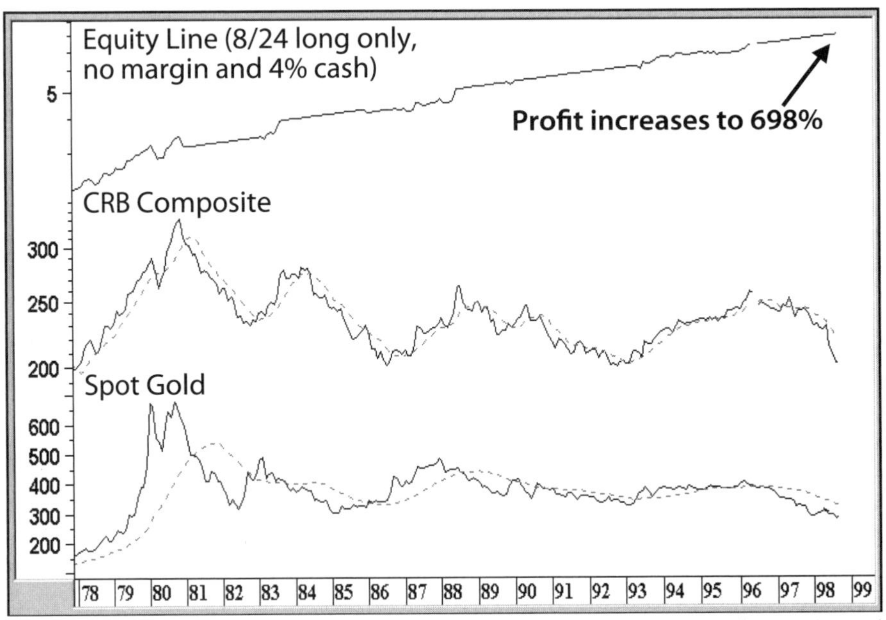

(Source: pring.com)

Now, if you study Chart 18-5 more closely, it is apparent the CRB itself was in many instances in a bear market. This made me think about running the test to include short positions. Remember, buy when gold is above its 24-month average and the CRB is above its 8-month MA, and sell when either falls below its respective MA. Short positions are initiated when *both* series are below their averages and covered when one of them goes positive. Then stay out until both are above their 8-month MAs, and so forth. Point A in Chart 18-6 is where the system goes into a cash position, the same way it did when we were just trading from the long side. Next, the gold price joins the CRB below its average (B) and the system now goes short. Finally, the position is covered (C), and the system once more moves to the cash side as the gold price rallies above its moving average. A couple of months later, the system goes bullish as the CRB crosses above its average by the next upward pointing arrow (D).

Given the sharp drops in the CRB during this period, the result was not as good as I expected. The overall return was increased to 794 percent, but so were the number of signals, from 17 to 31. The short sales produced 14 signals, half of which were losers. Remember, the longs had a 12 to 5 plurality favoring the winners.

Chart 18-6 CRB Versus Gold

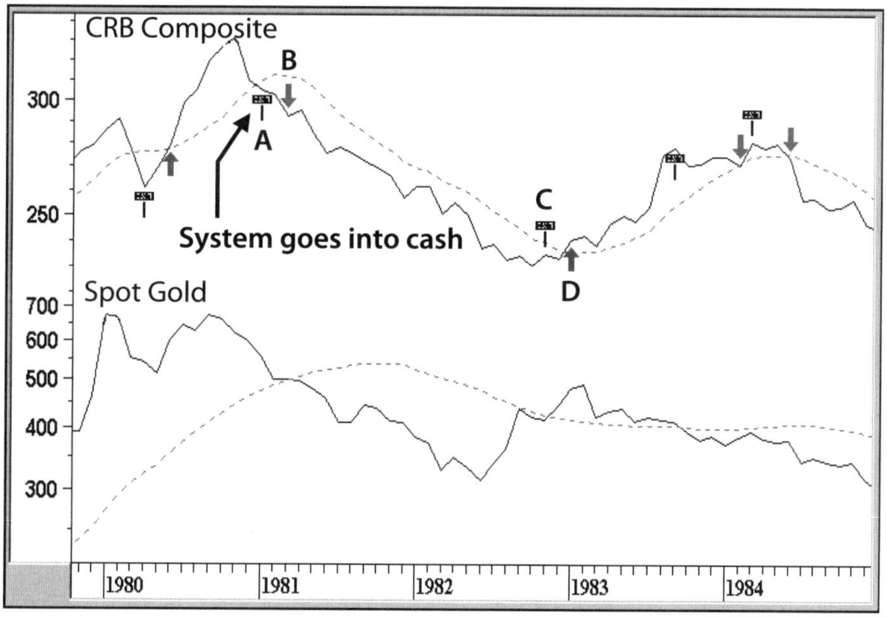

(Source: pring.com)

Finally, I decided to test the long-short reversal system with a 50 percent margin. In this instance, the return increased spectacularly where $1 increased to $38. Before you run off and try to duplicate it, note that the first signal in 1972 was the most profitable and that set us up for this stupendous performance. Chart 18-7 also shows the buy and sell signals. Look at the period in the ellipse and you can see that there were quite a few whipsaws. This was why the reversal system did not perform as spectacularly as you may have thought, given the sharp drops in the early and mid 1980s, and that of the late 1990s. Once again, remember the 8/24 combination was not the most profitable of those tested. It actually came in at number 19.

USING WEEKLY DATA

Another alternative is to use weekly data to see if the results can be improved. For this I tested for the 18 years, ending in 1998. This time, I optimized for three parameters, the two moving averages for the CRB and the gold price as before. Remember the monthly prices were 4-week moving averages plot-

Chart 18-7 CRB Versus Gold

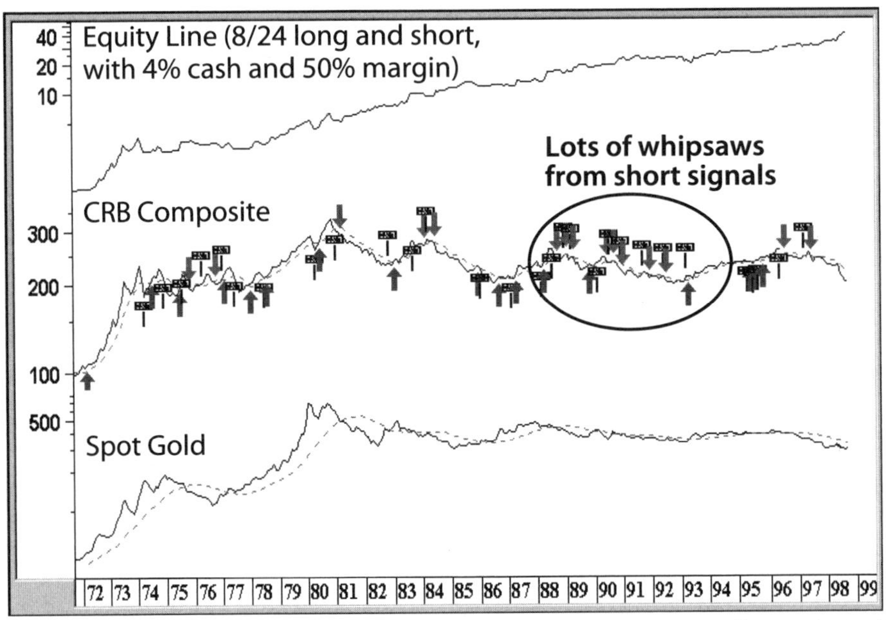

(Source: pring.com)

ted at the end of the month. This is where our third parameter comes in because I optimized for 1 to 30 periods. This variable was common to both series. The other variables were from 10–65 for the CRB and the same for gold. This was a massive test, so I had to do it in several steps. When the results came back, I narrowed the optimization and decreased the number of steps to one. The actual test was 20 to 30 for the first moving average, 35 to 45 for the long-term average for the CRB, and 60 to 75 for the long-term gold moving average. I also went crazy and traded using the assumption of a 50 percent margin. The results are shown in Table 18-2. As you can see, the parameters were very close together. I chose the 26/45/65 combination. It actually came in number 12 out of over 1,900 possibilities. The top few systems are not shown here. However, the 951 percent gain was not that much different from the 1,004 percent gain from the winning 23/44/65 combination. I chose these parameters since they represent 6 months and $1^1/_4$ years, and the 45-week span has often tested well for the stock market. It was perhaps an arbitrary choice but, nonetheless, a consistent one. Note that everything shown here had an extremely high win/loss ratio, making it one of the best intermarket systems I have ever seen. One important point to bear in mind is that all these gold-CRB systems are based on the cash

Table 18-2 CRB Versus Gold

CRB COMPOSITE							
Percent	Total Trades	Winning Trades	Losing Trades	Average Win	Optimization 1	Optimization 2	Optimization 3
983.53	13	12	1	8.3504	23	43	65
975.62	14	12	2	7.8721	23	40	65
971.84	12	11	1	9.3944	23	43	61
971.49	13	11	2	5.3945	23	43	62
965.25	12	11	1	4.9226	26	45	61
960.96	13	11	2	8.7324	23	40	61
960.63	14	11	3	6.0632	23	40	62
955.88	12	10	2	5.1672	26	44	63
951.84	11	10	1	5.2592	26	45	65

Chart 18-8 CRB Versus Gold

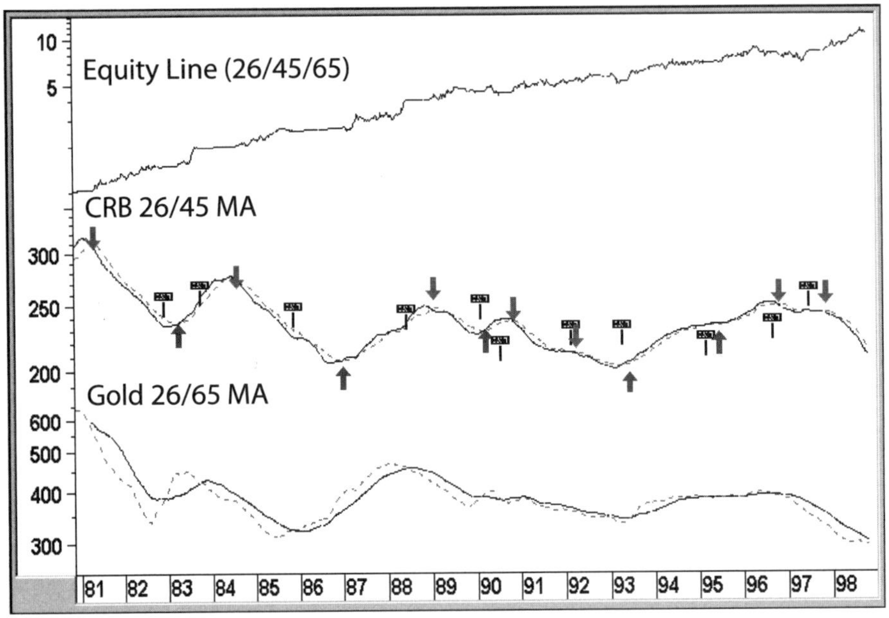

(Source: pring.com)

market, so application in the futures markets with differing carrying charges, and so forth, will not be quite the same.

The result in graphic form is shown in Chart 18-8. Both solid lines are 26-week averages. The dashed line for the CRB is 45 weeks and 65 weeks for gold. Chart 18-9 shows that the system works exactly the same as the one based on monthly data. It goes into a cash position from a long position as the gold price goes negative (A). Then the CRB 26-week MA crosses below its 45-week series and a short position is initiated (B). This is, then, covered as the gold price rallies above its average and a cash position established (C). Very shortly after, the CRB moves above its average and the system goes bullish (D). The actual return using no margin was 290 percent, quite a bit less than the over 900 percent using margin, but still comparable with the monthly systems considering that my weekly data did

Chart 18-9 CRB Versus Gold

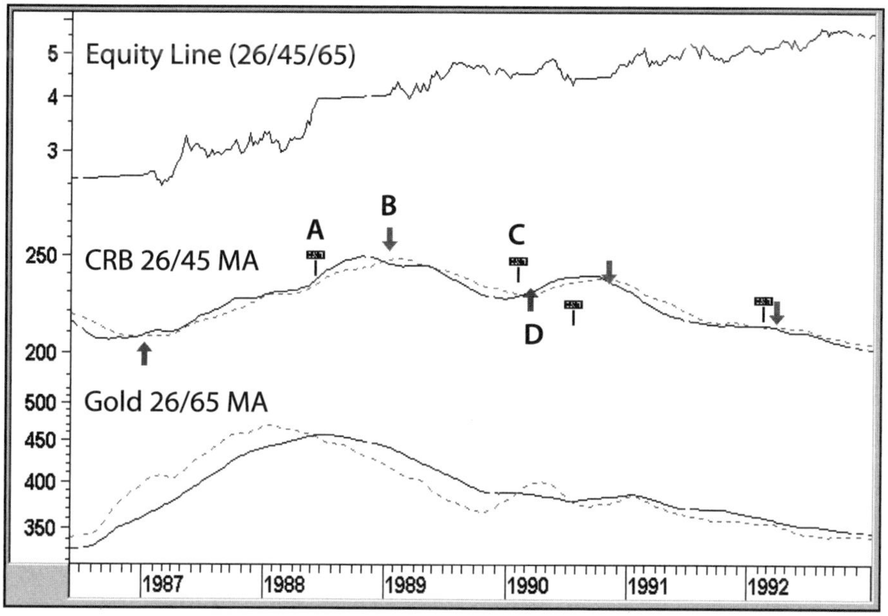

(Source: pring.com)

not include the sharp trending tune up in the late 1970s. I also tested for various combinations using daily data but was unable to come up with any combinations that worked as well as the weekly or monthly systems.

Chapter 19
Bonds Versus Commodities

THE RELATIONSHIP

Bond prices hate rising commodity prices, but love declining ones. The relationship between them makes a very good intermarket situation on which to base a system. Because major trends in bonds and commodities are determined by the course of the business cycle, this means the most consistently profitable intermarket relationships must also be based on longer-term trends. Chart 19-1 compares government bond prices to the CRB Spot Raw Industrial Price Index. This index only contains economically sensitive industrial commodity prices and is not prone to be weather driven as is the more widely followed CRB Composite. The arrows show, for the most part, commodities lead bonds, although there are exceptions such as the 1994–1995 experience. Commodities usually start to rise before bond prices fall, as we can see in Chart 19-2. Of course, there are exceptions, and the leads and lags vary in each cycle. That is why we use two moving averages as we did in the stock short-term interest rate system described earlier.

THE SYSTEM

Chart 19-3 shows a U.S. government bond series in the upper portion and the CRB Spot Raw Material Index in the lower one. The system is bullish when the trend of bond prices is up and commodities are down. The trend in this case is measured by a 9-month MA crossover for bonds and a 12-month moving average for commodities. Sell signals are triggered when

Chart 19-1 Bonds Versus Commodities

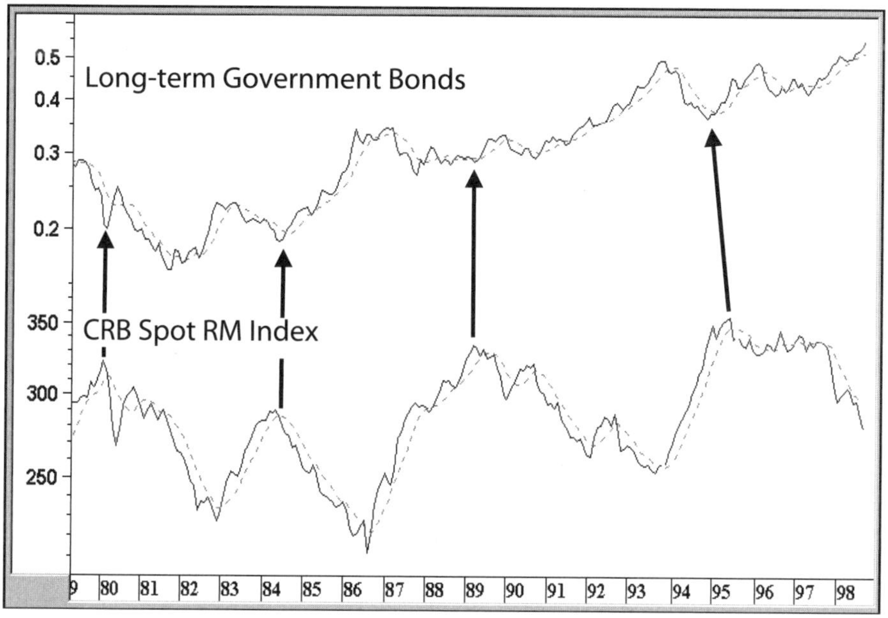

(Source: pring.com)

Chart 19-2 Bonds Versus Commodities

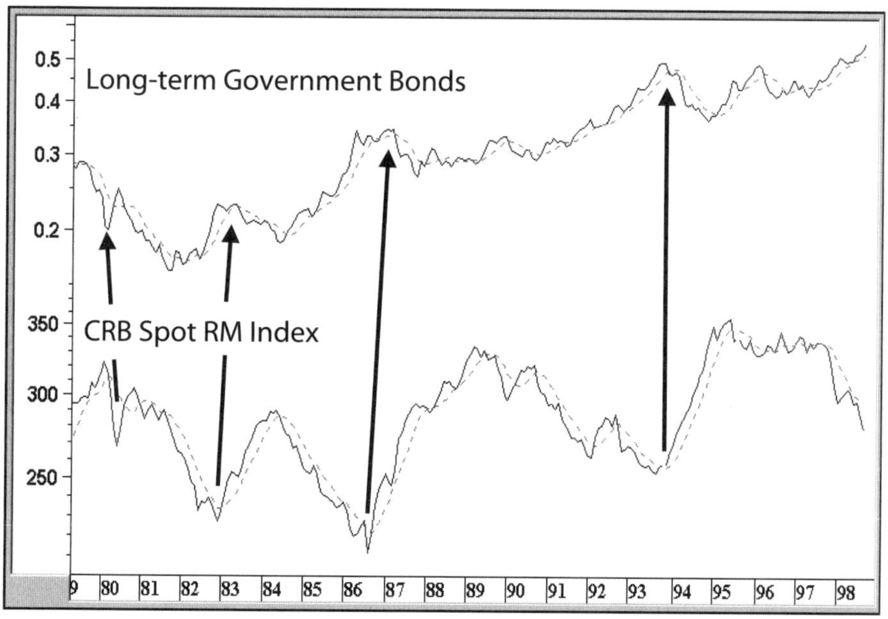

(Source: pring.com)

Chart 19-3 Bonds Versus Commodities

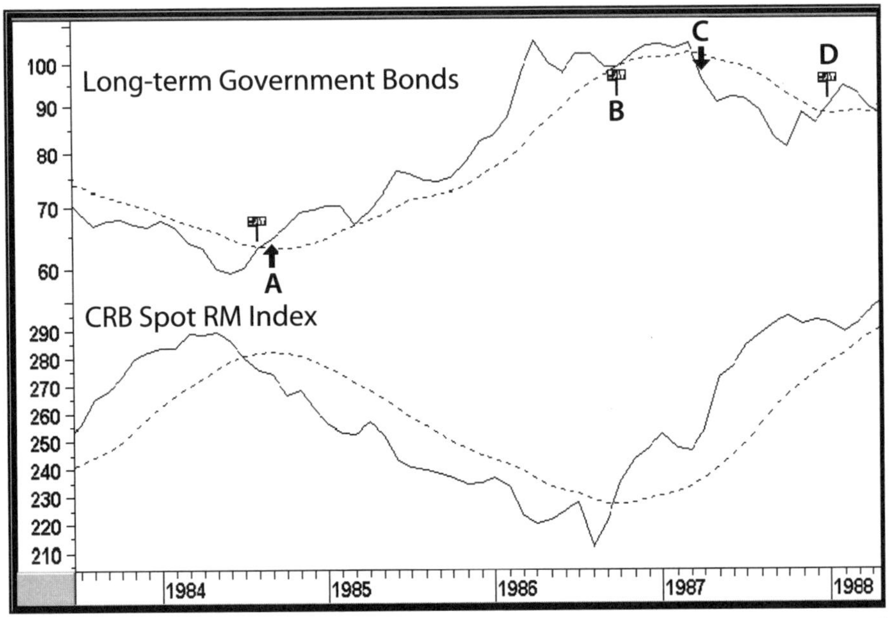

(Source: pring.com)

either series goes negative. Short signals develop when both are negative and covered when either goes positive. See how the bond price moves above its moving average in mid 1984 as it joins the CRB, which is declining and is, therefore, a bullish mode for bonds (A). The system stays bullish until mid 1986, when the CRB rises above its 12-month moving average (B). It is then in a cash position until the bond price falls below its average in early 1987, when it goes short (C). Finally, the short position is covered in 1988 as the bond moves above its 9-month moving average (D).

Looking at Chart 19-4, the equity line in the top portion shows the system worked pretty well between the 1950s and the close of the century. There was no serious drawdown throughout this period of bullish and bearish environments. Table 19-1 is the summary report of my optimization. I optimized for the two moving averages between 6 and 24 months in one-step intervals. I chose the 9/12 combination because it also tested reasonably high up on the list for a "longs only" test. This, I felt, gave it a better sense of consistency than the other parameters. These chosen parameters are also quarterly timespans, which makes them, in my mind, more palatable. The total return of over 2,000 percent was earned between the 1940s and 1998. Just about half the signals were profitable. However, this did not stop the risk/reward ratio from maintaining 100 percent and

Chart 19-4 Bonds Versus Commodities

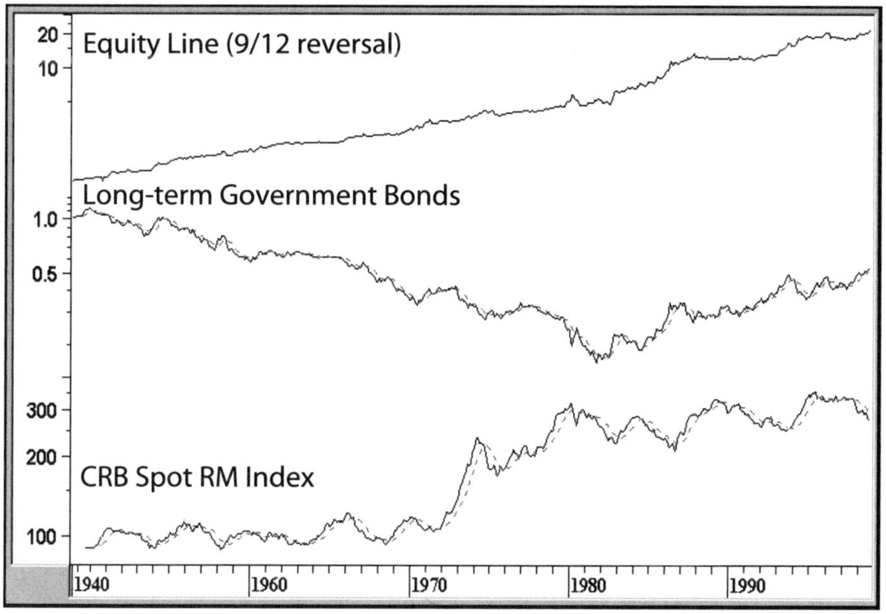

(Source: pring.com)

Table 19-1 Bonds Versus Commodities

Bonds Versus Commodities							
Net Profit	Percent	Total Trades	Winning Trades	Losing Trades	Average Win	Optimization 1	Optimization 2
22.0629	2206.29	61	31	29	3.6004	9	11
21.8429	2184.29	59	30	29	3.5649	9	12
21.8371	2183.71	55	28	27	4.0528	9	13
21.4416	2144.16	65	36	29	3.4765	8	11
21.2275	2122.75	63	34	29	3.3876	8	12
21.2206	2122.06	59	32	27	3.4081	8	13
20.5571	2055.71	59	31	28	3.5662	9	10
20.4897	2048.97	71	39	32	2.7289	9	6
20.4136	2041.36	57	30	27	3.2271	9	14

beating the buy-hold approach by a substantial margin. This was, of course, due to the system's excellent performance during the long post-war bear market that ended in 1981. Also, the average loss exceeded the average win by a large margin.

Once again, my suggestion for short-term traders is to use a system such as this to determine the direction of your trades. In a bullish bond-commodity environment just go long, and in a bearish one limit your activity to the short side.

Chapter 20

Systems Using Relative Strength (RS)

THE CONCEPT OF RELATIVE STRENGTH

It is a well-documented fact that the stock market experiences a rotation between various component industry groups. At the beginning of a bull market, defensive and interest-sensitive stocks tend to outperform the averages. As the cycle progresses, earnings-driven stocks, such as basic industry and resource-based equities, take over the leadership role. This is not, strictly speaking, an *intermarket relationship*, but it does build on the rotational process that results from a developing business cycle.

Chart 20-1 shows the smoothed long-term momentum of the relative strength of the Dow Jones Financial and Energy sectors. See how the financial momentum is the first of these two sectors to bottom in the cycle. As this series is in the process of peaking, the energy-relative momentum starts to bottom out. You can see this rotation of fortunes between the two is more or less a continuous process. Occasionally, it gets out of kilter, such as in the 1996–1997 period, when the financials experienced a rally simultaneously with the energy series, but for the most part, this is a pretty sound relationship. Actually, the financials paid for this exceptional strength by experiencing a sharper than normal correction in 1998.

Not all industry groups fit so well into the business cycle rotation process, but the concept of *relative strength (RS)* can, nonetheless, be used to an advantage when constructing mechanical trading systems.

Chart 20-1 Energy RS Momentum Versus Financial RS Momentum

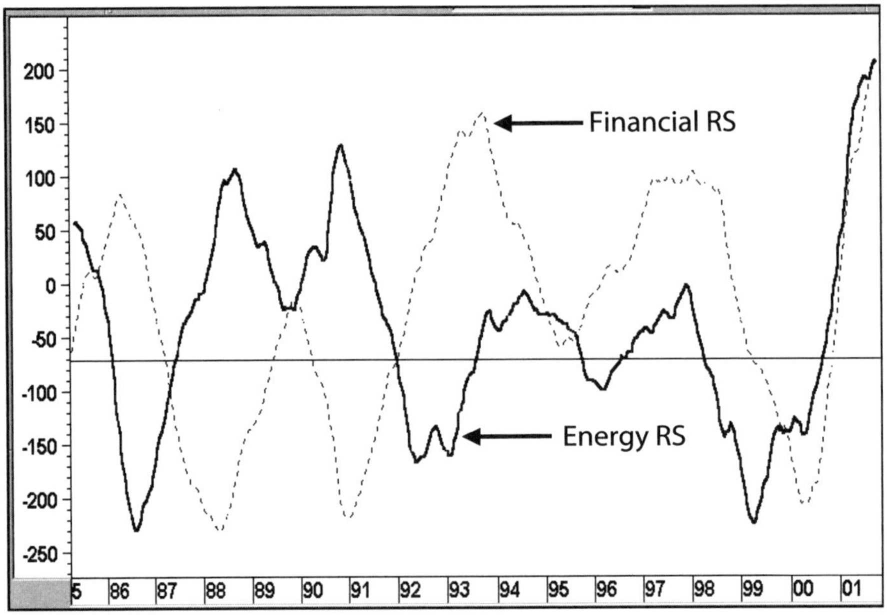

(Source: pring.com)

A *relative strength line* is calculated by dividing a stock or an industry group by a market average such as the S&P Composite. In Chart 20-2, we can see the Dow Jones All Banks Index together with its relative strength against the Dow Jones Composite, a broad-based measure of the whole market. If the relative strength (RS) line is rising, it means the stock or group in question is outperforming the average. If it is declining, this means it is the market that is performing better. In many instances, the RS line turns ahead of the absolute price of the stock or group, and this gives us a warning of strength or weakness under the surface.

Chart 20-3 shows a classic example as the RS line turns down well ahead of the 1987 peak. By combining indicators measuring the trend of both the absolute and relative price, it is possible to devise a system that helps us not only to purchase stocks, mutual funds, or industry groups that are rising, but that are advancing *faster* than the market. Greater profits can also be attained from short sales using the same criteria.

APPLYING AN RS SYSTEM

Chart 20-4 features the Dow Jones All Banks Index, again, in the center portion. The bottom portion is the relative strength of this group to the Dow

Chart 20-2 DJ All Banks Index

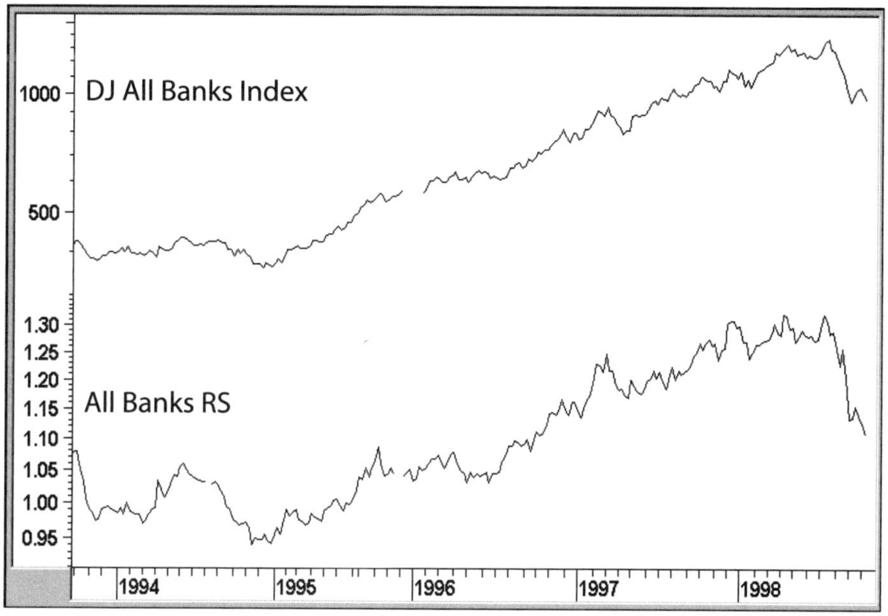

(Source: pring.com)

Chart 20-3 DJ All Banks Index

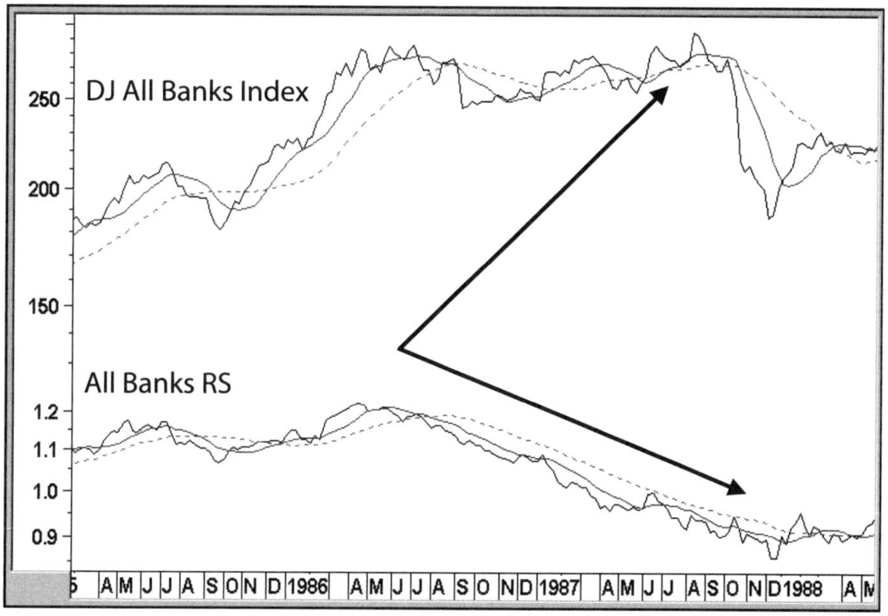

(Source: pring.com)

Chart 20-4 DJ All Banks Index

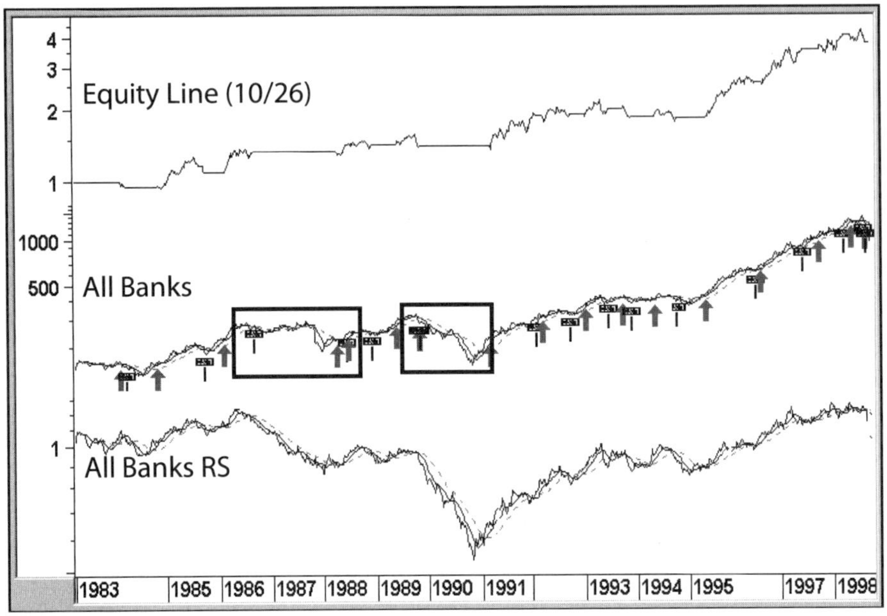

(Source: pring.com)

Jones Composite and the top portion is the equity line based on a 10/26-week crossover of both series. Buy signals are generated when the 10-week moving average of the Banks Index crosses above the 26-week simple MA. This is confirmed by a similar signal by the RS line. Sell signals are triggered when either of the 26-week averages is recrossed by their 10-week counterparts. The 10-week averages are displayed as a solid line, and the 26-week series are dashed lines. Commissions are assumed at .01 percent, and there is no margin or interest earned when out of the market. As you can see from the course of the equity line, the system worked reasonably well. We must remember, though, that this system was being tested during a very long-term bull market where a trend-based system ought to make money. Even so, there were two periods of real weakness; 1987 and the 1989–1990 period as shown in the rectangles. You can appreciate the leading characteristics of the RS line by the fact that the system was not bullish in either of them. It would have made more sense to go into a cash situation or invest in a group where the relative strength was positive during those periods.

Chart 20-5 includes a 4 percent interest for times when the system was in a cash position. You can see the results were even better. But, having said that, we must still be careful. For example, the precious metal group was one of the worst performers during this period, but as Chart 20-6 shows,

Chart 20-5 DJ All Banks Index

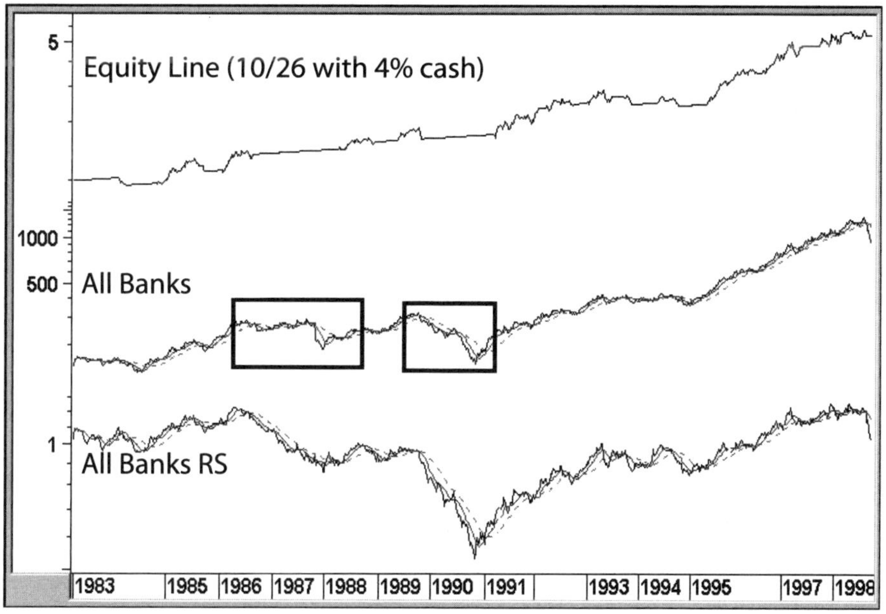

(Source: pring.com)

Chart 20-6 DJ Precious Metals Index

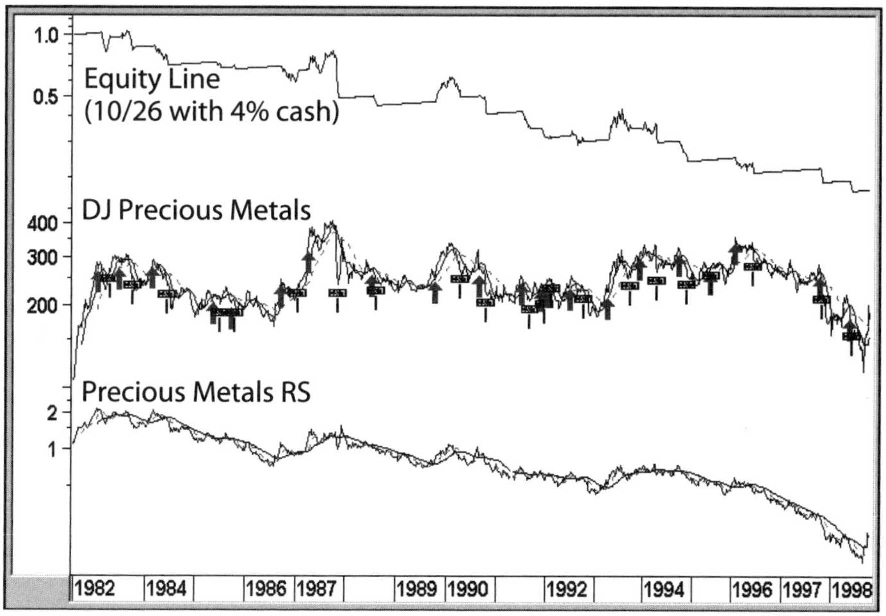

(Source: pring.com)

the equity line was not only volatile, but it was in a negative trend, even using the 4 percent cash return. This underscores the point that different stocks and groups have different characteristics.

Now take a look at Chart 20-7. It features the Australian Stock Exchange's Insurance Group together with its RS line against the ASE's Top 50 Index. The timeframes are the same for the moving average signals, but the data are daily, not weekly. This means the weekly numbers of 10 and 5 have multiplied 26 times, because there are 5 trading days to the week. A 4 percent interest rate has been assumed for cash positions. There are two points regarding this test. First, the system performed more or less as well for Australian insurance stocks as for U.S. banks. Second, the RS line was not weak enough to obtain liquidation prior to the 1987 crash, which is why the equity line took such a beating at that time.

Finally before we move on, Chart 20-8 shows the way a system ought to deal with a bear market. This is the T. Rowe Price Japan Fund, which was in a bear market throughout this whole period. The system is, again, similar with a 10/26-week crossover of the fund and RS line. The relative strength, in this case, is measured against the S&P Composite. It made money largely because of the assumed 4 percent return on cash during those long periods when the system was not bullish. However, in Chart 20-9,

Chart 20-7 ASE Insurance Index Versus Australian Top 50 Index

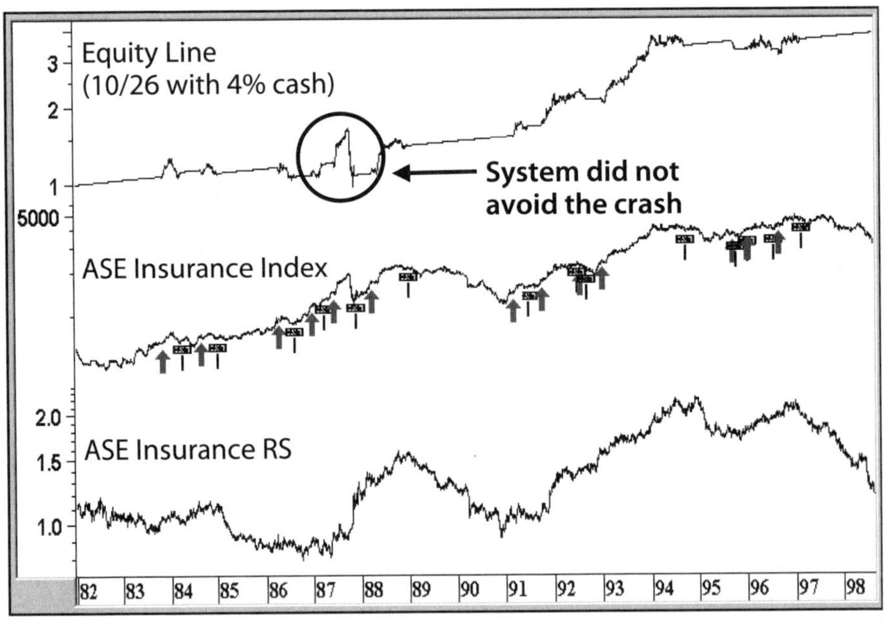

(Source: pring.com)

Chart 20-8 T. Rowe Price Japan Fund

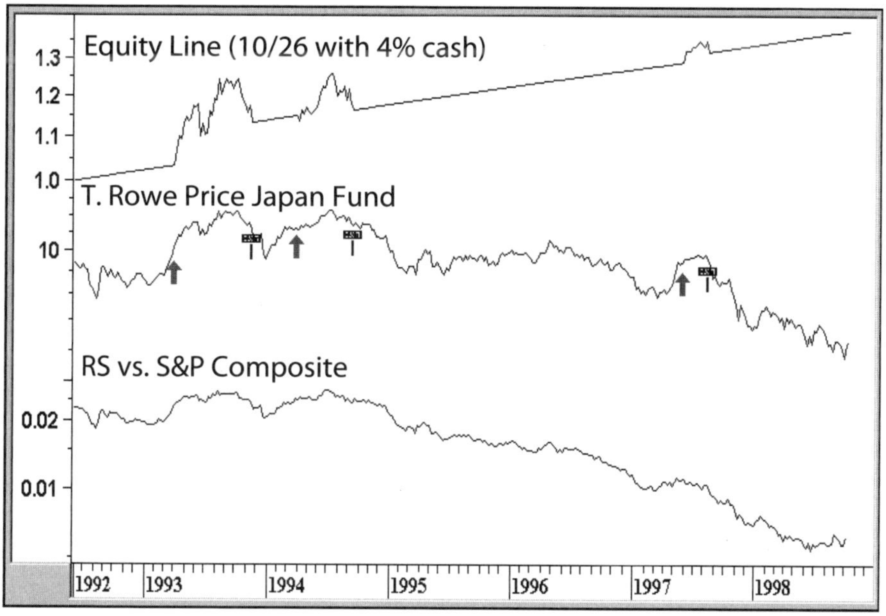

(Source: pring.com)

Chart 20-9 T. Rowe Price Japan Fund

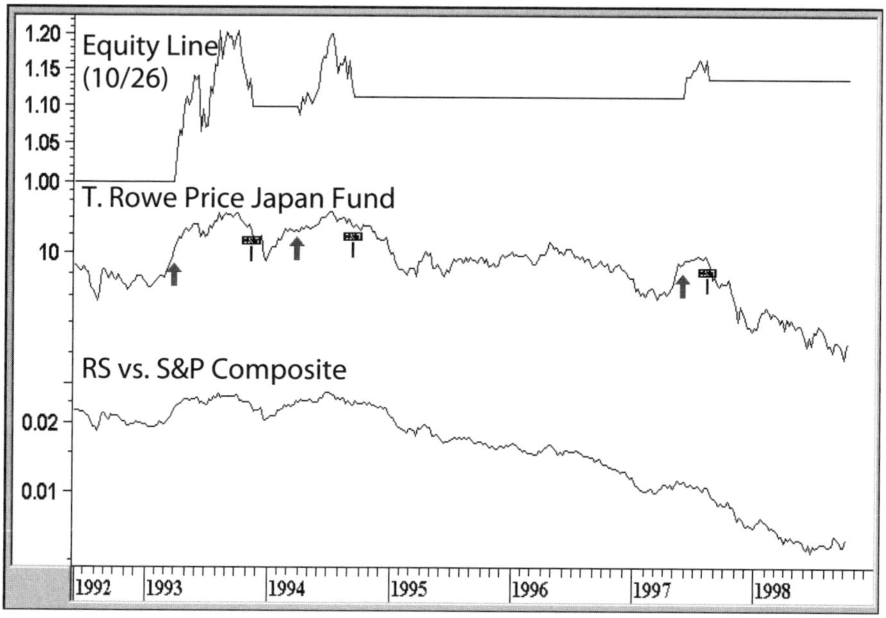

(Source: pring.com)

even if the cash positions had earned nothing, the system would have returned 13 percent compared with an approximate 30 percent loss for the buy-hold approach. Chart 20-10 is the Scudder Emerging Markets Fund. The principle is again the same, except that I have reverted to the 4 percent return on cash. See, once again, how the fund was basically unchanged during this period, yet the system returned a healthy 30 percent.

APPLYING A MORE SENSITIVE RS SYSTEM

Another combination using the same principles that seems to work very well on closed-end mutual funds uses the 3/10 parameters. Buy signals are generated when the 3-week moving average of the price and RS crosses above their respective 10-week MAs, and sell signals occur when either cross below their 10-week MA. Here, in Chart 20-11, you can see this for the T. Rowe Price Science and Technology Fund. It shows a wonderful consistently rising equity line, even during some difficult selling squalls. This system experiences more whipsaws than the 10/26 combination we saw earlier, but, because it is more sensitive, it liquidates positions more

Chart 20-10 Scudder Emerging Markets Fund

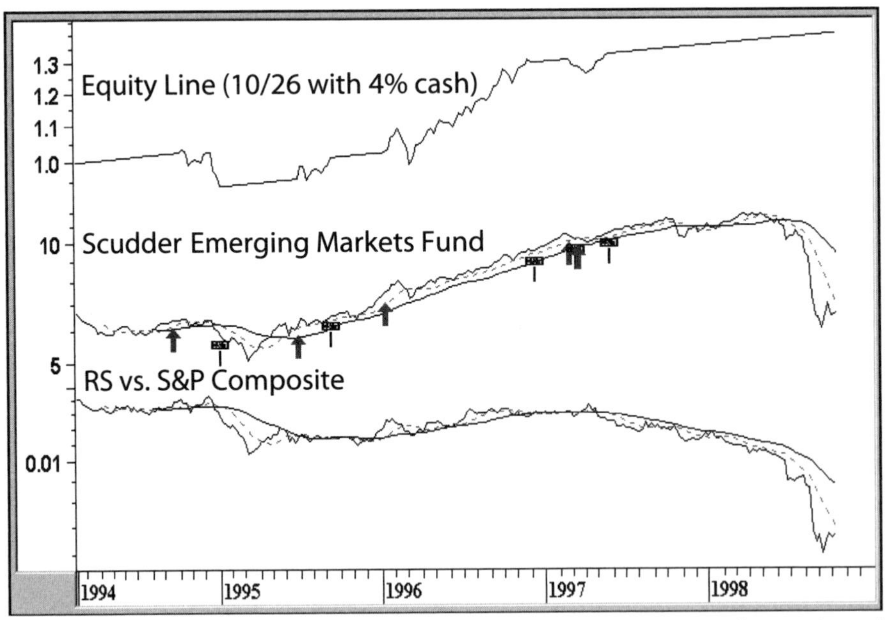

(Source: pring.com)

Chart 20-11 T. Rowe Price Science and Technology Fund

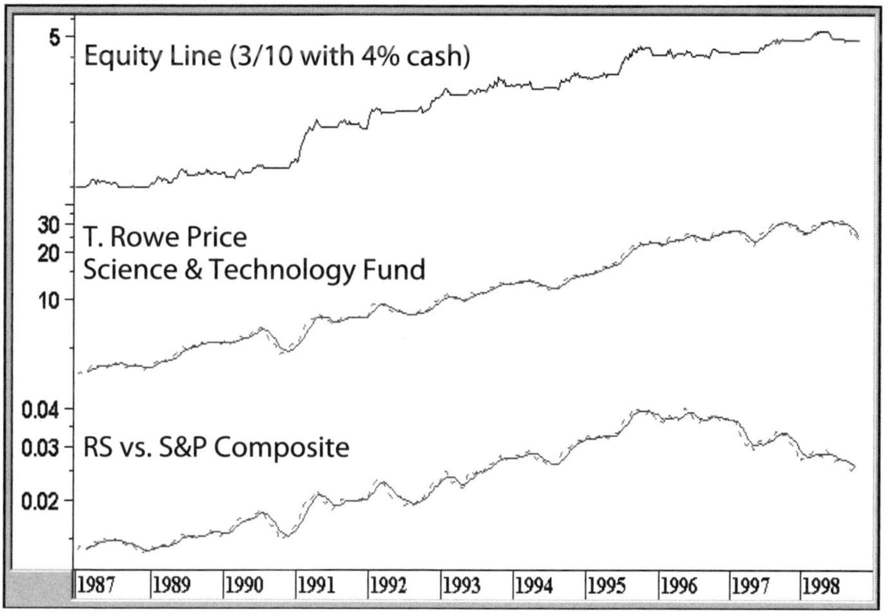

(Source: pring.com)

quickly when the market reverses on a dime. I have tried it with many funds and most of them perform quite well. Typically, wins outnumber losses and there are normally very small drawdowns. If you decide to apply this system, remember to backtest it over a considerable period of time, say 10 years for any security, to make sure that it has a good history.

SUMMARY

We may summarize the chapter as follows:

1. *The use of automated systems has the prime advantage of reducing emotion and encouraging greater discipline in the investment process.*
2. *No system will work all the time.* It is important to understand the disadvantage of a mechanical trading system so that some of the pitfalls can be programmed out.
3. *Mechanical trading systems may be used as a filter to identify important buy and sell junctures.* In this approach, actual market decisions are based on appraisal of *other* indicators. Alternatively, every signal of a mechanical

trading system may be followed consistently, to allow the system to stand on its own.

4. *Any system should be designed to take into consideration the fact that markets not only trend, but also undergo periods of volatile trading activity.* In appraising the results of the system, it is important to look for consistency and maximum drawdown (losses).
5. *Because no system is perfect, any approach should involve exhaustive testing over long periods and with many markets.*
6. *The use of any system should involve diversification to filter out periods when the system does not operate for a specific market.*

Appendix

The principles outlined in the CD and book are, of course, timeless, but since the production of the CD the great bull market of the 1980s and 1990s has ended. With this in mind several of the more promising systems described earlier have been updated to the end of 2001 in order to let you know how they performed in real time. Because the text in the book follows the script of the CD-ROM, these updates have been included in the form of an Appendix rather than as an addendum to the actual chapters.

THE "POUND" SYSTEM (TRIPLE INDICATOR)

This system was described in Chapter 15. You may recall that it requires three events to trigger a signal—a 10-week MA crossover and a zero crossover by the 6- and 13-week ROCs. Chart A1-1 shows the pound itself. After 20 years of excellent results this system began to fail in 1993 as it slipped below its 300-week MA. Since then, it—like the pound itself—has been flat. At first glance this may appear to be a weak performance, but when it is considered that the pound was in a narrow trading range between 1992 and 2001, in which countless whipsaw signals could have been given, this is not a bad performance.

Chart A1-2 updates the performance of the Nikkei using the same approach. Here the performance is far more impressive because the equity line was pretty close to its all-time high as the Nikkei sank to a new secular (or very long term) low in the fall of 2001. Certainly this system (which was traded from both the long and short sides) rose between 1990 and 2001, while the Nikkei itself lost more than 75 percent from its peak value in early 1990.

THE STOCK COMMERCIAL PAPER YIELD INTERMARKET SYSTEM

This system, which goes bullish when the S&P is above its 12-month MA and the commercial paper yield is below its 12-month MA, continued to

Chart A1-1 British Pound System

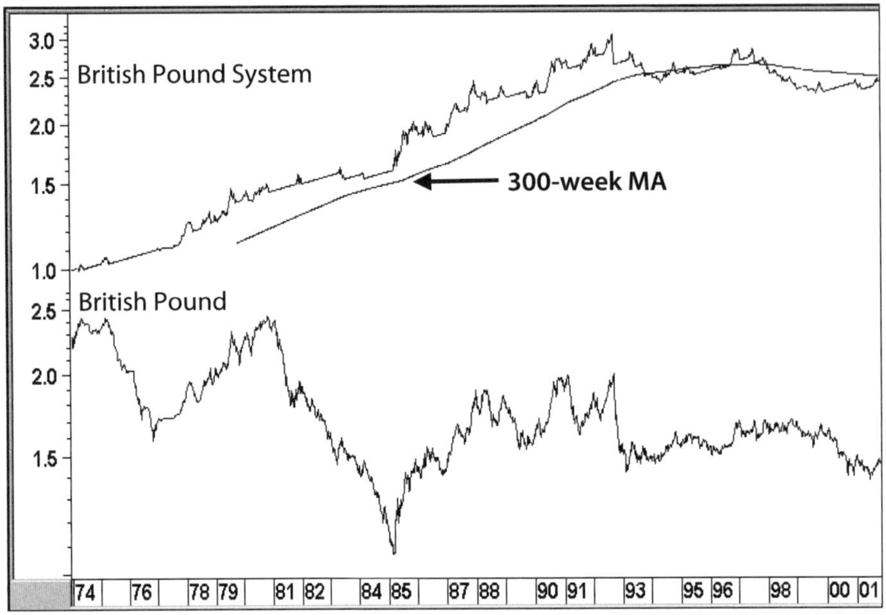

(Source: pring.com)

Chart A1-2 British Pound System Applied to the Nikkei

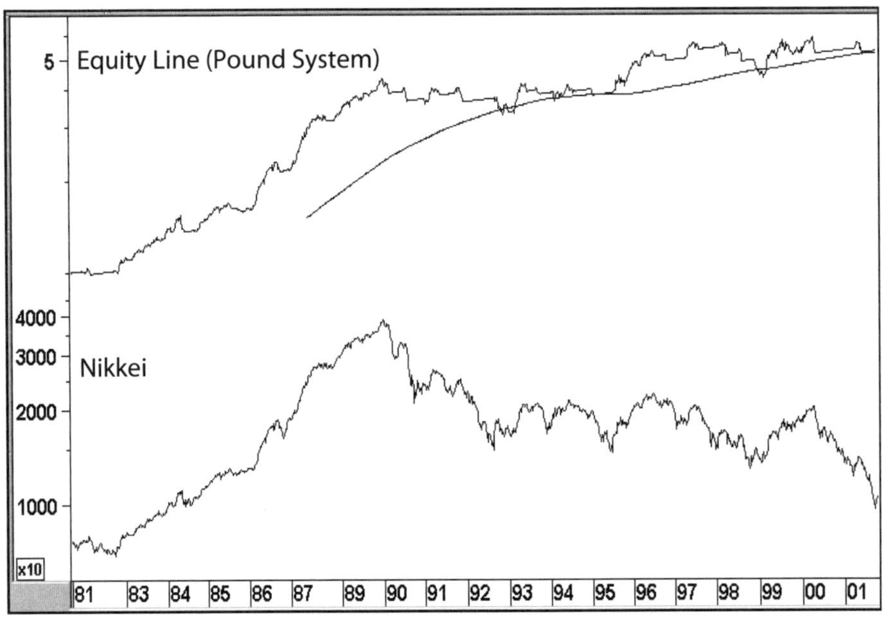

(Source: pring.com)

perform well in the late 1990s. Chart A1-3 shows that it failed to go liquid during the 1998 "Asian melt down," but triggered a sell signal pretty close to the high in 1999. It remained bearish in 2001 for despite the fact that rates fell precipitously in 2001 the market did not respond by rallying above its 12-month MA. Followers of the system were therefore in cash at the time of the September 11 attack on the World Trade Center and Pentagon.

THE CRB GOLD INTERMARKET SYSTEM

Chart A1-4 shows that this system continued to perform very well during the last part of the last century. Because it trades from both the long and short sides, it was able to take advantage of the sharp 2001 sell-off in the CRB Composite. Buy signals were triggered when the CRB 26-week MA was above the 45-week MA and the 26-week MA for spot gold was above its 65-week MA. Short positions were entered when both conditions reversed. Positions were liquidated when either series went bearish (bullish for short sales). The system returned an impressive 16 winners to three losing trades

Chart A1-3 S&P Composite Versus 3-Month Commercial Paper Yield

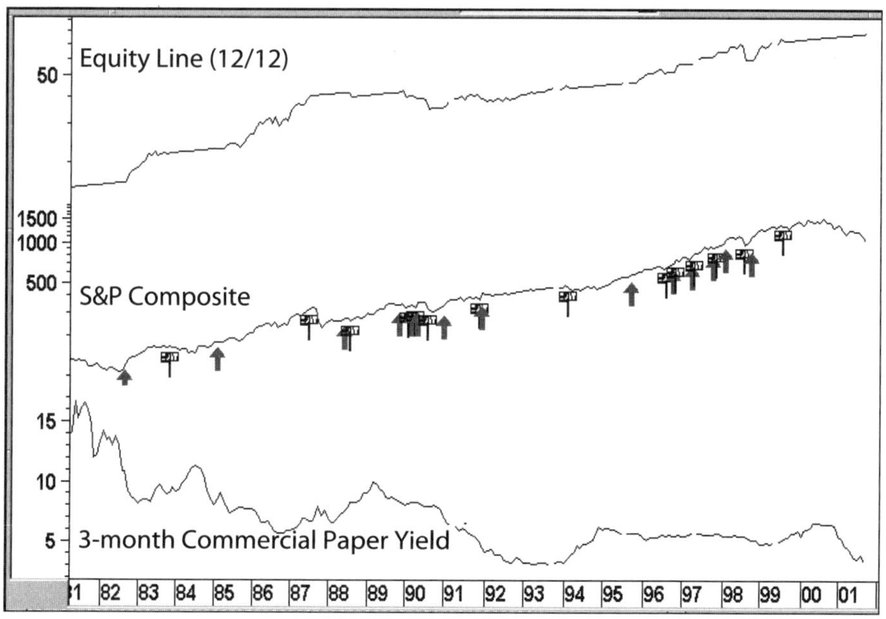

(Source: pring.com)

Chart A1-4 CRB Composite Versus Spot Gold

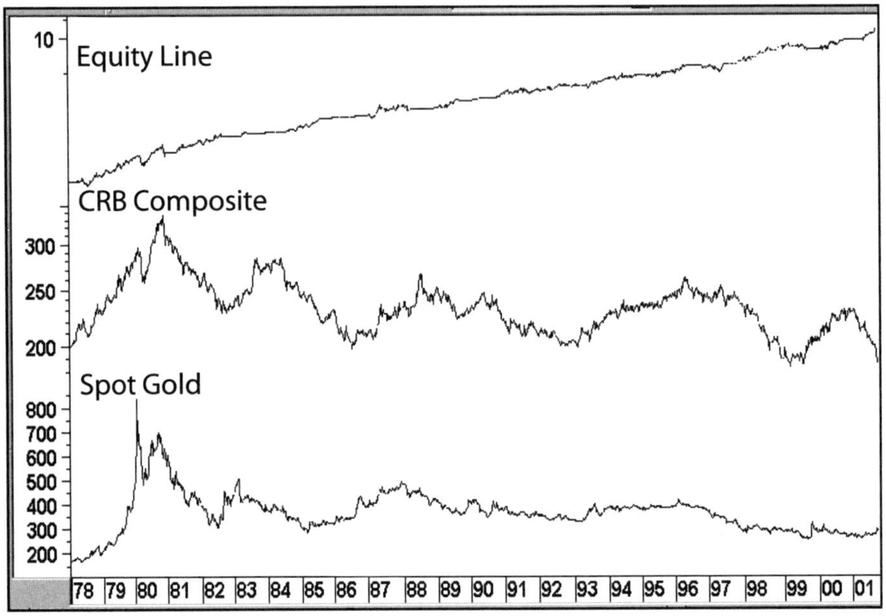

(Source: pring.com)

with an annualized rate of return of nearly 40 percent, when trading. We must add, however, that no commissions were assumed and no allowance was made for slippage. Because there were only 19 signals, and these were based on weekly closings, this would not have amounted to much anyway.

RELATIVE STRENGTH SYSTEMS

Chart A1-5 updates the T. Rowe Price RS system. This one only trades from the long side when the 10-week MA of the Fund and its RS line to the S&P Composite are both above their 26-week MAs. When either condition goes bearish, the fund is liquidated. A 4 percent interest rate is assumed when in a cash position. The chart shows that the system would have kept a trader out of the sharp 2000–2001 decline and ended up at the end of 2001 close to its all-time high. There were six signals in 9 years, only one of which lost money.

Chart A1-6 updates the same system for the Scudder Emerging Markets Fund. Until 1998 the system had performed quite well; however, the volatile

Chart A1-5 T. Rowe Price Japan Fund

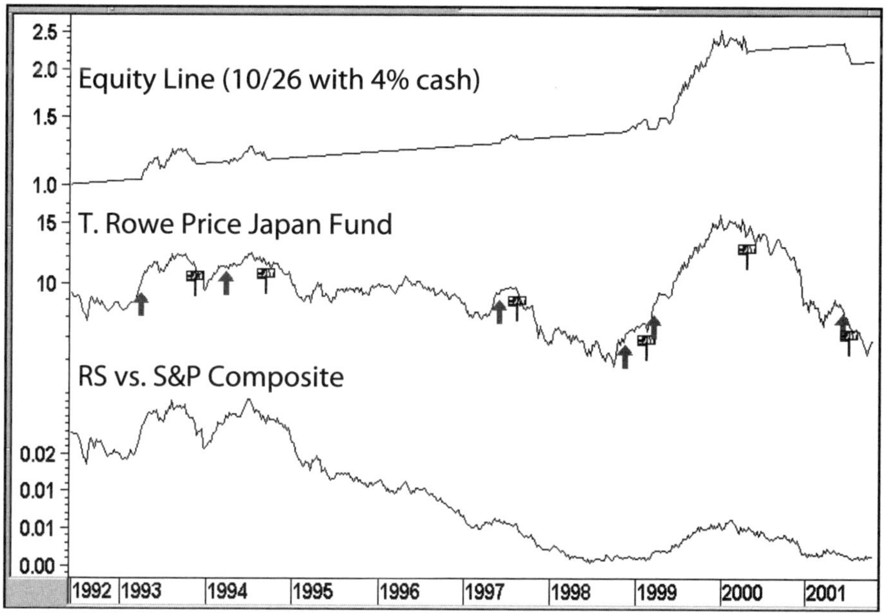

(Source: pring.com)

Chart A1-6 Scudder Emerging Market Fund

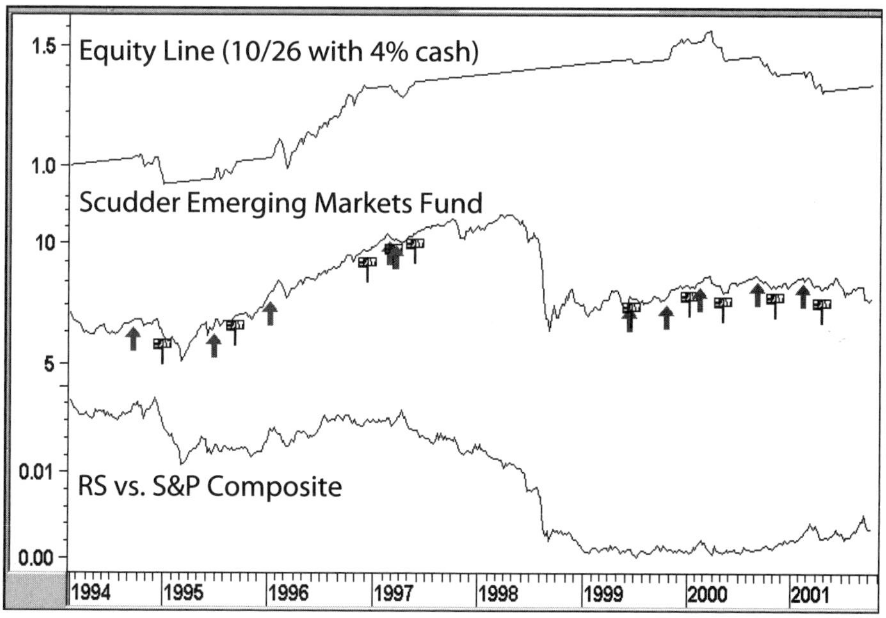

(Source: pring.com)

Chart A1-7 T. Rowe Price Science and Technology Fund

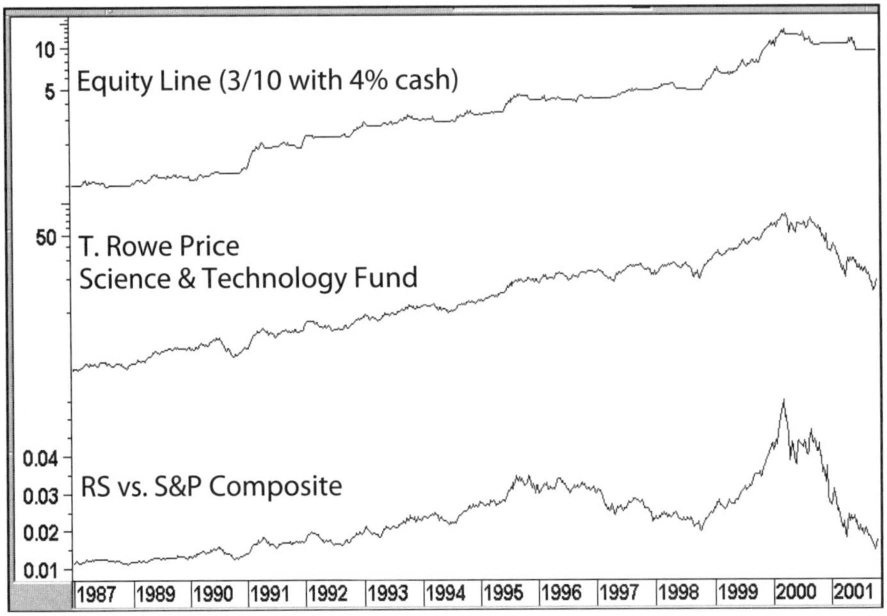

(Source: pring.com)

Chart A1-8 RS System Applied to NASDAQ

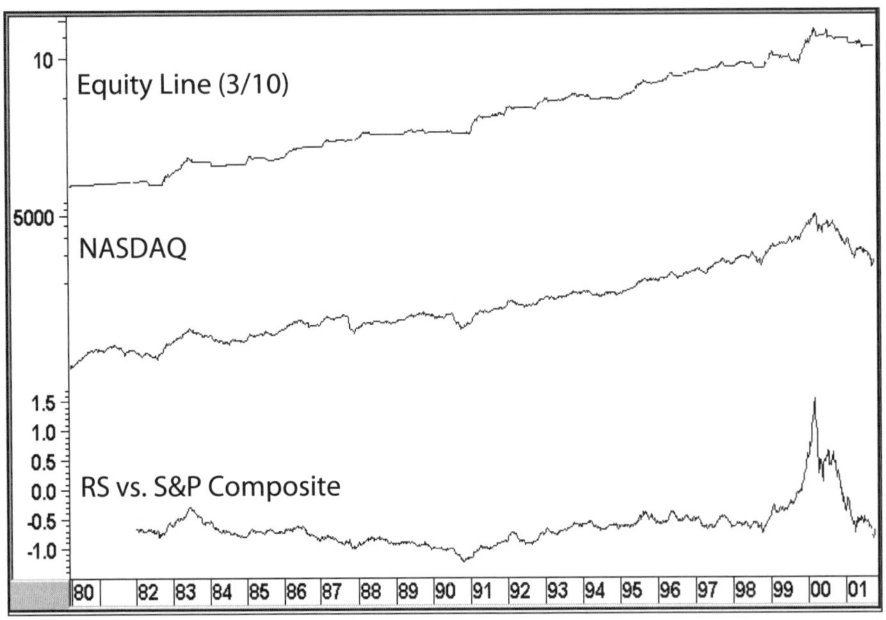

(Source: pring.com)

trading action between 1999 and 2001 resulted in numerous whipsaw signals. The system still beat the buy-hold approach, but the damage of the last 3 years shows how difficult it is to design a system that can successfully deal with volatile trading ranges.

The T. Rowe Price Science and Technology Fund is featured in Chart A1-7, using the more sensitive 3/10 RS combination. The fund declined sharply between 2000–2001, but because of the trending nature of the decline, the equity line remained close to its all-time high.

Finally, this same system was applied to the NASDAQ. This chart was not shown previously, but with the dramatic decline in this index between March 2000 and October 2001, I thought it would be a good idea to test one of the systems to see how it would react in a bear market. The result, as you can see from the equity line in Chart A1-8, was that it worked well during bull and bear markets alike.

Quiz

For answers, go to www.traderslibrary.com/TLEcorner

1. Mechanical systems should be:
   A.) Used at random.
   B.) Used only with a moving average.
   C.) Used as a filter among several indicators to draw a conclusion about the state of a current trend, or alternatively, every signal should be followed without question.

2. The best systems offer the largest profits.
   A.) True
   B.) False

3. A mechanical trading system should:
   A.) Fit the sample data set perfectly and then it will stand a better chance of being profitable in real time.
   B.) Test with consistent, rather than spectacular, profits.
   C.) Offer many signals, most of which are profitable.
   D.) Have as many parameters as possible so the results can be crosschecked.

4. Which is not an advantage of mechanical systems?
   A.) Remove emotion from trading.
   B.) Offer a great consistency of results.
   C.) Allow profits to run and losses to be cut.
   D.) Eliminate random events.

5. Backtesting is always a good way of simulating what would have happened.
   A.) True
   B.) False

6. A market if touched order is:
   A.) A form of market order.
   B.) A guarantee of a fill at the price when it is touched.
   C.) An order that will not be executed unless a sufficient quantity trades at the designated price.

7. The first step in designing a system is:
   A.) Finding a good broker.
   B.) Keeping it simple.
   C.) Trying to get a fix on the character of the security you are trading.
   D.) Establishing a timeframe you are going to be working in.

8. Which statement is true?
   A.) If you do not invent enough rules, the sample data will not be profitable and neither will be the real-time application.
   B.) The size of the drawdown is unimportant if the system is really profitable.
   C.) If your system starts out a big winner in real time, you know you have got it made.
   D.) None of the above is true.

9. It is most important to:
   A.) Cut profits and let losses run.
   B.) Cut losses and let profits run.
   C.) Cut losses.
   D.) All of the above.

10. Other things being equal, which is the best test?
   A.) One that covers a wide set of market conditions.
   B.) One that covers a wide set of market conditions with different securities over a long period of time.
   C.) One that tests profitability with a small data set.
   D.) One that is tested with many different securities.

11. Looking at the three equity lines below, which is the most likely to offer the best real-time results?

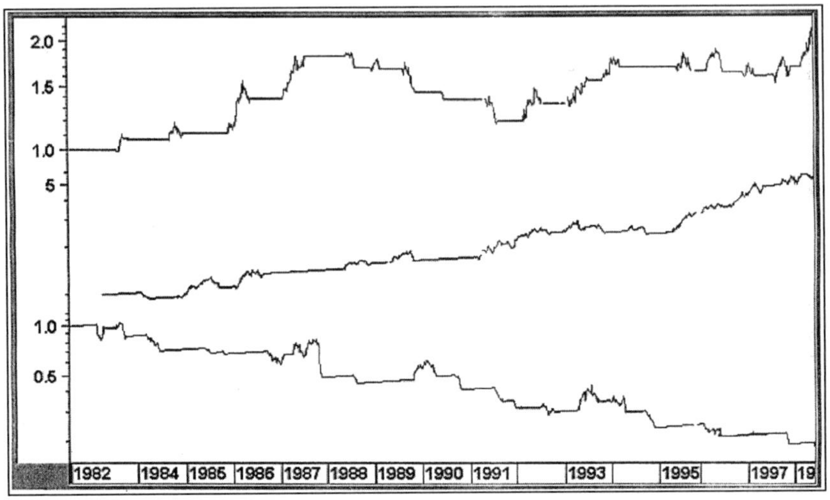

12. Since mechanical systems are designed to remove emotions, it is not important that they fit your personality.
A.) True
B.) False

13. Signals that develop in the direction of the main trend:
A.) Will always give better results.
B.) Will generally give better results than those that are contrary to the main trend.
C.) Are only relevant for primary trend signals.

14. Which statement is true?
A.) A system will fail because it has been improperly optimized.
B.) A system will fail because it is an inherently poor system to begin with.
C.) A system will fail because market conditions can and do fail.
D.) All of the above.

15. The best system will:
A.) Test extremely well on one market over a period of time.
B.) Offer the highest reward, but with the highest risk.
C.) Offer consistent profits and small losses over many markets in many different market conditions.
D.) None of the above.

16. Trading risk capital should be:
   A.) Greater than the greatest drawdown in the test period.
   B.) As small as possible so you do not lose too much money.
   C.) Something to test the system. When you lose it, bring more money to the table.

17. Setting stops:
   A.) Guarantees liquidation at the designated price.
   B.) Always results in a loss.
   C.) Should only be done to make sure you break even.
   D.) None of the above.

18. If the optimized results of a sample test offer good, consistent, profitable results with only small drawdowns you should:
   A.) Call your broker and start trading immediately.
   B.) Fine-tune the parameters to get even better results.
   C.) Walk forward with the test to see how well the results will be duplicated.
   D.) None of the answers are correct.

19. A trailing stop is:
   A.) One that is continuously moved in the direction of the position.
   B.) A stop that is only placed after a profit has been earned.
   C.) One that trails a market if touched stop.
   D.) None of the above.

20. A well-defined and tested filter will:
   A.) Not require any extended testing.
   B.) Be of little use if you are also using seven or eight other filters.
   C.) Both B and D.
   D.) Help to improve the overall results of the system.

21. If an optimization returns one extremely profitable system with an equal number of wins and losses, this is better than an optimization that returns several less profitable systems with a 6 to 4 win/loss ratio.
   A.) True
   B.) False

22. A walk forward test is:
   A.) One that returns good results.
   B.) One that precedes a testing of sample data.
   C.) A second test that is made after a first set of sample data returns promising results.
   D.) None of the above.

23. One advantage of a walk forward test is:
   A.) It always returns more reliable and better results than the sample test.
   B.) It would "smell out" curve fitted systems.

24. When a system is being applied in real time, what are the signs it is not performing correctly?
   A.) Losses are greater than the largest drawdown.
   B.) Profits are far greater than the tested data.
   C.) Both A and B.
   D.) The win/loss ratio is very similar.

25. If the real-time application of a system initially results in a large string of losses that are less than the worst string of the test data losses, you should:
   A.) Immediately abandon the system.
   B.) Margin the account because the odds favor a win on the next trade.
   C.) Suspend the application of the system, then wait for a profitable signal and re-enter the market.
   D.) Continue with the system.

26. Using leverage with a mechanical system will:
   A.) Always result in bigger gains.
   B.) Exaggerate the results both on the upside and downside.

27. When defining a system, it is important to:
   A.) Define it precisely so there can be no confusion as to the correct interpretation of the rules.
   B.) Define it precisely so there is always a countervailing signal that liquidates the position.
   C.) Make sure you get a best-fit curve for the data.
   D.) Both A and B.

28. True or False? A system can be used as a filter in conjunction with other indicators to identify important buy and sell junctures.
   A.) True
   B.) False

29. Overfitting:
   A.) Rarely happens when you have filters.
   B.) Will result in good test results and even better real-time results.
   C.) Occurs when too many rules are devised to make the historical test data profitable.
   D.) Both A and B.

30. If you test several decades of data on hundreds of securities with highly profitable results, when you trade real time:

A.) You are guaranteed success.

B.) The odds favor the application being profitable.

C.) The odds favor the application being profitable, so you should margin yourself to the hilt.

D.) The odds are about even that the application will be profitable.

For answers, go to
www.traderslibrary.com/TLEcorner

Glossary

For an extensive technical glossary with over 300 terms, please visit *www.pring.com.*

A

Arbitrage — The process of buying and/or selling in two or more different markets or contracts in order to profit from irregular price discrepancies.

Asymmetrical trading system—Occurs when the sell signal is different from the buy signal.

B

Backwardation—Shortages of product in the cash or spot market, which cause the spot month and other near-term contracts to trade at a price greater than the deferred contracts.

Breakeven stop—Closes an open position when the closed out value falls below the equity amount at the time the trade was opened.

Buy-stop limit order—An order to close out an existing position by buying when a price reaches a designated level.

Buy-stop order—An order that is placed at a price above the current level and executed when the price reaches that level.

C

Contango—The premium of a deferred futures contract that reflects the carrying cost.

D

Divergence—A discrepancy between two time series. The divergence may develop between two price series or a price series and oscillator.

Dollar profit target—An unconditional exit, at a profit, that is at a point equal to a dollar amount above or below the entry price.

E

Equilibrium line—A line that is frequently plotted on oscillators to reflect neutral momentum.

Equilibrium price—The market price at which the quantity supplied of a commodity equals the quantity demanded.

K

KST (know sure thing)—An oscillator developed by Martin Pring, calculated from the weighted summed rate of change of four smoothed rate-of-change indicators. KSTs can be calculated for any timeframe, including intraday. The most common are short, intermediate, and long-term (Primary trend). KSTs can also be very effectively applied to comparative relative strength.

L

Leverage—Controlling large dollar amounts of securities with a comparatively small amount of capital.

Limit moves—The maximum daily price swing in a futures contract as determined by the exchange.

Locked limit day—Develops when the open, high, low, and close for the day are the same and volume is low.

M

Margin—In stock trading, an account in which purchase of stock may be financed with borrowed money; in futures trading, the deposit placed with the clearinghouse to assure fulfillment of the contract. This amount varies daily and is settled in cash.

Margin call—The demand upon a customer to put up money or securities with a broker. The call is made if a customer's equity in a margin account declines below a minimum standard set by the exchange or brokerage firm.

Market if touched (MIT) order—An order that becomes a market order as soon as the security trades at the designated price.

Market order—Instructions to a broker to immediately sell to the best available bid or to buy from the best available offer.
Maximum losing run—The series of losing trades that has the largest dollar value.
Moving average (MA) crossovers—Occur where the price crosses a moving average, thereby triggering a buy or sell signal.
Moving average convergent/divergence (MACD)—An indicator constructed by relating two exponentially smoothed moving averages. It is plotted above and below a zero line. The crossover, movement through the zero line, and divergences generate buy and sell signals. Alternatively, crossovers of a signal line constructed from a smoothing of the MACD provide buy and sell signals.

O

Overbought—A condition in which an oscillator moves above a level that is well above its normal limit.
Overfitting—Involves the establishment of a profitable set of parameters for a specific sample of test data that has little or no forecasting value.
Oversold—A condition in which an oscillator moves below a level that is well below its normal limit.

P

Parabolic system—A stop system that moves progressively toward the price as the price moves in a parabolic fashion.
Price/earnings ratio—The ratio of the price of a stock to the earnings per share, that is, the total annual profit of a company, divided by the number of shares outstanding.
Price limit order—The price specified by a customer order at which a trade can be executed.

R

Required capital—The sum of the maximum drawdown margin and a safety factor needed to trade a system profitably.
Reversal system—When the original long position is closed out, a short position is immediately initiated; positions are reversed each time a signal is given.
Risk capital—Should be greater than the equivalent of the maximum drawdown of an established and tested system.

S

Selling short—Selling a security and then borrowing it with the intent of replacing it at a lower price. Selling short in a futures market occurs when the trader enters a position by assuming responsibility of the seller.

Sell limit order—An order that is placed at a price above the current level and must be filled at or above the price.

Sell-stop limit order—An order to close out an existing position by selling when a price reaches a designated level.

Sell-stop order—An order executed as a market order when the price declines to the designated level.

Slippage—The difference between the price where the stop was placed and where it gets filled; a transaction expense paid to the trading floor.

Stop loss—A means of limiting risk that is triggered only if certain conditions are met.

Symmetrical trading system—A sell signal that is the reverse of a buy signal.

T

Technical analysis—The art of interpreting a number of different and reliable scientifically derived indicators.

Trading risk—The minimum amount of capital to be put at risk in order to be able to trade long enough to establish a profit.

Trailing stop—Is placed at a dollar amount above or below a recent low or high, depending on whether you are short or long in the equity for the current trade.

Trendline—A line that connects a series of highs in a downtrend or a series of lows in an uptrend. Uptrendlines represent support and downtrendlines resistance. Trendline penetrations either result in consolidation moves or an actual reversal in trend. Their significance is determined by their length, the number of times they have been touched or approached, and the steepness of the angle of ascent or descent.

W

Walk-forward analysis—Evaluates performance by extrapolating the results of an earlier period.

For an extensive technical glossary with over 300 terms, please visit *www.pring.com*.

Index

B

C

D–E

G–I

K–L

M–N

O

P

R

S

T–U

W

About the Author

Martin J. Pring is the highly respected president of Pring Research (www.pring.com). A pioneer in the field of technical analysis, Pring is probably best known for his seminal *Technical Analysis Explained*, used by many technical societies around the world as a teaching tool for certification programs. In addition to 14 books and numerous articles (including contributions to Barron's and other national publications), he has held workshops for traders in Asia, Australia, Africa, Europe, and North America and has lectured at several universities, including Harvard Medical School, the Darden Business School, Golden Gate University, and the University of Richmond. He is also editor of *The Intermarket Review*, a monthly technical letter that forecasts the world's principal financial markets from a long-term perspective. He was awarded the Jack Frost Memorial Award from the Canadian Technical Analysts Society, as well as the Traders' Library Hall of Fame Lifetime Achievement Award for his groundbreaking contributions to the field.

Installation Instructions

This CD has an Autorun feature. Insert the CD into the CD-ROM drive and it will start automatically. Please allow sufficient time for loading.

If the Autorun feature does not work, insert the CD, open your CD-ROM drive and double-click on the Setup.exe icon. Then, access the program by clicking on Start, Programs, Pring and locate the icon for the tutorial title you are playing in the flyout.

1. We recommend not changing the default installation settings.
2. This program is best viewed using small fonts.
3. This CD is best viewed in 800 X 600 pixels and 256 colors.
4. For additional support, please go to Support at www.pring.com.

Advanced Technical Analysis CD Tutorials:

Learning the KST
Intro to Candlestick Charting
Tech's Guide to Day Trading
Breaking the Black Box
How to Select Stocks

MetaStock CD Tutorials:

Exploring MS Basic
Exploring MS Advanced
Super CD Companion
Indicator Companion
Market Analysis Companion
Selecting Stocks Using MetaStock

Visit ***http://www.pring.com*** for info on these and other products.

Pring Research, Inc.

4830 Sweetmeadow Circle, Sarasota, FL 34238
941-926-9664 • Fax: 941-870-0642
Web Site: www.pring.com • E-mail: info@pring.com

SOFTWARE AND INFORMATION LICENSE

The software and information on this diskette (collectively referred to as the "Product") are the property of Marketplace Books, and are protected by both United States copyright law and international copyright treaty provision. You must treat this Product just like a book, except that you may copy it into a computer to be used and you may make archival copies of the Products for the sole purpose of backing up our software and protecting your investment from loss.

By saying "just like a book," Marketplace Books means, for example, that the Product may be used by any number of people and may be freely moved from one computer location to another, so long as there is no possibility of the Product (or any part of the Product) being used at one location or on one computer while it is being used at another. Just as a book cannot be read by two different people in two different places at the same time, neither can the Product be used by two different people in two different places at the same time (unless, of course, Marketplace Books' rights are being violated).

Marketplace Books reserves the right to alter or modify the contents of the Product at any time.

This agreement is effective until terminated. The Agreement will terminate automatically without notice if you fail to comply with any provisions of this Agreement. In the event of termination by reason of your breach, you will destroy or erase all copies of the Product installed on any computer system or made for backup purposes and shall expunge the Product from your data storage facilities.

LIMITED WARRANTY

Marketplace Books warrants the physical diskette(s) enclosed herein to be free of defects in materials and workmanship for a period of sixty days from the purchase date. If Marketplace Books receives written notification within the warranty period of defects in materials or workmanship, and such notification is determined by Marketplace Books to be correct, Marketplace Books will replace the defective diskette(s). Send request to:

Customer Service
Marketplace Books
9002 Red Branch Road
Columbia MD 21045

The entire and exclusive liability and remedy for breach of this Limited Warranty shall be limited to replacement of defective diskette(s) and shall not include or extend any claim for or right to cover any other damages, including but not limited to, loss of profit, data, or use of the software, or special, incidental, or consequential damages or other similar claims, even if Marketplace Books has been specifically advised as to the possibility of such damages. In no event will Marketplace Books's liability for any damages to you or any other person ever exceed the lower of suggested list price or actual price paid for the license to use the Product, regardless of any form of the claim.

MARKETPLACE BOOKS SPECIFICALLY DISCLAIMS ALL OTHER WARRANTIES, EXPRESS OR IMPLIED, INCLUDING BUT NOT LIMITED TO, ANY IMPLIED WARRANTY OF MERCHANTABILITY OR FITNESS FOR A PARTICULAR PURPOSE. Specifically, Marketplace Books makes no representation or warranty that the Product is fit for any particular purpose and any implied warranty of merchantability is limited to the sixty day duration of the Limited Warranty covering the physical diskette(s) only (and not the software or information) and is otherwise expressly and specifically disclaimed.

This Limited Warranty gives you specific legal rights; you may have others which may vary from state to state. Some states do not allow the exclusion of incidental or consequential damages, or the limitation on how long an implied warranty lasts, so some of the above may not apply to you.

This Agreement constitutes the entire agreement between the parties relating to use of the Product. The terms of any purchase order shall have no effect on the terms of this Agreement. Failure of Marketplace Books to insist at any time on strict compliance with this Agreement shall not constitute a waiver of any rights under this Agreement. This Agreement shall be construed and governed in accordance with the laws of Maryland. If any provision of this Agreement is held to be contrary to law, that provision will be enforced to the maximum extent permissible and the remaining provisions will remain in force and effect.